AESTHETICISM AND DECONSTRUCTION

AESTHETICISM
AND DECONSTRUCTION

PATER, DERRIDA, AND DE MAN

Jonathan Loesberg

PRINCETON UNIVERSITY PRESS   PRINCETON, NEW JERSEY

Copyright © 1991 by Princeton University Press
Published by Princeton University Press, 41 William Street,
Princeton, New Jersey 08540
In the United Kingdom: Princeton University Press, Oxford

All Rights Reserved

Library of Congress Cataloging-in-Publication Data
Loesberg, Jonathan, 1950–
Aestheticism and deconstruction : Pater, Derrida, and De Man /
Jonathan Loesberg.
p. cm.
Includes bibliographical references and index.
ISBN 0-691-06884-4
1. Deconstruction. 2. Aestheticism (Literature) 3. Pater,
Walter, 1839–1894. 4. Derrida, Jacques. 5. De Man, Paul.
I. Title.
PN98.D43L64 1991   90-19139
801'.95—dc20

This book has been composed in Adobe Palatino

Princeton University Press books are printed
on acid-free paper, and meet the guidelines
for permanence and durability of the Committee
on Production Guidelines for Book Longevity
of the Council on Library Resources

Printed in the United States of America by
Princeton University Press, Princeton, New Jersey

10 9 8 7 6 5 4 3 2 1

TO THE MEMORY OF MY FATHER

Burton Loesberg

Art for Art

The smiling of women and the motion
Of great waters, these alone disturbed
Leonardo, who enjoyed what was left:
The brilliant sins highlighting the dark,
The exquisite fevers of the Borgias,
The canvases which took the place of God.
Careless with time, he never wondered why
Saint John went to the waste for food,
Or Saint Anne praised an unnatural child,
Or man not man broke bread that was not bread—
All beyond him, perfectly beyond him.
So he painted, took any stand, chose any side,
And his indifference grew till he was French,
Married to their valley, past unsettling waters
And the smile that was neither his nor hers.

—Edward Kessler

Contents

Acknowledgments	xi
Introduction The Aestheticism of Deconstruction	3
One What Is Art for Art's Sake and How Could It Be Anything Else?	11
Two Studies in the Histories of *The Renaissance*	42
Three Deconstruction: Foundations and Literary Language	75
Four Deconstructive Aesthetics: Literary Language, History, Ideology	122
Five Aesthetic Analysis and Political Critique	160
Afterword Aestheticism, Journalism, and de Man's *Wartime Writings*	190
Notes	201
Works Cited	223
Index	231

Acknowledgments

FIRST THANKS go to Ed Kessler, who, in a persistent attempt to force me to write readable prose, has gone over this manuscript as many times as I have. Asking me about every element of its analysis, he also helped me to clarify what I wanted to say about aestheticism and political discourse. I also want to thank him for permitting me to reprint his poem "Art for Art" as an epigraph. I would also like to thank the anonymous reader to whom Princeton sent a preliminary draft of the chapters on Pater. In extensive, sympathetic close argument, that reader asked key questions, the answering of which helped me shape the final manuscript. Helena Michie also read and offered valuable comments on the manuscript. A conversation with Jerry Christensen helped me to think out why I had avoided addressing the controversy over de Man's *Wartime Writings* and how I ought to confront them. Discussions with Jeff Reiman, who would no doubt disagree with every word in this book, have nevertheless also been helpful to me. The American University, through summer grants and a sabbatical leave, offered financial support.

Portions of Chapter 5 also appear as "Deconstruction, Feminist Criticism and Canon Deformation" in the November 1991 issue of *Paragraph*.

Gail Grella's support of various kinds is beyond thanking.

AESTHETICISM AND DECONSTRUCTION

Introduction

The Aestheticism of Deconstruction

IT WAS INEVITABLE that Walter Pater would be deconstructed. Partly it had to happen because any complex author writing on subjects that concern literary theorists would seem to call forth the application of a reading method implied by a new theory. But Pater did not elicit particular attention from the New Critics. He interests current literary theorists, surely, because his concerns pertain to the problems they address. His skeptical theories of perception and aesthetics, explicitly informed as they are by various and contradictory philosophies, foreshadow the deconstructive interest in the corrosive links between philosophy and aesthetic form. Moreover, the hazy line between his ostensibly impressionistic art criticism and the critically and intellectually dense but narratively immobile genre of fiction he invented, the imaginary portrait, calls into question the line between literature and criticism in a way that further anticipates deconstructive concerns.[1] But that means that a deconstructive reading applied to Pater as its own end somehow misses the point, making of his work, as it inevitably must, yet another example of the way literature either may be deconstructed or deconstructs itself.

If Pater's ideas already foreshadow elements of deconstruction, the more pertinent question might be how the appearance of those elements in a necessarily different context may elucidate current theoretical debate. In discussing this issue, I do not want particularly to make Pater seem relevant, to show that he was really talking about the paradoxes of language or the perils of interpretation all along.[2] Instead, through the particular issues raised by the problems he saw in Victorian cultural criticism, precisely because of their different context, I hope to cast light on a theoretical movement that we now frequently condemn as aestheticist. Not wanting to use contemporary literary theory to elucidate Pater, I will use Pater to elucidate contemporary literary theory. In effect, by reading deconstructive theory, as formulated by Jacques Derrida and Paul de Man, in the light of Pater's *Renaissance*, I begin by accepting what is frequently the most virulent charge against deconstruction, its aestheticism. Aestheticism, at least for many critics, stands as a vague synonym for imagining a realm of art entirely separate from social or historical effect and then advocating an escape into that "unreal," aesthetic universe. Starting with Pater, and proceeding to a discussion of deconstruction, I will argue that, on the contrary, aestheticism has always operated as a central mode both of engaging in and of interpreting philosophy, history, and politics. By outlining the connection between Pater's aestheticism and deconstruction, I will show what it really means to construe deconstruction as aestheticist.

Before outlining aestheticism's mode of engagement and interpretation here, I want to specify the charges made against both Pater and deconstructive theory and identify the common ground of their ostensible theoretical failure. When *The Renaissance* first appeared in 1873 under the title *Studies in the History of the Renaissance*, reviews, though generally favorable, repeated a series of related critiques. First, one critic claimed that the book was not historical because its formalism detached the art it discussed from its contexts: "the work is in no wise a contribution to the history of the Renaissance. For instead of approaching his subject, whether Art or Literature, by the true scientific method, through the life of the time of which it was an outcome, Mr Pater prefers in each instance to detach it wholly from its surroundings, to suspend it isolated before him, as if it were indeed a kind of air-plant independent of ordinary sources of nourishment" (Seiler, *Walter Pater, The Critical Heritage*, 71–72). Nor are critics surprised that Pater treats art and literature in this way. Since his skepticism reduces all reality to individual sensation, it makes the only valuable activity the intensifying of pleasurable sensation. Thus another critic laments that the book's "philosophy is an assertion, that no fixed principles either of religion or morality can be regarded as certain, that the only thing worth living for is momentary enjoyment" (Seiler, *Walter Pater, The Critical Heritage*, 62). And while this skepticism might seem to ally itself with the liberal interrogation of established institutions, even a receptive liberal reviewer like John Morley worries about an aestheticist passivity, concluding that "directly effective social action" is "calculated to give a higher quality to the moments as they pass than art and song, just because it is not 'simply for those moments' sake.'"[3]

As a school of literary criticism, deconstruction has faced precisely the same charges, posed with the same vehemence one sees in the Victorian reviews. Thus one finds that "if one takes seriously Miller's deconstructionist principles of interpretation, any history which relies on written texts becomes an impossibility."[4] Moreover, "American poststructuralist literary criticism tends to be an activity of textual privatization, the critic's doomed attempt to retreat from a social landscape of fragmentation and alienation. Criticism becomes, in this perspective, something like an ultimate mode of interior decoration whose chief value lies in its power to trigger our pleasures and whose chief mea-

INTRODUCTION   5

sure of success lies in its capacity to keep pleasure going in a potentially infinite variety of ways" (Lentricchia, *After the New Criticism*, 186). And so, just as Morley found Pater's aesthetics wanting in comparison to directly effective social action, "deconstruction translates into that passive kind of conservatism called quietism; it thereby plays into the hands of established power. Deconstruction is conservatism by default" (Lentricchia, *Criticism and Social Change*, 5). Deconstruction, then, is guilty of all the moral, philosophical, and political sins of Pater's aestheticism.

All of these criticisms are variants of three related charges that contain the basic assumptions critics make about aestheticism (Pater's and that of deconstruction), and their objections. The first accuses aestheticism of relativism or nihilism. This charge arises from the presumption that one could base a claim about the philosophic centrality of art or literature only on a belief that no theory can found a value that would supersede or regulate the subjective pleasures one takes in artistic indulgence. Stanley Fish made the exemplary version of this ostensibly aestheticist argument when he claimed that his theory relieved him of the responsibility to be right, replacing it with the responsibility to be interesting (Fish, 180).[5] But the same presumption leads to the constant inference that if Derrida and de Man show that literature deconstructs philosophy, they must mean that philosophy reduces to literature and is merely fictional. The second charge finds in aestheticism an inauthentic search for an ahistorical stance in a pure aesthetic perception outside the confusion of historical and social judgment and event. The inauthenticity of the search inheres in the relativist or nihilist grounds by which, presumably, aestheticism values its perception in the first place, since logically one cannot ground a position, pure or not, on nihilism. Finally, and as a consequence, aestheticism must entail political quietism. By espousing art or literature as an escape from any extra-aesthetic or extra-literary concerns and by contending that all political commitment or belief is delusory, aestheticism implicitly cooperates with any ruling institutional or social power. The common ground beneath all of these charges is a belief that art and literature are defined by their absolute alterity to discourses concerned with truth—either abstract and foundational truth as in philosophy or specific truths as in history and political criticism. Espousing aestheticism must, therefore, entail a nihilist attitude toward the constraints of truth upon discourse and a desire for a position outside the effects of history and politics. This book will contend that both Pater's aestheticism and deconstruction confront precisely that common ground. Those theories argue for the centrality of aesthetic experience both to philosophical understanding and to the interpretation of history and politics.

In my readings of both Pater and deconstruction, then, my argument divides into two parts. One concerns the relationship between aestheticism and the philosophy it both critiques and redefines. The second then extends that philosophically refined aestheticism to an articulation of its historicist and ideological implications. Pater's philosophic critique begins in the "Conclusion" to *The Renaissance*, where he connects his notorious espousal of art for art's sake with empirical philosophy's grounding of all knowledge in physical sensations. Arguing that sensations themselves depend for their existence on change and thus on the friction between one sensation and another, Pater imbeds an abstraction—friction as a necessary form of sensation—within a self-contradictory founding sensation. That self-contradictory friction within sensation, an abstract form of sensation that is also itself a sensation, has its exemplary occurrence, Pater argues, in the sensations that art evokes. Far from being an escape from reality or a refutation of philosophy, then, art is the founding mode of knowledge precisely in its formal embodiment of friction. In effect, Pater finds empiricism's foundational moment contradictory, but, instead of abandoning it, he recognizes the necessity of both the foundation and the contradiction. He then uses this duality to fashion a philosophy that includes all others, thus binding Ruskin's scientific claims for aesthetics with Arnold's urbane cultural criticism as an alternative to science. Aesthetics, for Pater, is not a hermetically enclosed discourse but one that encompasses all others by accepting the contradiction within the foundation of knowledge delineated by empirical philosophy. Reproducing the foundational moment of empiricism, which reduces all knowledge to a starting point in the sensation that evokes perception, then finding a contradictory, foundational necessity for abstraction in the form of friction, Pater never expands his idea of sensation back out but proceeds to find all other forms of interpretation and knowledge comprehended within that founding contradiction. This definition of Pater's connection between philosophy and aestheticism leads, in my second chapter, to a discussion of how Pater uses aestheticism to connect philosophical abstraction with historical particularity; in an ultimate act of inclusiveness, he joins Hegel's idealist historicism with empiricism through an aestheticism that depends on and makes sense of historical difference. This chapter addresses the form of Pater's narrative as well as his explicit argument because his aestheticism acts out its own abstract claims in the experience his narrative affords.

While my opening chapters offer a rather more complex and philosophic Pater than the solipsist who appears in many critical works, I most pointedly do not deconstruct Pater. These chapters do not apply a particular method of reading his works in order to show that, either

INTRODUCTION 7

with or without his prior knowledge, their unifying form contains certain vital contradictions, thus exemplifying the validity of deconstructive philosophy. Indeed, my discussion of Derrida will question whether this method is a logical consequence of Derrida's theories. Rather, in my analysis of Pater's aestheticism, I trace a series of connected themes that elucidate the aestheticism of Derrida and de Man. First, Pater's finding of a contradiction within empiricism's founding moment, his articulation of that contradiction as a comprehensive mode of inclusion, accommodating the contradictory claims of various theories of art, literature, and social criticism, and his definition of aesthetic sensation as the exemplary form of that contradiction, all recur in the deconstructive connection between philosophy and literary language. Derrida's philosophical analysis, I will argue, does not undo all constraints of logic and reason in favor of a nihilist free play, but rather identifies a necessary contradiction within philosophy's ambition to offer foundational rules governing all knowledge. The contradiction that Derrida finds within the exclusionary activity of foundational rules does allow one to articulate particular truths. Indeed, it does not even do away with foundational philosophy. It entails recognizing the conflicting necessities both to ground thought and knowledge and to include within that grounding its own negation. As the third chapter will note, the foundations Derrida analyzes pose problems of meaning and reflection rather than problems of sensation and perception, as in Pater. Accordingly, deconstruction follows a very different thematic itinerary from Pater's, one that has considerably confused its American readers. Because Pater's language of sensation and perception is more familiar, the structure of his philosophical analysis may aid in articulating Derrida's philosophic project.

But Pater's service becomes more vital in analyzing the issue of aesthetic sensation and its exemplary role. Concerned with meaning and reflection, Derrida uses literary language rather than our perception of the artwork to exemplify the problems he outlines within the foundational moments of Continental philosophy. But, as with aesthetic sensation in Pater, literary language serves as a central crux of a philosophic situation; its status does not prove that philosophy is fiction or that all truth is relative to the beholder. This crux connects Derrida's project with that of de Man. As we will see in the third chapter, critics now commonly distinguish between Derrida and de Man as if the serious philosophical projects of the one were aestheticized, thus domesticated or trivialized, by the other. I will argue, however, that while Derrida brings philosophy to bear on literary language and de Man approaches philosophic issues from the problem of literary language, ultimately their work does participate in a coherent intellectual project, distinguishable from theories that have transformed it into a mere method of reading. Pater outlines that coherence for us by binding together the two concerns of philosophy and art in his aestheticism. The aestheticism Derrida and de Man share with Pater does not entail relativism, nihilism, or even an ultimate epistemological knowledge of the impossibility of knowledge. Instead, like Pater, they show how an aesthetic issue—the status of literary language—rather than being classed and defined by philosophy, works to explain problems in philosophy's ostensibly more primary discourse.

The second chapter's discussion of Pater's aesthetic connection of philosophical abstraction with historical particularity leads to two further themes that elucidate the workings of aestheticism in deconstruction's confrontation with history and ideology. First, as I have been arguing, Pater does not see aesthetics in terms of an alterity to philosophy, history, or politics, or see the connection as making those other discourses somehow less real. Instead, he construes aestheticism as a mode of historical and social interpretation. Then, because aesthetic sensation works as an embodiment of the meeting place between the philosophical and the historical, he embodies that form of sensation in his own aesthetic form: the narrative of *The Renaissance*. Following Pater's construction of aestheticism as a mode of historical understanding, in the fourth chapter I analyze Derrida's connection between philosophical generality and historicist particularity and de Man's formulation—from the topic of literary language—of a historicized rhetoric that reads both history and ideology. Accordingly, I argue that deconstruction's aestheticism, rather than escaping history into a formalist mode of reading, acts to open itself to the issues of historical causation and ideological influence. The status of narrative in Pater's argument will recur in my treatment of rhetoric in the form of de Man's essays. In contrast with the first chapter's articulation of Pater's philosophy, and discussions in the third and fourth chapters of Derrida's philosophy and historicism, in discussing Pater's and de Man's confrontations of aesthetics with history and ideology, I read their thematic conclusions back onto the form of their writing precisely because their writing demands such a deployment of reflection. In both cases, this is not solely a literary analysis but an explication of the theoretical implications through that analysis, an enactment of the book's presiding contention that aestheticism and aesthetic interpretation *are* historical analysis and ideological comment.

These four chapters outline the connections between philosophy and aestheticism, and between aestheticism and socially directed discourses such as history and ideological criticism, first in Pater, then in the deconstruction of Derrida and de Man. They also respond to the first two charges against aestheticism discussed above—its relativism and its supposedly inauthentic desire to enter a discourse free from historical and political concerns. Both these charges pertain to the content of the theories common to Pater and deconstruction, and so the response to them in terms of an analysis of that content forms the central task of this book. But there is a final charge, that of political quietism, which I respond to in my fifth chapter's discussion of the political implications of aestheticism. I have claimed here, and I will argue in the rest of this book, that the critics of Pater and of deconstruction, in claiming that aestheticism inauthentically resists the historical and political connections of art and literature, themselves assume a constitutive alterity between the aesthetic and the real, or those discourses that address and analyze the real directly. This assumption of alterity on the part of critics who are supposedly ideologically and historically attuned may seem paradoxical, but its logic is not that abstruse. When these critics discuss connections between literature, for instance, and history or ideology, they connect form as an event with historical or ideological cause; when they discuss the political or historical effects or intents of works, they do so in terms of the represented content, distinguishing among works that do intend social consequences from those that do not.[6] They never argue the political implication of aesthetic form itself, except to assume that a concern for intrinsic form must also be antagonistic to political or historical significance. My fifth chapter extends the analysis of the first four chapters by discussing the political ramifications of aestheticism as reformism and resistance to institutional structures of power. It thus addresses precisely the political significance of aesthetic form, as identified by Pater in terms of aesthetic sensation and by Derrida and de Man in terms of literary language. Once one learns to take aestheticism as inherently an interpretation of historical and ideological issues, one can start to see what kind of interpretation it will offer.

As this introduction indicates, this is a rather determinedly polemical book. Taking as its thesis an admission of a charge of aestheticism and the project of reversing the terms of that charge, and structuring itself at least partly as a response to and argument against the particulars of that charge, it certainly courts dispute as much as it attempts persuasion. To the extent that critical dispute enacts one type of the contradiction I identify as the paradoxically founding moment of both Pater's and deconstruction's aestheticism, I could hardly do other than cheerfully encourage it. And yet, readers may be somewhat surprised to find the book's polemic carried on frequently in terms of some extremely close reading of the theories involved, of their forms, of the implications of details in wording and turns of argument. I do not justify the closeness of the readings merely as rectifications of past errors in reading, though many of them do work in that way. Rather they are this book's own attempt to embody its polemical intentions in its aesthetic interpretations—not aesthetic interpretation as impressionistic commentary or fictive remarks, but as a detailed working out of conflicts within and between form and argument as its own form of argument. Thus, through a discussion of aestheticism and deconstruction, the book offers a polemical analysis of the aestheticism of deconstruction.

One

What Is Art for Art's Sake and How Could It Be Anything Else?

I ASK the question in this chapter's title neither idly nor rhetorically. Misreadings of aestheticism in Pater start with misreadings of this phrase. Only by removing it from its context can critics respond to the phrase with the accusations against aestheticism touched on in the Introduction. Thus, T. S. Eliot takes Pater's view of art to be "not wholly irresponsible for some untidy lives" and specifies that while the theory of "art for art's sake," as applied to the artist, has a certain value, "it never was and never can be valid for the spectator, reader or auditor" (Eliot, 392).[1] Pater's view could be responsible for untidy lives, of course, only if it espoused an indulgence in an art that opposed itself to "tidier" or more responsible activities or attitudes. Such an art would oppose reality and therefore encourage relativism by espousing an interest in its own unreality. But an art that actually espoused hedonism, for instance, assuming hedonism to be one of the causes of untidy lives, would actually be art for hedonism's sake. And the claim that no reader, spectator, or auditor ought to experience art for art's sake, though it espouses extra-aesthetic relevance, does so in terms of the content of particular artworks rather than in terms of art's status as a discourse or mode of perception: if artists ought to have no extra-aesthetic interests in creating their art, then an audience's other interests cannot be connected to the art itself as art; those interests will be concerned with the issues, ideas, or feelings that a specific work of art happens to reflect or represent. In fact, Eliot, not Pater, implicitly contends for a prophylactic separation of art from other forms of experience. He connects this separation with the dictum that one should attend to art only for the sake of other forms of knowledge or experience from which it has first been separated. Pater's sin, from Eliot's perspective, does not involve positing a separation that Eliot seems to take as self-evident but originates in his claim that the separation has value for its own sake, thus turning the prophylaxis into an artificial barrier.

In using the phrase "art for art's sake," however, Pater claims the centrality of art to all other forms of experience, not its separation from them. The problems with the phrase have to do with the basis of that connection. If Pater offers the "Conclusion" to *The Renaissance* as an "ethical point of view," albeit one that led Benjamin Jowett to label him a "demoralizing moralizer," why would he end his advocacy of a certain philosophical position, even a radically skeptical one, with a statement on art?[2] Or, to take the issue in reverse: what is a "Conclusion" promoting an ethical philosophy doing at the conclusion of *The Renaissance*, a work of art criticism? We may start to answer these questions, and see the distance between Pater's aestheticism and the beliefs of which he is accused, by looking at the famous last lines of the "Conclusion," and those answers will bring us to the core problem with the phrase and its importance to understanding Pater's philosophy:

> we have an interval, and then our place knows us no more. Some spend this interval in listlessness, some in high passions, the wisest in art and song. For our one chance lies in expanding that interval, in getting as many pulsations as possible into the given time.... High passions give one this quickened sense of life, ecstasy and sorrow of love, political or religious enthusiasm, or "the enthusiasm of humanity." Only be sure it is passion—that it does yield you this fruit of a quickened, multiplied consciousness. Of this wisdom, the poetic passion, the desire of beauty, the love of art for art's sake, has most; for art comes to you proposing frankly to give nothing but the highest quality to your moments as they pass, and simply for those moments' sake. (*Renaissance*, 190, 274)[3]

The paradox here is that the value of art is instrumental, but only to the extent that it cannot be perceived instrumentally. Like political and religious enthusiasm, it is good to the extent that it gives us "a quickened sense of life." But it has this instrumental value more surely than those other activities because, unlike them, it cannot be experienced instrumentally, but only for its own sake. The connection between the philosophy of the "Conclusion" and the art criticism that comprises the body of *The Renaissance* is precisely that between aestheticism and philosophy mentioned in my Introduction: the experience of art for its own sake embodies a primary value to which philosophy, either religious or political, can only refer.

This passage indicates two other elements of Pater's aesthetics and his ethics, and their connection leads to the central working of the perceptual and aesthetic theory stated in the "Conclusion" to *The Renaissance* and enacted in its art criticism. The first element relates to what Pater values about art. The second relates to Pater's attitudes toward the other discourses he finds secondary. Together, they define the real work of Pater's aestheticism as a philosophy. First, then, "art for art's sake" in the above sentences says nothing about the proper way of creating art, perceiving it, or evaluating it. It makes no separations between one kind of art and another or one kind of aesthetic experience and another. It simply describes what all art does, what all aesthetic experience is. "Art for art's sake" does not refer to the content of art but to the way in which art is experienced. And indeed, Pater has markedly catholic tastes in art; he lauds works of literature by such noticeably "unaesthetic" writers as Victor Hugo, William Thackeray, and Robert Browning.[4] He is, in fact, very rarely critical of an artist, except in some minor details. Even on the face of it, the phrase will distinguish one kind of art from another only if there could be an art not for art's sake to which good art might be opposed. In its initial use, the phrase did have such a reference, one that links it to the more traditional views of art that Pater's aestheticism redefined and absorbed. Understanding the difference between Pater's aestheticism and this earlier version will provide a clearer definition of the workings of Pater's philosophically informed theory.

One of the clearest sources of the phrase is Algernon Swinburne's *William Blake*.[5] Swinburne uses the phrase, though, in the way Eliot does: "Art for art's sake first of all, and afterwards we may suppose all the rest shall be added to her (or if not she need hardly be overmuch concerned); but from the man who falls to artistic work with a moral purpose, shall be taken away even that which he has—whatever of capacity for doing well in either way he may have at starting" (Swinburne, 91). Directing the phrase "art for art's sake" at the artist, rather than the audience, Swinburne argues that art not created merely to do good on its own grounds can do good on no other. Further, Swinburne cannot mean that the content of this art does not refer to extra-aesthetic, moral, or spiritual values. The phrase introduces an explanation of how to evaluate Blake, whose poems clearly endorse certain religious meanings that have to do with more than just art. But art for Swinburne does not refer solely to the object of perception. Just as he directs the phrase "for art's sake" at the artist's motivation, he uses the term "art" to describe a mode of perception on the part of the artist: "No one again need be misled by [Blake's] eager incursions into grounds of faith or principle; his design being merely to readjust all questions of such a kind by the light of art and law of imagination—to reduce all outlying provinces, and bring them under government of his own central empire—the 'fourfold spiritual city' of his vision" (Swinburne, 94). Swinburne essentially predicts the work of modern Blake criticism since Northrop Frye's *Fearful Symmetry* in seeing Blake's concern to be the power of the romantic imagination. That imagination, for Swinburne, constituted the aesthetic propriety of Blake's art, its quality of being for its own sake.

Following the Romantics, Swinburne essentially saw art in terms of a radically separated form of perception, one entailing imagination rather than reason. He thus differentiated art, as a discourse, from science or philosophy, in addition to distinguishing it as a mode of perception in the artist: "Poetry or art based on loyalty to science is exactly as absurd (and no more) as science guided by art or poetry. Neither in effect can coalesce with the other and retain a right to exist. Neither can or (while in its sober senses) need wish to destroy the other; but they must go on their separate ways, and in this life their ways can by no possibility cross" (Swinburne, 98). The reasons for this separation are clear enough. Evaluating art in terms of the religious, philosophic, and political ends it may have puts it in a losing competition with those discourses. At least in the case of philosophy and any claims regarding the state of the physical world, nineteenth-century science seemed to Victorians a much firmer basis for knowledge than did art or poetry. To avoid this competition, Swinburne proposed a special mode of artistic perception—imagination—and then demanded of art, for its own safety, that it stay within that mode. This version of art for art's sake, this form of aestheticism, does imagine a realm of art that is both pure and in an obvious way opposed to physical perception and the reality it registers. And it may well be the form of aestheticism endorsed by figures like Eliot and opposed by critics of Pater and deconstruction who want to delineate art's political and historical involvement. But, since Pater does not in fact distinguish proper from improper art with the phrase, it is not his version.

Later I will address in more detail the relation of art to science in Pater, Ruskin, and Arnold. Here it is enough to note that Swinburne's separation would destroy the claims in the last sentences of the "Conclusion." Pater there talks about all forms of perception and thought, and although he does not refer to science directly in the last sentences, his earlier remark—"the service of philosophy, of speculative culture, towards the human spirit, is to rouse, to startle it to a life of constant and eager observation"—would seem to include science and to evaluate its purpose in the same way. For Pater, art is a primary form of perception among all forms of perception. Since art is not merely the romantic imagination in Pater, and since it is placed amid all other forms of seeing and knowing, it can seem to be less easily justified than Swinburne's art for art's sake at the same time that Pater makes far greater claims for it. Thus perhaps the sting of the phrase in Pater. He can look as if he wants a special form of art, but then wants to measure all life by it. Pater means to sting. His view of the relationship between art and living in the world intends to challenge our categorical preconceptions. But the challenge is not in a narrow definition of art nor in some refined or exclusive mode of aesthetic perception. Pater claims that all art exalts perception, and it does so precisely because all art entails self-justifying perception, and thus concentrates on the general act of perception itself. Science, philosophy, political and religious enthusiasms are not different kinds of discourse or perception but simply kinds of perception leading to other ends; art is perception leading to perception itself.

The second element of Pater's aestheticism indicated by the closing lines of the "Conclusion" involves its relationship to the discourses he labels as secondary, particularly philosophy, religion, and politics. If "the love of art for art's sake" is not a love of one kind of art as opposed to another, neither does the goal of "a quickened, multiplied consciousness" oppose itself, as critics usually assume, to religious or political ideals in any direct way. Pater defines art as a central enactment of a perception engaged in for its own sake to respond to the foundational principles of empirical philosophy. In claiming that, stated briefly, our mortal lives are comprised entirely of our sensations, Pater simply restates more pointedly empiricism's founding of knowledge on physical perception, sensation. This founding claim of empiricism does not preclude our reaching conclusions from the evidence of our sensations about values that transcend the mere obtaining of sensation. For reasons we shall see, however, Pater refuses to allow empiricism's grounding in sensation to function as a foundation on which reliable, abstract truths, separable from those sensations, can be constructed. In effect, Pater finds the form of sensation itself too contradictory to be a firm base. Pater's art has its central value because it enacts the problematic and contradictory sensation that founds empiricism. We will see in Chapter 3 how literary language serves this central role in Derrida's analysis of the foundational reflection in Continental philosophy. Pater constructs an art that embodies rather than opposes philosophy and science; by embodying the contradiction within its founding moment, this theory begins Pater's expansive aestheticism.

Central to his philosophical analysis, Pater's aesthetic sensation also works to include within itself, rather than to expel, other forms of knowledge and the discourses to which they lead. Pater's sensation would be describable as "intense self-stimulation through visual perception, for the moment's sake" (DeLaura, 226) only if he were seeking one kind of sensation rather than another. Religious or political enthusiasms, however, are also forms of experience, forms of sensation, and cannot be excluded from the sensations Pater finds valuable. Nor could any other experience or sensation. Moreover, to the extent that religion and politics become passions, we have no reason to want to exclude them, since passions yield a quickened sense of life. Only to the extent that they themselves either exclude or distract would we want to avoid them: "the theory or idea or system which requires of us the sacrifice of any part of this experience, in consideration of some interest into which we cannot enter, or some abstract morality we have not identified with ourselves, or of what is only conventional, has no real claim upon us" (*Renaissance*, 189, 274). In short, having acts of perception, experience, or sensation as a goal does not allow us to exclude some kinds of perceptions, experiences, or sensations in favor of others.[6] No doubt, from a religious or political perspective, the experience of religious or political enthusiasm as its own end is false to the goals of religion or politics. But one cannot discriminate between the kinds of experiences themselves on this basis. Thus, Pater justifies abstract thought, philosophy, politics, or religion on the basis of the sensations they offer. In precisely this way, he intends his values to include all others. He wants to reduce reality to its component parts, base an ethic purely on the result of that reduction, and then claim that everything real in any other ethic must therefore exist within his own.

In short, Pater values art for art's sake as an embodiment, in its own self-sufficiency, of the paradoxical sensation founding empiricism. He does not deny value to other discourses but rather includes their values within his own analysis of the paradox. Thus, far from showing everything to be relative by claiming an unreal art as the only value, Pater's aestheticism builds an analysis of empirical philosophy from an aesthetic perception. To show how this process of building works, this chapter will first analyze Pater's discussion of sensation as the basis of knowledge in the "Conclusion" to *The Renaissance* and show how that discussion places art at the center of sensation. Then, discussing his absorption of Ruskin and Arnold, I will show how Pater's philosophic aestheticism included the positions it seemingly undercut. In this process, I will introduce a set of categories—the analysis of foundational philosophy, the relevance to that analysis of a reflexive aesthetic perception, and the consequent and contradictory goal of complete inclusiveness—that will operate centrally as well in the book's subsequent discussion of deconstruction.

II

Asserting the centrality of aesthetic perception, however, does not explain it. If perception in itself is the primary value, we would have no particular reason to prefer art's noninstrumental perception over any other kind. After all, if any sensation, any pulsation, has value, even if aesthetic experience were a model for a form of perception that knew itself as intrinsically valuable, that self-knowledge would not by itself create any higher value. Nor ought it to be able, more than other experiences, to give us a "quickened sense of life, ecstasy and sorrow of love," since these are not qualities linked in any clear way with the essence of aesthetic experience. A contemporary of Pater's, S. R. Brooke, who did not accuse him of being a hedonist, rather pointedly wondered why he was not one: "To sit in one's study all [day] and contemplate the beautiful is not a useful even if it is an agreeable occupation, but if it were both useful and agreeable, it could hardly be worth while to spend so much trouble upon what may at any time be wrested from you. If a future existence is to be disbelieved, the motto 'Let us eat and drink for to-morrow we die,' is infinitely preferable" (Monsman, *Walter Pater*, 30). This passage typifies the confusion over Pater's aesthetics and his ethics. A carpe diem philosophy does indeed follow more naturally from the claim that this life is all there is and we should enjoy it than does an intense interest in art. But, as we have seen, Pater wants to expand the interval of our existence by multiplying pulsations and quickening our sense of life. Indulgence in mere physical sensation will not multiply our pulsations and may even deaden our sense of life; therefore, Brooke's complaint misses Pater's point. He might still ask, however, why art should achieve Pater's ends any better than the usual physical indulgences.

To determine the connection between Pater's inclusive aesthetics and his inclusive ethics, a connection the "Conclusion" and, through it, *The Renaissance* as a whole take as their project, we must look further at Pater's method of expanding the interval of existence and his idea of experience: neither the method nor the idea is entirely straightforward. Pater's method seems neither self-evident nor coincident. The word "pulsations" recalls the physiological topic of the first paragraph as well as the claim that "a counted number of pulses only is given to us of a variegated, dramatic life" (*Renaissance*, 188). But if Pater means that just as there is a physiological limit to our existence, there is a limit to our experiences, how can we get more of them? We can seek different experiences from the ones we have ordinarily, but if experiences come like pulsations, whatever we do we will have some kind of experience, just as we will always have pulsations as long as we are alive, and we will have those experiences or pulsations only as long as we are alive. We can no more get more pulsations, strictly speaking, than we can actually expand the length of the interval given us. Indeed, if we truly have a counted number of pulses, by increasing their rate of occurrence, we would only shorten our life. Moreover, having a quickened sense of life would not multiply any experiences but would merely change our relationship to them. Indeed, to the extent that the quickened sense of life applies to a stance we could take toward all experience, then in itself it is not an experience, a sensation, at all, but an abstract idea of how we should use or react to our sensations or experiences. Thus Pater's goal as applied to experience per se does not make immediate sense, but as applied to a desire to intensify experience contradicts its own project of maintaining itself on the minimalist ground of sensational reality. The contradiction, however, is not in the ends of Pater's philosophy but in empiricism's foundations. And it is a contradiction that Pater analyzes rather than one he succumbs to.

Pater defines physical perception not only as the experience of a sensation but also as a friction between sensations, a friction necessary for an experience to take shape. Here, for instance, is the sensation that opens the "Conclusion": "Let us begin with that which is without—our physical life. Fix upon it in one of its more exquisite intervals, the moment, for instance, of delicious recoil from the flood of water in summer heat" (*Renaissance*, 186). One could summarize this passage as "Pater begins with the sensation of wetness," but the inaccuracy of the summary would entail more than merely excising the exquisitely charged language. Pater fixes not upon a sensation, precisely, but upon a moment of physical life, a moment defined by recoil. In other words, the sensation of wetness itself may be further broken down into component parts—"flood of water" and "summer heat"—whose relationship, "recoil," causes the sensation. Even the recoil itself is not univalent. It is a "delicious recoil," an experience both pleasurable and painful. Thus for Pater, as indeed for most nineteenth-century empiricists, there is a necessary friction or contradiction within each unitary act of sensation.

One might argue that the poetry of the passage calls into question the exemplariness of the sensation it describes. But, in fact, the definition is firmly embedded in the empirical tradition on which Pater is basing himself. Indeed, even before Hume, Berkeley, and Locke, Hobbes offers at the beginning of *The Leviathan* this compact definition of sense: "The cause of sense is the external body or object which presses the organ proper to each sense, either immediately as in the taste and touch, or mediately as in seeing, hearing, and smelling; which pressure, by the mediation of the nerves and other strings and membranes of the body continued inward to the brain and heart, causes there a resistance or counter-pressure or endeavor of the heart to deliver itself, which endeavor, because outward, seems to be some matter without" (Hobbes, 25). Later empiricists, of course, did not all follow Hobbes's primitive physiology of resistance between inner core, brain and heart, and outer object. But the later empirical theory maintains the friction in Hobbes by making awareness of sensation depend on changes between sensations.[7] Pater's "delicious recoil" then merely embodies in a specific example a definitive aspect of sensation from which his ideas derived. The specific embodiment, however, also has the effect of stressing the necessity of friction within sensation.

This necessity explains the seeming contradiction between Pater's claim that we have a limited, counted number of pulses and his desire to enjoy as many pulsations as possible. All experiences or sensations may be equally desirable in this view, but the necessity for friction in order for sensation to occur suggests that habitual response may actually be the absence of sensation, thus the absence of perception, rather than careless perception or less intense sensation: "Failure is to form habits; for habit is relative to a stereotyped world; meantime it is only the roughness of the eye that makes any two persons, things, situations, seem alike" (*Renaissance*, 189, 273-274). When the roughness of the eye smooths the roughness of the world, blindness inevitably results. Thus habit can be called failure in life (the phrase immediately follows Pater's example of "success in life"), since it halts life to the extent that life is synonymous with mere sensation. If sensation depends upon difference, though, difference also leads to an inability to hold onto sensation. The sentence that immediately precedes Pater's "delicious recoil" asserts that "to regard all things and principles of things as inconstant modes of fashions has more and more become the tendency of modern thought" (*Renaissance*, 186). Pater then immediately dissipates the moment of intense pleasure that follows into various physical forces outside and within the body that change constantly, carrying away the sensation as soon as it arrives. In effect, any given sensation depends on simultaneous, multiple, conflicting sensations. But that conflict then disperses the first sensation across the space created by the difference between sensations that first gave rise to it.

Thus the difficulties in Pater's goals of getting as many pulsations as possible and of achieving a quickened sense of life arise from his empiricist definition of sensation and flux, coupled with a desire to hold onto life by abstracting sensation from that flux. To deny the flux would deny the source of sensation and life within friction. To accept it is to drown in it. From one standpoint, Pater wants to open himself to that flux, to experience "the greatest number of vital forces," because more forces create more friction which creates more sensations, more pulsations. But he also wants to stand apart from those forces, to stand at their focus, because within them is the flux that dissipates life. This contradictory desire explains the dispute between those who stress Pater's empiricism and those who stress his idealism, his sources in Hegel.[8] Pater defines his world in the empirical terms of flux, seeing those who do not accept flux and relativity as blind to "the tendency of modern thought." Yet he also clearly wants to define a position from which to savour sensation, one that accepts friction but that is not caught up within it, a position that transcends sensation. Accordingly, Pater wants a form of sensation that is also an act of sensation, a form that allows a position from which to observe flux and yet may still be quickened, vitalized by that flux—since nothing else will quicken or vitalize.

In desiring an ideal form within sensation, Pater does not contradict empiricism. Rather, he responds to the problem within the empirical definition of sensation. If sensation depends upon change, it depends for its existence, at least momentarily, on its own absence. Empirical philosophy starts with physical sensation because it attempts to posit as little as possible in its founding moment. It eschews all innate ideas, all necessary forms of thought, trying to build all knowledge up from the incremental addition of one irreducible, undeniably real sensation to another.[9] And, yet, that irreducible minimum to reality, it turns out, depends for its identity upon its own absence, not merely as a logical possibility, but as a constant and actual occurrence. If sensations did not constantly leave us, we would never be aware of them. But we are in danger of being aware only of their departure. Pater's desire both to observe flux as an abstract necessity and to experience it reproduces explicitly the implicit contradiction in empiricism's founding definitions. At this point, one might be tempted to find a stable point in the self that has sensations and that perceives flux. Traditional empiricism builds the self from its experiences rather than the reverse.[10] And Pater continues to follow empiricism in its skeptical view of a stable self. But in a reflection upon self-dissolution, he finally identifies a genuinely irreducible sensation, one that is nevertheless constituted by the very contradictions that make sensation such an unstable foundation in empiricism. At once a stabilizing form of sensation and an actual and self-contradictory sensation, this articulation imbeds a necessary abstraction within a primary physical sensation of self. With this sensation that is also an abstract form, Pater marks the necessary and contradictory idealism within empiricism. And this leads him to posit a self-validating aesthetic perception, in its own contradictory reflexiveness, as central.

So, following empiricism and having broken up the world into a series of discrete elements and forces, all in constant flux, Pater turns to the "inward world of thought" to enact the same dismantling. At first, however, he does not dismantle the self but locks us within its walls:

> And if we continue to dwell on this world, not of objects in the solidity with which language invests them, but of impressions, unstable, flickering, inconsistent, which burn and are extinguished with our consciousness of them, it contracts still further: the whole scope of observation is dwarfed to the nar-

> row chamber of the individual mind. Experience, already reduced to a swarm of impressions, is ringed round for each one of us by that thick wall of personality through which no real voice has ever pierced on its way to us, or from us to that which we can only conjecture to be without. (*Renaissance*, 187, 273)

This passage has become something of a critical battleground recently, and since the battle concerns issues of vital relevance to Pater, it will help to approach the passage by working our way back through the criticism. One school finds the solipsism in this passage entirely characteristic of Pater and the mark of his distinctiveness as a critic. Seen in the context of J. S. Mill's empiricism, Pater's solipsism seems to agree entirely with Mill's belief in what one critic describes as "the relativity of knowledge."[11] But, more recently, critics have wondered how this solipsism can coexist with the firmly asserted empirical vision of the external world in the first paragraph. If no real voice ever reaches us, how can we know that the outer world is in flux? Moreover, what in empiricism allows the division between outer and inner here? And can solipsism ultimately even coexist with the deindividuating view of the self implicit in empiricism's definition of it as a bundle of sensations?[12]

The answer to these questions comes with the continuation of Pater's description of the self and the realization that the wall of personality has no more solidity than the sensations from which it seemingly walls us away. To be a relativist or a solipsist, one needs, paradoxically, to believe in an absolute and objective—if internal—self. In the same way, those who believe art to be a discourse defined by its separateness from reality and also preferable to it need, paradoxically, to believe in the solidity and reality of the art they think they oppose to reality. But Pater is neither solipsist nor relativist, aesthetic or philosophical. He proposes a resting place within the self, but he shows as little belief in it as does the empiricism he both inherits and analyzes. Having retreated behind the wall of the personality, he proceeds to crumble that wall:

> Analysis goes a step farther still, and tells us that those impressions of the individual to which, for each one of us, experience dwindles down, are in perpetual flight; that each of them is limited by time, and that as time is infinitely divisible; each of them is infinitely divisible also; all that is actual in it being a single moment, gone while we try to apprehend it, of which it may ever be more truly said that it has ceased to be than that it is. To such a tremulous wisp constantly re-forming itself on the stream, to a single sharp impression, with a sense in it, a relic more or less fleeting, of such moments gone by, what is real in our life fines itself down. (*Renaissance*, 188, 273)

The wall of the personality is itself an impression, one of "those impressions of the individual." Pater's revision in 1888 of "individual" into "individual mind" makes his point even more clearly. Far from being a retreat, the mind, like a sensation of the physical world, immediately becomes subject to dispersal into flux, so that each of its experiences or impressions divides into moments, one different from the other, none stable or even fully apprehensible. Thus flux enters everywhere, even within the personality, and what is real in our life has been fined down to wisps, moments that leave as soon as we notice them. At first, change, contrast, friction, created the possibility of sensation and its intense pleasure. But now, as one looks at sensation, that difference between two moments causes it to disappear. Nor will Pater stop flux anywhere. His analysis starts with the world and ends with our awareness of self slipping through our fingers. His empiricism follows neither Berkeley's solipsism nor Mill's objectification of sensation. It rests completely on the spaces of difference and contrast between and within sensations.

Thus Pater fines life down to a moment of awareness that sees itself only as it passes. The awareness of the contrast within sensation threatens to lose itself in awareness only of empty spaces, thus turning to no awareness at all. At this point, Pater ends his analysis with an image of arresting sharpness: "It is with the movement, the passage and dissolution of impressions, images, sensations, that analysis leaves off—that continual vanishing away, that strange, perpetual, weaving and unweaving of ourselves" (*Renaissance*, 188, 273). Most empiricists accept the dissolution of the self into discrete sensations only because it seems a necessary consequence of their theory. Pater, however, at the end of analysis, seems to experience that dissolution as itself a lush sensation. The "strange, perpetual, weaving and unweaving of ourselves" entices almost as much, in Pater's exotic description, as does that first sensation, the "delicious recoil from the flood of water in summer heat." Philosophically, of course, this sensation of self-dissolution has no special status. If all sensations pass momentarily, this one will be no less fleeting. But analysis leaves off here, Pater states, perhaps because it has started to repeat itself. An analysis of dissolution creates a sensation of dissolution. That sensation may lead to further analysis, but as the analysis dissolves, it will just become a sensation again. In effect, Pater has combined both analysis and sensation. In this sensation of dissolution, then, Pater also has a sensation of pure contrast that cannot be dissolved without repeating itself. Here then is a sensation of flux that can be held onto, dwelt on, intensified without its own flux being denied. It is an arrival at the abstract form of sensation in contrast that is also itself a sensation.

A loss of self figures frequently in contemporary criticism as the ultimate abyss before which we must totter in speechless terror, and this sensation of the self unweaving is indeed central to the workings of the philosophic aestheticism in Pater that I will argue also operates in deconstruction.[13] But the melodramas that deconstructive readings of Pater create around this moment elide rather than illuminate Pater's relevance. First, since self-reflection is not a foundational moment in empiricism as it is in Continental philosophy after Kant, since it is always secondary to sensation, a sense of self-loss, personally unsettling as it might be, simply would not create the philosophic unsettling that, as we will see later on, it does in Derrida's analysis of phenomenology. And, as we see, the concept's strangeness as a sensation pleases Pater more than he fears its creating some abyss of thought. Following empiricism, Pater finds an instability in individual sensations far more unsettling in its implications than an instability in a self that would always be reducible to its sensations in any case. Because of duality in the foundational moment it creates, this moment matters both in analyzing Pater and as a model for my subsequent analysis of deconstruction. And that duality rests squarely on the pleasure Pater finds in watching himself dissolve. In that pleasurable sensation that arises from skeptical analysis, Pater creates a founding sensation for empiricism that that philosophy can neither accommodate nor expel. And this sensation carries within itself the necessity for reflection and analysis that empiricism always classes as secondary. We will later see Derrida, from an opposite direction, delineate the existence in phenomenology of contradictory empirical possibilities within its founding moments of ostensibly pure reflection. From opposite directions, both Pater and Derrida perform the same analysis, each finding the contradictions within foundational moments. They place within foundations precisely what those foundations must exclude in order to maintain a theoretical consistency. The result is hardly the total exclusion of nihilism. It is rather an opening for the working of realizations in those philosophies that their contradictory foundations compel them to exclude. Here, Pater opens empiricism to its dependence on abstract reflection, even as he depicts abstract reflection as itself a sensation.

This description of a contradictory founding sensation also helps explain Pater's claim for art's centrality. As we have seen, art plays a central role in giving us a quickened, multiplied consciousness because it elicits perception for the sake of perception rather than subordinating it to some ultimate conclusion. Having worked through a definition of perception and sensation as based on contrast and friction, we have arrived here at an essential sensation of self-dissolution that embodies the form of sensation as friction or contrast. The problem with this sensation of self-dissolution, though, is not that it is too terrifying to behold—Pater gives us numerous images through which to behold it—but that if we dwelt on it constantly, we would be locked in a sameness as dulling as any habit. As a moment of unweaving, self-dissolution has all the "delicious" shock of recoiling from a flood of water. As an abstract philosophic point, however, like any sensation constantly repeated, it loses its force.

I opened this section by asking why art, as a reflexive perception of perception, a noninstrumental perception, has any particular status that would lead us to prefer it to nonreflexive, instrumental perceptions. We can now answer that question in terms of Pater's founding sensation of a reflexive awareness of self-dissolution. In order for that sensation to embody the contrast or friction that all sensations need, Pater had to create as primary the empirically secondary act of self-reflection while maintaining that reflection's secondariness by showing it dissolve into prior sensations. These logical contradictions vex philosophy's foundational ambitions, but they cement Pater's view of aesthetic perception. Aesthetic reflexiveness assumes its primary value because it re-creates the reflexiveness of the paradoxical, founding sensation. At the same time, aesthetic sensations are even less categorizable than their philosophic model; they exist only in reaction to particular artworks. Any abstract definition of beauty, Pater insists in his "Preface" to *The Renaissance*, deceives by removing us from the very perceptions that created the beauty: "the definition of [beauty] becomes unmeaning and useless in proportion to its abstractness. To define beauty, not in the most abstract but in the most concrete terms possible, not to find a universal formula for it, but the formula which expresses most adequately this or that special manifestation of it, is the aim of the true student of aesthetics" (*Renaissance*, xix, 208). Art, then, creates a continual series of different sensations, each of which in its own immediate, noninstrumental value enacts a different version of the self-contradictory, foundational, dissolving self-reflection.

Pater's "Preface" offers the description of aesthetic criticism that corresponds to the central role in his philosophy of aesthetic perception. We should see that opening discussion of criticism in the context of his reworked empirical epistemology rather than trying to extrapolate from it directions for engaging in a proper practical criticism of art. We can thereby understand Pater's aestheticism as embodied epistemology rather than as an attempt to replace philosophy with relativist, impressionistic art or an artificial unity that imposes a fictive order upon a chaotic universe, the goals critics frequently ascribe to aestheticism. To distinguish Pater from relativist impressionism, we may start with the statement that seems most clearly to assert that relativism: "'To see the object as in itself it really is,' has been justly said to be the aim of all true criticism whatever; and in aesthetic criticism the first step towards seeing one's object as it really is, is to know one's own impression as it really is, to discriminate it, to realise it distinctly" (*Renaissance*, xix). By shifting Arnold's famous dictum from the object to our impressions, Pater seems at first to turn Arnold's cultural object inward toward subjective impressionism.[14] In fact, though, this reference does not quite oppose subjectivism to Arnold's objectivism. In the first place, to know one's impression as it really is would be as objective a task as to know the object as it really is. Knowledge of an impression can be just as objective as knowledge of an external artwork. Pater turns our attention to our own impressions—here of beauty specifically—precisely as he does in the "Conclusion," because our impressions ground our knowledge of reality.

Aesthetic perception, we have seen, has as its epistemological purpose the capturing of sensation within a form that allows one to sense the act of sensation. Accordingly, aesthetic criticism reacts to the art object only insofar as that object evokes those perceptions. The reporting and interpretation of those perceptions become primary, not because they lead to impressionistic pleasure, but because they are the *raison d'être* of art. If one tried to extrapolate a method of art criticism from Pater's discussion, no doubt it would contrast with Arnold's method because it stresses subjective impression. That stress would lead to relativism, since one impression would be as good as another as long as both were impressions of an artwork. But Pater does not concern himself primarily with particular impressions of artworks as a matter of theory; he criticizes artworks, but he does not offer a theory of how to criticize them. He focuses on the status of impressions resulting from artworks in general. And those impressions, in accord with their role in Pater's epistemology, have a special solidity. When we turn to our impressions of artworks, we do not find that they evaporate before us as do our impressions of impressions and our impressions of ourselves. Instead they become self-justifying: "he who experiences these impressions strongly, and drives directly at the discrimination and analysis of them, need not trouble himself with the abstract question of what beauty is in itself, or its exact relation to truth or experience" (*Renaissance*, xx, 208). When we turn to impressions of artworks at least, we can analyze them and discriminate among them, since they do not dissolve but partake of the stability that reflexive perceptions achieve by recognizing their own fluctuation. Art for art's sake means, finally, the aesthetic perception of perception; art criticism is an activity leading to that perception, not an objective of it.

The special solidity of aesthetic perception, however, its ability to grasp a form of sensation, arises, as we have seen, because it recognizes how contrast both creates and dissolves that form. Pater's aestheticism cannot impose an order on a chaotic reality, either an ideal order or a fictive one, because the form it perceives is that of chaos. And this chaos is not merely one of multiple sensations; it is a chaos within each individual perception caused by the friction that first sparks sensation. Aesthetic perception has preference in Pater over the original sensation of a dissolving self precisely because of a variety that foils habit-forming stasis. That variety occurs in the contrasts Pater finds essential to the value of art: contrasts within works in terms of the opposition between an artist's genius and the untransformed mass of his work surrounding that genius (*Renaissance*, xx–xxi, 208); contrasts between artists and their time;[15] and finally contrasts between the critic and the artwork that make the perception of the artwork possible in the first place. Frequently, we think of aesthetes as seeing art in terms of an escape from the chaos of reality into a world of pure form.[16] And some aesthetes may well think of art in this way. But Pater's art, I have been arguing, was not an escape from but an intense form of engagement with reality, so the solidity of aesthetic perception never transcends its immersion in sensational friction. It may sound paradoxical or self-contradictory to insist that aesthetic perception both has a solidity that allows its objective analysis and rests entirely on the contrasts and frictions that created the evanescence of sensation in the first place. But I have been arguing that that self-contradiction makes of aesthetic perception the founding sensation of empiricism, unsettling as that foundation is. Pater's philosophy comes to rest in an art criticism because he has created an aestheticism that materially embodies the frictions he finds within empiricism's foundational moment. His analysis of foundations foreshadows Derrida's by finding necessary to empirical foundation an element—contrast as form or abstraction—that empiricism had to exclude as secondary to be coherent. Pater's placement of aesthetics as central to his analysis of foundational contradiction also predicts the importance of literary language to deconstruction and hence the common ground between Derrida and de Man. Critics who allow Derrida's philosophic import sometimes construe de Man as a literary degradation of Derrida's philosophic deconstruction, charging him with the aestheticism that either escapes reality or denies it in favor of relativism or subjectivism. The analysis here of an aestheticism that at least intends to embody and allow to emerge clearly philosophy's central definitions of reality creates a model for understanding how de Man's concern with literary language works in deconstruction and how determining a common ground between Derrida and de Man does not transmogrify the philosophy of one into the literary criticism of the other. Pater's empirically informed aestheticism and his aesthetic empiricism form an early version of that common ground.

In effect, the "Conclusion" offers a method of perception, responsive to the truths (we will see that Pater does not shy away from this concept even as he uses it to refer to his world of corrosive flux) modern thought teaches, but still promising the value of an enhanced life. In the "Preface," he foreshadows that discussion by defining aesthetic criticism as a privileged form of that perception. Between these brackets, *The Renaissance* embodies a series of examples of aesthetic criticism that, taken together, form a narrative enacting the theme laid out in the book's opening and closing. In my next chapter, I will discuss the role of that narrative in Pater's aesthetic philosophy and analyze its workings. In order to complete this analysis of Pater's design to include the fruits of other philosophies within his reduced ethic of sensation, however, I will look briefly at the end of "Winckelmann," a more expansive description of the effects of aesthetic perception, one that makes Pater's inclusive claims explicit. Then, discussing how Pater reworked, combined, and revised the most significant contemporaneous English writers who combined aesthetics and social criticism, Ruskin and Arnold, the chapter will show Pater's philosophic inclusion by reduction in action.

III

This discussion of Pater has so far followed the "Conclusion" in defining his aesthetic perception at least partially by its opposition to abstract philosophy and political and religious enthusiasms. In order to define it fully, however, Pater had to include within it the abstract philosophy it ostensibly expelled, finding it necessary to experience the form of sensation as friction in order to hold onto the ability just to perceive, just to have a sensation. Pater's inclusion of that which empirical foundation tries to expel also encompasses the claims of political and religious enthusiasms. We can see Pater extending his aesthetic perception toward the social and political in "Winckelmann," where he discusses art's cultural value. Pater here captures Arnold's Culture within his perceptual definition through an acceptance of the science Arnold rejects. Insisting, against Ruskin, on the value of the Renaissance, Pater moreover accommodates Ruskin's Gothic value of individualism as a proper communal ethic without linking that claim to a theological exclusion of the more sensual individualism in the Renaissance. Pater thus claims the sacral value Ruskin gives to art while basing it as always on empirical sensation. In effect, Arnold and Ruskin offer the kinds of supposedly extra-aesthetic values that critics frequently accuse Pater of eliminating: social efficacy in Arnold and a significance that transcends personal pleasure in Ruskin. Including science within Arnold's Culture and secular empiricism within Ruskin's theological aestheticism, Pater insists that his own aestheticism, rather than eliminating those values and retreating from the world, captures them and functions as a primary mode of understanding and operating within the world.

Pater's ending to "Winckelmann," the essay immediately preceding the "Conclusion," moves aesthetic perception toward Arnoldian Culture by making it, as well as a response evoked by artworks, a concomitant mode of perceiving and interpreting society and culture. In the "Conclusion" and the "Preface," Pater discussed the condition of perception and the special place of perceiving art adequately. In the last pages of "Winckelmann," he turns mode and object around:

> the proper instinct of self-culture cares not so much to reap all that these various forms of culture can give, as to find in them its own strength. The demand of the intellect is to feel itself alive. It must see into the laws, the operation, the intellectual reward of every divided form of culture; but only that it may measure the relation between itself and them. It struggles with those forms till its secret is won from each, and then lets each fall back into its place, in the supreme, artistic view of life. (*Renaissance*, 183, 270)

Not a proper perception of art, but an artistic view of life. The artistry of this view does not reside in a view of ideas and cultures that drains them of ethical implication, evaluating only their aesthetic form, the usual notion of aestheticism. Following an instinct of "self-culture," the intellect seeks other ideas for its own ends, but not for a mere aesthetic thrill. The mind intends to measure its own distance from different forms of culture as if that difference would automatically entail an enrichment of self-culture. This cultural meditation replicates at the intellectual level the fixing upon friction and contrast within sensation. And this intellectual act reproduces the duality of sensation by avoiding both the purely sensory as insufficient and the metaphysical as "a fancied gift of absolute or transcendental knowledge" (*Renaissance*, 183–184). Making of aesthetic perception a mode of intellectual apprehension, Pater thus expands its relevance to historical and cultural analyses.

Although this definition of a supreme, artistic view of life expands Pater's claims and clearly distinguishes his special form of perception either from hedonism or indulgence in sensation, it can still look simply like a more refined form of self-indulgence. The intellect, which can measure other cultures with the most rigorous care, does so finally only to "feel itself alive." On the last pages of the essay, though, Pater proceeds to define a service art performs for modern culture. Labeling "the sense of freedom" as the chief need of the spirit "in the face of modern life" (*Renaissance*, 184), Pater then claims that art provides this need:

> For us, necessity is . . . a magic web woven through and through us, like that magnetic system of which modern science speaks, penetrating us with a network, subtler than our subtlest nerves, yet bearing in it the central forces of the world. Can art represent men and women in these bewildering toils so as to give the spirit at least an equivalent for the sense of freedom? . . . In [Goethe's] *Wahlverwandtschaften* this entanglement, this network of law, becomes a tragic situation, in which a group of noble men and women work out a supreme *dénouement*. Who, if he foresaw all, would fret against circumstances which endow one with those great experiences? (*Renaissance*, 184–185, 271)

Pater hardly initiated the idea that humanity, when confronted by the concept of necessity, needs to feel itself free. Forty years before the appearance of *The Renaissance*, Carlyle had found history's primary value in its portrait of the perpetual struggle between free will and material necessity, an idea he drew no doubt from Goethe and German Romanticism (*Works*, 18: 44–45). And, as we will see in a moment, Arnold claimed for Culture a similar "deliverance." To the extent that his art provides that freedom, Pater responds to the need defined by socially engaged theories of art and history.

This sense of art's possibilities does not yet involve anything we might reasonably call political or social activity. Art's service remains tied to its ability to offer an artistic *view* of life. It does not offer a sense of freedom by representing men and women acting freely. Instead, it creates a vision of their "entanglement" within the "network of law" as "a tragic situation" leading to "a supreme *dénouement*." In other words, when the law of necessity takes on aesthetic form, it becomes tragic inevitability, leading to the narrative experience of *dénouement*. The sense of freedom occurs only with the reader—the viewer—who, having experienced the work, foresees all and ceases to fret against circumstances. The later revision of circumstances into "the chain of circumstances" (*Renaissance*, 185) makes clear that freedom occurs within an aesthetic view that accepts necessity, having seen it in artistic terms. That view creates freedom rather than explaining how actually to avoid the laws of necessity. The artist neither acts freely in creating nor creates a vision of freedom, precisely. Pater does not exempt artistic creation from the laws of necessity, and art does not depict freedom. Freedom exists in the view of necessity that art affords. And, finally, the friction embedded within artistic perception occurs in the concept that a vision of necessity provides freedom. In a sense, Pater enacts that freedom implicit in aesthetic transformation by imaging "the magnetic system of which modern science speaks" as "a magic web woven through and through us." As we will later learn to gaze at the weaving and unweaving of ourselves with a curious fascination, we here learn to see with equanimity the magic web woven within us. From the conceptualization of the friction or contrast that allows sensation comes first aesthetic sensation, then the supreme artistic view of life, and ultimately the sense of freedom that serves modern culture. Even with these expanded claims for aesthetic perception, then, Pater's artistic deliverance still seems a very subjective affair. We oppose as purely subjective the sensational apprehension of freedom to social or political activity, however, only by presuming that those activities must be something in addition to sensation or experience. But Pater wants to challenge the contention that something transcends or supersedes mere sensation. His challenge, however, rests on his ability to include what we perceive as vital in philosophies to which we might turn as salutary examples of an alternative to Pater. By encompassing the cultural and political effects of Arnold and Ruskin, in particular, Pater claims an artistic view as a social act.

We see Pater's reading of Arnold in pervasive references to him in "Winckelmann."[17] Pater and Arnold share a belief that culture affords a principle of liberation. Arnold makes that claim in "On the Modern Element in Literature," a lecture he delivered in 1857 but did not publish until 1869. Pater did not come up to Oxford until 1858, and he first published "Winckelmann" in the *Westminster Review* in 1867. A direct link between the two essays is thus unlikely. After Pater arrived at Oxford, however, a few months after Arnold gave that first lecture, he followed the rest of the lectures on modern literature (an uncompleted and unpublished series) and began to read Arnold closely (Levey, 67–68). The echo of "On the Modern Element" in "Winckelmann" may thus be a matter of elective affinity. It is, in any case, a good place to start a discussion of Pater's revisions of Arnold. In that lecture, Arnold argues that "an intellectual deliverance is the peculiar demand of those ages which are called modern," and that "in the enjoyment of both [intellectual and moral deliverance] united consists man's true freedom" (Arnold, 1: 19). He then proceeds to identify the cause of the demand for intellectual deliverance and the content of that deliverance:

> The demand arises, because our present age has around it a copious and complex present, and behind it a copious and complex past; it arises, because the present age exhibits to the individual man who contemplates it the spectacle of a vast multitude of facts awaiting and inviting his comprehension. The deliverance consists in man's comprehension of this present and past. It begins when our mind begins to enter into possession of the general ideas

> which are the law of this vast multitude of facts. It is perfect when we have acquired that harmonious acquiescence of mind which we feel in contemplating a grand spectacle that is intelligible to us. (Arnold, 1: 20)

Although the issues of freedom and necessity do not figure here, the idea of a viewpoint that liberates or "delivers" merely by the spectacle it affords foreshadows closely Pater's claim that the vision of necessity afforded by a work of art liberates by the perspective it gives us. Although Pater finds his liberation in literature and Arnold in a more generalized spectacle, it cannot really be said that Pater's liberation has any less social extension or that Arnold's spectacle exists any less within the individual mind that comprehends. Why then is Pater often pictured as an etiolated Arnold, narrowing Arnold's Culture down to refined sensations available to a hypersensitive elite?[18]

From one perspective, at least, the picture has an element of truth. Arnold can maintain the social relevance of his cultural view because of his crucial insistence on the idea of a best self. Eliminating any such idea from his aestheticism, Pater's version of Arnoldian Culture may at first look more subjectivist than Arnold's because Arnold's concept makes his liberating cultural view more than a subjective impression: "By our everyday selves ... we are separate, personal, at war.... But by our *best self* we are united, impersonal, at harmony" (Arnold, 5: 134). In other words, Arnold proposes a self, an element of our psyche, which we nevertheless share with all other human beings. Every individual will naturally share in the perceptions afforded by the best self of each individual. This concept is vital to *Culture and Anarchy*. Since Culture is a way of seeing or meditating upon society rather than a system for acting, its value cannot be measured by the efficacy of actions it espouses. For the way of seeing not to reduce to merely individual impression, it must be tied to some element beyond subjective perception: the best self. But Pater begins by limiting us to subjective impression, to our individual sensations, to one's own impression of the object before the generalized seeing of the object as it really is. Pater's elimination of Arnold's best self may justify itself by the absence of any foundation for that concept within Arnold's argument, but it also seems to reduce fatally the relevance and appeal of Arnold's Culture. Doesn't a culture without a general base become just a refined sensation?

Pater's elimination of Arnold's foundational best self, and his consequent insistence that general culture rests on individual and differentiated sensation, may skew our reading of "Winckelmann" away from its broader claims and toward those moments that seem to stress sensation exclusively. Pater seems to narrow Arnold, however, only if we do not attend to the differing ground to his theory, its absolute openness to what both critics take to be the truths of modern science and empirical philosophy. Arnold bases his claims for literature, poetry, and Culture, his sense that they will replace religion, on a discursive difference between these fields and science, thus following Swinburne and, more directly, the Romantics to whom Swinburne was heir. Thus his famous prediction for the future of poetry rests on poetry's detachment from fact:

> The future of poetry is immense, because in poetry, where it is worthy of its high destinies, our race, as time goes on, will find an ever surer and surer stay. There is not a creed which is not shaken, not an accredited dogma which is not shown to be questionable, not a received tradition which does not threaten to dissolve. Our religion has materialised itself in the fact, in the supposed fact; it has attached its emotion to the fact, and now the fact is failing it. But for poetry the idea is everything. . . . Poetry attaches its emotion to the idea; the idea *is* the fact. (Arnold, 9: 161)

Religion has faltered because science has shown the historic facts on which it grounds its faith to be untrue, "the fact is failing it." Poetry cannot be shaken by science in the same way because it grounds itself on the idea, rather than the fact. Arnold does not define "the idea," but his essay "Literature and Science" makes it clear that it appeals to a human need that is independent of knowledge.

In that essay, Arnold argues that literature ought to be included in education because it responds to human need even though, unlike science, it does not teach knowledge of the world: "Following our instinct for intellect and knowledge, we acquire pieces of knowledge; and presently, in the generality of men, there arises the desire to relate these pieces of knowledge to our sense for conduct, to our sense for beauty,—and there is weariness and dissatisfaction if the desire is baulked. Now in this desire lies, I think, the strength of that hold which letters have upon us" (Arnold, 10: 62). By locating the importance of letters in their ability to connect our knowledge with our senses for conduct and beauty, Arnold suggests that letters matter because they interpret scientific knowledge so that it becomes responsive to human need. His example of how literature makes the connection, however, shows that the relationship is not a close one: "under the shock of hearing from modern science that 'the world is not subordinated to man's use, and that man is not the cynosure of things terrestrial,' I could, for my own part, desire no better comfort than Homer's line . . . 'for an enduring heart have the destinies appointed to the children of men'!" (Arnold, 10: 68). Accepting the evaluative conclusions of Huxley that he quotes as scientific knowledge, Arnold offers a line from Homer as an interpretive response. But that line has noticeably little to do with the particular scientific evaluation it follows. Homer's comfort would apply to any negative conclusion and does not apply in any specific way to Huxley's remark. It has the power, though, of that poetic quality that Arnold never defines but always thinks self-evident in the touchstones he offers.[19] For Arnold, science threatens us with a depiction of a barren, merely physical world, and poetry braces and consoles as it has always done. His connections of science with beauty and conduct are not therefore specific interpretations of science but turnings away from it to statements about beauty and morality whose persuasive strength resides in that undefinable but self-evident quality that makes them great poetry, that makes them touchstones.

Pater learns from science much the same lesson that Arnold does. But the relationship he draws between literature, the arts, and aesthetic experience, on the one hand, and the truths of science, on the other, differs entirely. We have seen that Pater wants to ground his ethics and aesthetics on a description of basic perception. The "Conclusion" breaks down the solidity of those perceptions to a core beyond which "analysis leaves off." The original opening paragraph to the "Conclusion" marked a transition from Pater's interpretation of William Morris's poetry to the more general statement. That transition makes clear the relationship between the "Conclusion" and Arnold's concerns and Pater's different tack to the problem Arnold sees science raising:

> One characteristic of the pagan spirit these new poems have which is on their surface—the continual suggestion, pensive or passionate, of the shortness of life; this is contrasted with the bloom of the world and gives new seduction to it; the sense of death and the desire of beauty; the desire of beauty quickened by the sense of death. "*Arrière!*" you say, "here in a tangible form we have the defect of all poetry like this. The modern world is in possession of truths; what but a passing smile can it have for a kind of poetry which, assuming artistic beauty of form to be an end in itself, passes by those truths and the living interests which are connected with them, to spend a thousand cares in telling once more these pagan fables as if it had but to choose between a more and a less beautiful shadow?" It is a strange transition from the earthly paradise to the sad-coloured world of abstract philosophy. But let us accept the challenge; let us see what modern philosophy, when it is sincere, really does say about human life and the truth we can attain in it, and the relation of this to the desire of beauty. (*Renaissance*, 272)[20]

The paragraphs we now read as the "Conclusion" Pater originally presented as what modern philosophy, drawing from its "possession of truths," says about human life and the desire of beauty. He thus opens with a direct discussion, in his own charged language, of contemporary principles of biology and physiological science.[21] For the next three pages, as we have seen, starting from science and empirical philosophy, he does his utmost to reduce our certainties to a bare minimum. If we follow his logic, when these pages conclude with the claim that "the wisest" spend their interval "in art and song," then he can offer this conclusion as the statements modern philosophy and science actually make about human life, rather than as an escape from their knowledge. Indeed, we find that the definition of a life haunted by the nearness of death, responding to that haunting by a more intense engagement in the sensuous experience of living, applies both to Morris's poetry and to science and philosophy.

Pater's reduction of Arnoldian Culture—from that which enlightens to the interpretations of aesthetic critics who insist on knowing their own impressions as they really are before they see the object as it really is—finally does not narrow the claims of that Culture at all. We should read the last pages of "Winckelmann" not as reducing Arnoldian claims to subjective response but as basing those claims on that empty, reduced physical universe science has left, on the uncertainty from which Arnold recoiled, asserting instead notions of a "best self." Pater includes all the values of Arnoldian Culture that do not depend on Arnold's turning away from science and philosophy, that do not depend on Arnold's exclusions. Arnold's Culture may seem more relevant than Pater's aesthetics because it insists on an objective basis in a best self. But Arnold rather than Pater founds his claim on a separation between art and science, between discourses that make knowledge claims and those that appeal to subjective response. Thus some critics of deconstruction see Arnold as a positive alternative to its skepticism, while others see his acceptance of art's discursive difference as the beginning of the deconstructive problem.[22] Whatever the significance of Arnold's cultural criticism, though, it has a far more circumscribed view of art than Pater's ostensibly more narrow aestheticism. Pater's theory opens itself deliberately to scientific discourse, thus claiming a wider relevance for his artistic view, even based as it is on impression.

Pater revises Arnold in Arnold's own urbane terms. His relationship to Ruskin is grittier, more vexed, both closer and more antagonistic. On the one hand, Ruskin was the most prominent aesthetic theorist of Pater's time, and his appreciation of art's sensuous qualities was far closer to Pater's sensibility than was Arnold's essentially intellectualized evaluation. Moreover, since Ruskin, like Pater, grounded art's value on its coincidence with science and natural reality, neither critic felt the need for suppositions of a best self whose perceptions were in any way different from empirical, sensual apprehension. But Ruskin's aesthetic sensibility embraced an evangelistic desire to remold society in a constrictive moral image, and that desire was just as alien to Pater as Arnold's view of liberation through culture was congenial. Like Arnold, Ruskin had a firm sense that art has moral and political significance. To give it that significance, though, he had first to insist on the sacral quality of aesthetic perception and then also give that sacral quality a specific theological and historical meaning. He thus drew certain aesthetic and political conclusions that forced constraints and preferences, for instance his praise of the Gothic and his condemnation of the Renaissance. Sharing Arnold's view of the liberating social role of art, Pater had to capture Ruskin's sense of the implicit value of aesthetic apprehension, which was, of course, crucial to his own theory, without letting a theological extension of that value start to operate exclusively. In the terms of the "Conclusion," he would experience Ruskin's religious enthusiasm as a passion but not as a dogma.

Ruskin's position on the relationship between art and science changed over the course of his career as geology, evolution, and the Higher Critics, the "dreadful hammers," chipped away at Victorian beliefs, and Ruskin tried to find in art a ground of truth opposed to the materialistic sciences.[23] But he always insisted that art be truthful to natural reality, even, perhaps especially, in minute detail. Throughout his early writing and sporadically to the end, he argues for a necessary coincidence between art and science. Thus, a typical early statement in *Modern Painters*: "Now there is but one grand style, in the treatment of all subjects whatsoever, and that style is based on the perfect knowledge, and consists in the simple unencumbered rendering, of the specific characters of the given object, be it man, beast or flower. Every change, caricature, or abandonment of such specific character is as destructive of grandeur as it is of truth, of beauty as of propriety" (Ruskin, 3: 25). A couple of pages later, Ruskin implies the connection between this perfect knowledge and rendering of natural detail and scientific knowledge : "The great masters of Italy, almost without exception ... are in the constant habit of rendering every detail of their foregrounds with the most laborious botanical fidelity" (Ruskin, 3: 29).

The explicit ground of dispute between Ruskin and Pater emerges in Ruskin's definition of the sense of beauty in the second volume of *Modern Painters*. There Ruskin disclaims the term "aesthesis" as a proper one to describe the apprehension of the beautiful because aesthesis applies purely to sense perception and "I wholly deny that the impressions of beauty are in any way sensual; they are neither sensual nor intellectual, but moral: and for the faculty receiving them, whose difference from mere perception I shall immediately endeavor to explain, no term can be more accurate or convenient than that employed by the Greeks, 'theoretic'" (Ruskin, 4: 42). One's apprehension of beauty of course derives from a sense perception of nature, but Ruskin insists that it does not rest with that perception:

> when, instead of being scattered, interrupted or chance-distributed, [pleasures of the senses] are gathered together, and so arranged to enhance each other as by chance they could not be, there is caused by them not only a feeling of strong affection towards the object in which they exist, but a perception of purpose and adaptation of it to our desires; a perception, therefore, of the immediate operation of the Intelligence which so formed us, and so feeds us.... Now the mere animal consciousness of the pleasantness I call Aesthesis; but the exulting, reverent, and grateful perception of it I call Theoria. For this, and this only, is the full comprehension and contemplation of the Beautiful as a gift of God; a gift not necessary to our being, but added to, and elevating it, and twofold: first of the desire, and secondly of the thing desired. (Ruskin, 4: 47)

The connection between the moral and the artistic in Ruskin does not at first involve embedding ethical codes within the laws of beauty. The apprehension of beauty is moral because it entails recognizing that the sensual pleasures in nature result from an arrangement serving no instrumental purpose, existing only for the satisfaction of those pleasures, and that recognition in turn infers that the arrangement was designed solely for our benefit. This inference, since it must also be an act of gratitude for the gift, is the moral act of the theoretic perception. Valuing the scientific accuracy of painting follows as a consequence, since any distortion of a divine gift would be a misuse of it.

Pater's scorn for abstract theories of beauty in his "Preface," and his notorious remark in the "Conclusion" that "with this sense of the splendour of our experience and of its awful brevity, gathering all we are into one desperate effort to see and touch, we shall hardly have time to make theories about the things we see and touch" (*Renaissance*, 188), may well respond more directly to this distinction between aesthesis and theoria in Ruskin than to theory in general. And certainly when Ruskin reprinted this volume in 1883, he intended the distinction as a rejoinder to the aesthetic movement, as a footnote added at that date makes clear (Ruskin, 4: 35). Still, the usual critical notion that Pater revised Ruskin by draining him of his moral claims and insisting on the sensual and hedonistic side of art simplifies more than it explains.[24] First, it ignores the odd connection between the writers' positive correlation between science and art. More important, it fails to see that since Ruskin's moral lesson in nature is not an abstraction added on but an intrinsic aspect of its apprehension, indeed dependent upon a recognition of the noninstrumental, self-justifying aspect of the sense gratification within the beautiful, Pater had less to revise than it might seem at this point. Both theories argue for an acceptance of beauty for its own sake; both argue that acceptance as the basis for their ethics. In effect, Ruskin's theological language exists in the service of a powerfully secular theory. Pater's refusal to grant Ruskin's secular apprehension a theological inference, in the first instance, merely recognizes that the theology is extraneous to the aesthetics.

Ruskin's real dilemma, though, was that he combined a secular vision that remained theocratic in its social structure with an egalitarian sense that aesthetic perception was universal. The reason he evaluates aesthetic perception theologically thus becomes evident only when it manifests itself in a specific historical and social theory. Ruskin's explanation of "the Nature of Gothic" ties aesthetic evaluation directly to social ethic by taking the artistic object as the sign of its manner of production. In *Modern Painters*, art taught the morality of gratefully enjoying nature. This enjoyment opposed a degraded understanding of the world in solely instrumental terms. This position remains the foundation of Ruskin's moral view of art, repeated throughout his writing in its moments of paean to the psychological, aesthetic, and religious value of simply appreciating the sight of nature and of art. And this concept informs Pater's evaluation of the senses and the intense language he uses to discuss that evaluation. Without Arnold's concept of culture, however, Ruskin had to look elsewhere for the social value of aesthetics. By interpreting great communal works of art, a society's architecture, in terms of their mode of production, he enabled himself to connect the aesthetic object with the morality of the social situation that produced it. Gothic architecture, as opposed to earlier Greek and Egyptian and later Renaissance building, reproduced in its treatment of its workmen the values of individual enjoyment leading to a humble gratitude before the divine:

> The Greek gave to the lower workman no subject which he could not perfectly execute. The Assyrian gave him subjects which he could only execute imperfectly, but fixed a legal standard for his imperfection. The workman was, in both systems, a slave.
>
> But in the mediaeval, or especially Christian, system of ornament, this slavery is done away with altogether; Christianity having recognized, in small things as well as great, the individual value of every soul. But it not only recognizes its value; it confesses its imperfection, in only bestowing dignity upon the acknowledgment of unworthiness.... And it is, perhaps, the principal admirableness of the Gothic schools of architecture, that they

thus receive the results of the labour of inferior minds; and out of fragments full of imperfection, and betraying that imperfection in every touch, indulgently raise up a stately and unaccusable whole. (Ruskin, 10: 189-190)

Gothic architecture reproduces the aesthetic values of *Modern Painters* in its qualities of naturalism and variety (Ruskin, 10: 205-238). These qualities lead Gothic buildings to include statuary of various aspects of nature, and finally make a Gothic cathedral resemble a mountain that a landscape painter might have painted. Naturalism and variety occur in Gothic buildings because those buildings come from the hands of many different workmen, each being allowed to express his own individuality and accept his own imperfection. The acceptance of imperfection both recognizes and mimes a divine guidance that allows the imperfect variety to end in a stately whole. Thus Ruskin's artistic value of gratefully enjoying the pleasures of the senses extends itself into a picture of a society arranged as a democratic theocracy.

The inherent contradiction between learning to enjoy nature noninstrumentally and responding to that enjoyment gratefully as a divine gift, thus seeing what was first an inherently valuable gift in terms of a mediation, starts to emerge more clearly here. Ruskin's picture of society fits both a reactionary interpretation stressing theocratic control and a radical one focusing on the picture of workers in control of their own production (and, of course, Ruskin's social vision has been interpreted both ways). As against his picture of pre-Christian enslavement of the workmen to false laws of perfection and false visions of nature resulting from false religion, Ruskin's Gothic makes coherent sense. In contrast to the normal picture of the Renaissance as the time of humanism and the valuing of individuality in its human embodiment, though, Ruskin pictures an age of pride and infidelity. And here his theory runs into trouble. After all, if the primary aesthetic values of Gothicism are the naturalism and variety that result from the individuality of the workmen, then would not Renaissance humanism lead to more valuing of the individual, and more of these qualities? Ruskin argued that it would not, because Renaissance pride in human achievement led to articulating standards of perfection that general workmen could not achieve:

Men like Verrocchio and Ghiberti were not to be had every day, nor in every place; and to require from the common workman execution or knowledge like theirs, was to require him to become their copyist. Their strength was great enough to enable them to join science with invention, method with emotion, finish with fire; but in them the invention and the fire were first, while Europe saw in them only the method and the finish. This was new to the minds of men, and they pursued it to the neglect of everything else. "This," they cried, "we must have in all our work henceforward:" and they were obeyed. The lower workman secured method and finish, and lost, in exchange for them, his soul. (Ruskin, 11: 17–18)

First Ruskin divides human achievement of perfection from human individuality by aligning the first with science, method, and finish and the second with invention, emotion, and fire. Since these traits are not mutually exclusive, he must propose a historical contingency: Europe decided to have one rather than the other. Although this may well be what happened, the narrative explanation breaks the necessary connection between Christian humility and Christian individuality that founded his claim that the Gothic exemplified the standard of aesthetic form and social arrangement.

We can now see the outlines of Pater's revision of Ruskin, the way his insistence that aesthesis includes theoria and is the primary term extends back into their differing treatments of science and forward to his different historical evaluations. For Ruskin the coincidence of science and art does not come from art's role being founded on scientific and philosophic knowledge, as it does in Pater, but rather from the manifestation of scientific accuracy within artistic representation. Art, in Ruskin, must found itself upon gratitude for the gift of nature or it becomes an expression of human pride and infidelity. Art must be accurate in order to express that gratitude for the gift of perceptual pleasure. Within the pure terms of Ruskin's argument for theoria, Pater changes little but the description of what pleasure in perception entails. Once perceptual pleasure becomes truly an intrinsically valuable end, it comprehends all of Ruskin's intellectual as well as sensual apprehension without presuming divine intention. The cause of aesthetic pleasure then fades as a matter of concern, accuracy of reproduction ceases to matter, and art may found itself on scientific knowledge, rather than on religious humility and scientific accuracy of representation. Pater's revaluation of the Renaissance, then, does not, as we will see in the next chapter, involve denigrating the Gothic but including it as an aspect of the Renaissance. His revisionary interpretation rests on a more consistent appraisal than Ruskin's of Renaissance humanism. He values its rediscovery of the individual and the sensuous without worrying over theological implications.

Pater's insistence on aesthesis as including theoria reduces Ruskin, as his refusal to ground Arnold in a best self reduces him. But he no more narrows Ruskin's aesthetic, scientific, or social claims than his revision of Arnold narrowed his cultural goals. Pater's aestheticism may look narrower than Ruskin's because it refuses to credit Ruskin's moral and dogmatic messages, as it denied Arnold's extra-scientific best self. Because of Pater's revision, however, art remains an inclusive and liberating form of cultural interpretation rather than a reproduction of scientific knowledge serving a conservative politics. Again, Pater's aesthetic actually includes more rather than less here, accommodating Ruskin's intense pleasure in aesthetic apprehension and his historical interpretation of the Gothic, without allowing his theological extension to deny the values of the Renaissance. By identifying theoria with aesthesis, Pater included Ruskin's real ground without following him into the theological difficulties that, after all, caused Ruskin himself so much pain when science later betrayed him, when the art of Veronese and an unconversion experience made him reevaluate the role of the senses.

These summaries of Arnold's and Ruskin's influences on Pater and his revisions of each no doubt simplify each situation. Looking at both relationships at once, though, shows how Pater completely digested both writers, creating an amalgam that included the largest claims of each within his own distinctive aesthetics. From Ruskin, Pater drew the insistence upon art's grounding in perception and thus the continuity between art and science that forms part of the argument of the "Conclusion." But he refused to accept Ruskin's theological justification of art, a justification that was also a limitation and a problem within Ruskin's own theory. Instead he defined art's importance as a perceptual act through the terms of Arnoldian Culture. But that Culture's power depended in part on its absolute difference from science, its grounding in a transhuman psychological state labeled "the best self"—a justification as theological in its own way as was Ruskin's. Rooting that Culture in Ruskin's perceptual theory meant rethinking the relation between art and perception so that the artificed cultural achievements within the artwork—Goethe's depiction of necessity as a tragedy whose understanding frees the observer and thus gives the impression of freedom—need not reflect a reality. At the same time, Pater justified the act of aesthetic perception, the supreme artistic view of life, as the founding reality of modern science and philosophy.

This chapter began with the question "what is art for art's sake?" and has ended with the answer that it is everything Ruskin said art is, everything Arnold said Culture is, while at the same time assuming the most hesitant and even corrosively minimal limiting of the reality to physical perception that Pater could draw from science and empirical philosophy. If Pater really did mean to build so much on so little, why has he been described as a reductive theorist with a hedonist ethic and a definition of art that drains it of all value? My answer to this question must wait until my fifth chapter, which addresses the pertinence of

Pater's thought to the politics of aestheticism and deconstruction. But Pater's revisions of Arnold and Ruskin suggest that one version of the answer would be that the most inclusive philosophy is the most challenging because it questions the exclusions other arguments depend on for their foundation and breadth and therefore always faces, ironically, the accusations of exclusivity and narrowness. Pater wanted a theory that would encompass Arnoldian Culture without depending on Arnold's exclusion of science and its consequent but unfounded supposition of a best self. He wanted to encompass Ruskin's reawakening of the pure value of perception without depending on that theory's exclusion of the Renaissance and the extraneous theology Ruskin thought he needed. Unsurprisingly, those who felt the necessity of exclusion believed that by leaving the best self out, in other words by leaving science in, Pater had made art and philosophy relative and subjective; by leaving theology out, in other words by leaving the Renaissance in, he hermetically enclosed art and narrowed philosophy to hedonism.

Pater's aestheticism, by operating as a way of analyzing the philosophic foundations of empiricism, turns out to be an extensive mode of perceiving and understanding, rather than a narrow alternative to more expansive discourses or a relativist refusal to engage in more serious discourses. While the most general criticism of aestheticism, charging it with narrowness and relativism, may seem now less forceful, the more specific criticism that it ignores historical and social reality for a transhistorical stance still has a certain weight. We have seen that even in the middle of describing his aestheticism's cultural role or social value, Pater relentlessly limits his discussion to an individual perception that seems to stand outside of history and social constraint. In fact, in the body of *The Renaissance*, Pater gives his essentially epistemological description of aestheticism historicist resonances. This chapter has analyzed aestheticism's ability, through its critique of foundational contradiction, to bind empirical particularity and philosophical abstraction, thus connecting Ruskinian aesthetic perception with Arnoldian cultural deliverance; my next chapter will then extend that analysis to a discussion of how aestheticism connects the philosophic urge toward transhistorical generalization with a historicist insistence on particularity and difference between cultures, time periods, and ideologies.

Two

Studies in the Histories of *The Renaissance*

CRITICS argue that the aestheticist desire to enclose oneself in a hermetically sealed art results in a theoretically flawed attempt to define a pure, transhistorical stance that ignores rather than evades the central causative powers of history and ideology. We have seen that Pater's aestheticism, at any rate, rather than providing an escape from reality, located aesthetic perception centrally in empirical philosophy's foundational theories. But philosophy itself is an ahistorical discipline, seeking foundational truths that ground knowledge regardless of historical period. Aestheticism's openness to philosophical analysis, therefore, though it would make relativism a false charge, might connect it with philosophy's transhistorical ambitions. In this chapter, I will argue that aestheticism's skeptical analysis of philosophic foundation contrasts it with those ambitions in its acceptance of historical differences and its ability to interpret those differences and the problems they raise. This argument draws fairly abstract connections between three topics: Pater's philosophy, his historicism, and the narrative structure of *The Renaissance*. Abstract as they are, these connections also explain Pater's aestheticism as a mode of historical interpretation and the particular form that historicist aestheticism takes as the art criticism of *The Renaissance*.[1]

The connections between Pater's aesthetic philosophy and his claims to be offering historical analysis start with the dependence, discussed in the first chapter, of aesthetic perception on various contrasts within artworks. Pater's definition of sensation as absolutely individual and yet as needing friction as a formal necessity led to his defining aesthetic perception as the founding sensation because it alone embodies friction and yet constantly experiences it in different versions; every aesthetic perception contains both the form of sensation and a distinctive actual sensation, individuated by its response to a separate artwork. Artworks, themselves, take form from contrasts and, moreover, produce them as aesthetic impressions on the part of the spectator. These contrasts constitute artistic value. The logic that leads Pater to think of art in terms of history begins with his definition of artistic value as resulting from characteristics in friction, emerging to our perception in art's friction with the medium it transforms. One can find the contrasts of art in a number of places. For example, in the "Preface," we find it in a friction between aesthetic essence and formal medium. This may quickly become a friction between form and content, which, as we have seen, far more characterizes Pater's definition of aesthetic effect than do theories that stress formal unities. In order for there to be either contrast or unity between form and content, though, both have to evoke sensations, to have a sensational content, that can act as a ground of comparison. This content may be drawn from various possible places. The artist's personality, for empiricism, exists as sensations and, as reflected in the artwork, may evoke further sensations. But also the historical context may be reflected in the artist's personality, his work, or both. And it may contrast with the personality, the work, or both. A contrast between the form of a work and its content prior to its aesthetic reworking can either differentiate the work's artistic value from that aspect of the artist's personality that had to be transcended or reworked or it can identify form with artistic genius and personality entirely and differentiate it from some aspect of reflected reality that the artistic genius transformed. In either case, historical context will connect with that which is contrasted with form. The aspect of the artist's personality that contrasts with his productive genius will be some empirical, biographic aspect ultimately referable to historical context. Or, if his entire personality becomes identified with the productive genius, then the reality he transforms will have even more obvious roots in his and the work's historical context.

Thus both the separateness of each artwork and the unifying value of artistic perception come to rest on the working of historical context. In between the artist's psychology and the aesthetic object exists historical context as a background against which the two may emerge. We see this pattern in the "Preface" even in a moment in which Pater seems to deny the importance of historical context: "To [the aesthetic critic] all periods, types, schools of taste are in themselves equal. In all ages there have been some excellent workmen, and some excellent work done. The question he asks is always:—In whom did the stir, the genius, the sentiment of the period find itself? who was the receptacle of its refinement, its elevation, its taste?" (*Renaissance*, xxi, 208). Although all periods are equal here, when the aesthetic critic locates the transcendent artistic genius, he defines it in terms of the period it transcends. And it transcends its period by working upon it rather than expelling it, by including as well as refining it. Thus historical context exists to be transcended, but the transcendence into the ideal state of aesthetic genius exists only as a result of historical period. The separate essays in *The Renaissance* constantly confirm this process. They define an artist in terms of his relationship to his period and then define the artwork in terms of relationships with both the artist, whose desires, intentions, and personality it may or may not reflect, and his historical period.

In effect, history, so far, plays a largely negative role, as a context to be evaded or transcended. This is not a feature of Pater's aestheticism, however, but is common to the larger empiricist context in which his theories operate. There is, of course, a connection within nineteenth-century intellectual history between empiricism and historicism, between the concept that knowledge depends on material sensation and the slightly more generalized determination of knowledge by historical context.[2] But there is also a deep schism between the epistemological bases of empiricism and historical concern. In order to found a social program on a theory of human perception, the utilitarian empiricists of the first half of the century attempted to base social practice on universal, ahistorical truths. Macaulay attacked this stance in his critique of James Mill's *Essay on Government* and Utilitarian social theory generally: Mill and the Utilitarians, Macaulay complained, tried to found a social system upon a psychology of human need and motivation without attending to the historical realities that might force them to refine their notions of how their theories worked (Macaulay, 1: 381–495). Although J. S. Mill felt that his father never adequately answered Macaulay (*Autobiography and Literary Essays*, 165–167), his own attempt to offer a science of history in the last section of *A System of Logic* enacted the same ambition to escape historical entrapment by finding a transhistorical explanation of history. Even Macaulay, however, thought that his refusal to elide historical specificity only made him the better empiricist, because it meant he valued historical experience as a source of knowledge. If he avoided formulating general laws, he nevertheless drew lessons. Those lessons gave history its value and thereby made history, again, a context from which conclusions were drawn. Pater's use of empirical epistemology in his theory of aesthetic sensation, then, would seem to imply a desire to make that perceptual situation transhistorical, true for all human situations and a basis for judging all of them.[3] Pater resists this empiricist tendency to the same extent that he resists the straightforward empirical foundation in sensation, and for the same reason. Precisely because he will not deny the truth of sensation, and particularly the truth of its absolute specificity, he resists any empirical movement from sensations to general laws that control or explain their significance. Seeing a formal need for contrast within each sensation, he undercuts the empirical separation of a sensational datum from an abstract, general explanation that allows that philosophy to move from a specific event to a controlling law. Thus even as a negative context, the role of history can never be separated in Pater from the artistic value it creates by contrast. After all, the contrast being part of artistic value in the first place, the historical specificity producing that contrast cannot really be reduced to a secondary role as a background or cause of an event. But Pater connects historicism even more deeply with his aesthetic philosophy by applying to the subject of historical interpretation the reflexive method of aesthetic interpretation. Taking an earlier historian, Pico della Mirandola, Pater applies to his writing the interpretive practices of a more contemporaneous historicism. But he thereby produces a reflexive situation that results in aesthetic impression rather than simply historic conclusions even as it shows the implicitly ahistorical quality of those ostensibly historical conclusions. Thus both historical events and historical analysis come to play central roles in the art criticism and the epistemology of *The Renaissance*.

We can see how reflexiveness generates both historical and aesthetic complication in "Pico della Mirandola" more easily because, at first, the essay depicts the most simple of historical situations involving an artist or writer, one in which the artist reflects his age, the work reflects the artist and the age, and both exist in instructive contrast with another age. Attempting to reconcile Greek and Christian religious myth, Pico exemplifies his age for Pater. We define the Renaissance, at least at first (even if for Pater ultimately falsely), by its rediscovery of Greek art and literature, and Pico's project of reconciliation follows naturally from that discovery in a Christian age. Pater then defines Pico's method of reconciling the two religions by its distinctive difference from the modern method. Knowing that "all religions may be regarded as natural products, that ... they have common laws, and are not to be isolated from the other movements of the human mind in the periods in which they respectively prevailed," a modern historicist might then "observe that each has contributed something to the development of the religious sense, and ranging them as so many stages in the gradual education of the human mind, justify the existence of each" (*Renaissance*, 25–26). Pico, however, not having modern historicism at his disposal, reconciles through allegory, showing that beneath their surfaces Christianity and Homeric epic offer the same meanings, the Homeric epic embodying the Christian meaning in allegoric figures.

Pater's modern analysis of Pico, however, partakes of both the historicist and the allegorical method. Pater first looks at Pico's ideas entirely in their historical context:

> as a curiosity of the human mind ... allegorical interpretation of the fifteenth century has its interest. With its strange web of imagery, its quaint conceits, its unexpected combinations and subtle moralising, it is an element in the local colour of a great age. It illustrates also the faith of that age in all oracles,

its desire to hear all voices, its generous belief that nothing which had ever interested the human mind could wholly lose its vitality. It is the counterpart, though certainly the feebler counterpart, of that practical truce and reconciliation of the gods of Greece with the Christian religion, which is seen in the art of the time. (*Renaissance*, 27)

Pater understands Pico's work here as a reflection of the trends of its age. It provides an element of local color, sharing the work of great art in reseeing the gods of Greece in Christian terms. The evaluations he offers at the start of the passage are the historicist ones of curiosity and interest. These evaluations shift, though, as he defines the qualities of the age. The Renaissance faith in all oracles, desire to hear all voices, belief that nothing human loses its vitality, are attitudes that Pater shares. Indeed, they fuel historicism and its desire to let past ages speak for themselves. At that point, the Renaissance is no longer a curious interest but a model.

This duality of evaluation becomes more complex when Pater turns from the work to Pico himself because he analyzes the history of Pico's life analogically: "And it is for his share in this work, and because his own story is a sort of analogue or visible equivalent to the expression of this purpose in his writings, that something of a general interest still belongs to the name of Pico della Mirandola" (*Renaissance*, 27). Note that Pico's life does not interest Pater as a historical cause of Pico's work. His life does not reflect his work because the work expresses his mind precisely but because the events of the life symbolize the purpose of the writings. Pater thus connects Pico to his work in the same way that Pico connected Homer and Moses. The splicing together of historicist and analogical analysis in effect reproduces the duality of Pater's evaluation of Renaissance attitudes: historicism demands that one see the period in terms of its own intrinsic attitudes. But these attitudes form the basis for a historicist analysis, thus turning that analysis back toward Renaissance analogy.

Pater does not really force this conflicting method on his subject, moreover. The subject of Pico's historicism pressures his analysis into its use of conflicting method. We can of course subject any historical topic to a historically relative analysis of its contemporaneous causes and relationships that refuses to ask ahistorical questions of ultimate validity. But if modern historical critics subject Pico's historical analysis to this purely relativist analysis, they will be unable to differentiate it from their own ostensibly more advanced practice, thus giving us no particular reason to accept their conclusions. If, however, they judge Pico's practice in terms of its historical insufficiency, the judgment loses its historical quality, since it subjects both Pico's history and modern history to a transhistorical standard. And as a consequence, Pico's history loses its interest, becoming significant only for the fact of its wrongness. In addition, Pico's history partakes of a Renaissance humanism that also informs modern history. One cannot thus adequately judge Pico's context without also judging our own. And that judgment will have to stand outside our own historical context. In effect, historicism's judgment not merely of itself (the normal trap into which critics thrust historicism) but of any historical analysis immediately produces neither historical nor ahistorical analysis, but that doubled interpretation that the previous chapter identified as aesthetic.

And indeed the final judgment of Pico, conflating historical curiosity with an analogical marking of transhistorical significance, is ultimately aesthetic. Pater analyzes Pico's real interest, which he contrasts with the scholastic quality of his writing but connects with the beautiful motivation that led to those writings (*Renaissance*, 34, 217). From either a purely historical interest or a purely transhistorical judgment about validity, neither Pico's life nor his work will have much interest. But one can conflate historicist and analogical reading to find an aesthetic piquancy in the relationship between Pico's life and his work. This moment of aesthetic appreciation exists only by virtue of all the contrasting analyses and evaluations that have gone before, the explanations of the differences between historicist and allegorical analyses, and the dual view of the Renaissance that forces Pater to mix those methods in his own analysis. We understand the difference between Pico's life and his work only in those terms. But that understanding finally leads us to a completely aesthetic evaluation of the work that succeeds in a reconciliation neither Pico's allegories nor historicism foresaw. This moment contains, indeed depends upon, the various historical and methodological differentiations that surround it. It is, in fact, as much a historical remark as an aesthetic evaluation. But the moment's final status is separate from historical context, since Pater offers essentially a transhistorical estimate of Pico's work. This is Pater's idiosyncratic historicism, one designed to produce an understanding of a historical event from within that also transcends the historicist context that constructs it.

The attitude toward sensation that we saw in the first chapter thus leads to a paradoxical form uniting historical and aesthetic interpretation. Pater accepted the empirical insistence on the primacy of sensation but coupled that acceptance with an analysis of empiricism's unrecognized need to internalize formal abstraction as a universal need for friction or contrast in every individual sensation. He refused to allow empiricism to expel abstraction from sensation; but that expulsion enabled sensation to function as a grounding fact evidencing and supporting secondary but still reliable general laws. Thus Pater undercut empiricism's transhistorical urge toward abstract explanation. Equally, by insisting on the inherence of transhistorical and analogical interpretation within historical analysis, Pater kept his interpretation of Renaissance event concentrated on its absolute historical specificity. That contrast between historical specificity and transhistorical evaluation reproduced the reflexive aesthetic perception discussed earlier. Indeed the friction within the historical interpretation coincides with the friction of aesthetic interpretation, since every aesthetic interpretation, by perceiving contrast, will suppose historical context, as we have seen, and that historical context will immediately become itself an object of aesthetic interpretation. In purely abstract terms, this extension of aesthetic interpretation into a mode of historical interpretation responds to the accusation that aestheticism constructs its hermetically enclosed art as an escape from history. To show how an aesthetic interpretation functions as a form of historical analysis, however, rather than showing at an abstract level merely that Pater proposes such a functioning, we have to turn to an analysis of Pater's narrative. The narrative structure of *The Renaissance* shows in action how aesthetic perception functions as historical interpretation.

In order to connect Pater's aesthetic philosophy and his historicism with narrative structure, I want first to propose some variations on the standard terminology of narrative theory. Narrative theorists commonly distinguish between *fabula*, the basic events of a story, and *sjuzet*, the arrangement by which those basic events become a story.[4] We must further distinguish between sjuzet and theme, however, since, as a purely formal arrangement, a sjuzet need have no final significance or ideational content of any kind. Narratives may exist without explicit themes, though a theme of a narrative will obviously have a close connection with its sjuzet if the narrative is coherent. I want to reserve the term "narrative structure," which some theorists also use as a synonym for sjuzet, to correspond to the working of all three elements, fabula, sjuzet, and theme. In Pater, the fabula of *The Renaissance* will be of course the separate essays of art criticism, and the separate events within those essays. The best candidate for theme, clearly, will be the philosophy of the "Conclusion," which, according to Stein, "organizes *The Renaissance* by defining most explicitly the attitude according to which the rest of the essays should be interpreted" (Stein, 226).[5] We can immediately see the first problem with this connection in its elision of sjuzet as organization with theme as attitude. On the face of it, the attitude of the "Conclusion" does not provide any means of arranging the essays, of connecting one with another into a narrative. In fact, though, the "Conclusion" does correspond to both theme and sjuzet because its aesthetic philosophy articulates, in a different terminology, the basic problem of narrative arrangement, and its philosophy of sensation thus tells us how to construct a narrative within and among the separate essays of art criticism. Moreover, since the specific content of Pater's narrative in the essays is historical, this connection between Pater's philosophy and his narrative also extends to his historicism. To see all of these connections at work, however, we must first see the basic narrative paradox that allows the alignment of all these topics.

Peter Brooks, in his book *Reading for the Plot*, outlines the central paradox of narrative arrangement that Pater's "Conclusion" also addresses. He starts with a statement by Walter Benjamin: "If in Benjamin's thesis ... 'Death is the sanction of everything that the storyteller can tell,' it is because it is at the moment of death that life becomes *transmissible*. The translations of narrative, its slidings-across the transformatory process of its plot, its movements forward that recover markings from the past in the play of anticipation and retrospection, lead to a final situation where the claim to understanding is incorporate with the claim to transmissibility" (Peter Brooks, 28). Benjamin's thesis partakes of a familiar connection: since only from the perspective of the end of a life, death, can the life be seen whole, it follows that thematic perspective upon narrative event bears the relationship to that event that death bears to life. Thus the perspective of death leads to "the claim to understanding" (the theme). Brooks goes a step further and connects a "claim to transmissibility" with "the claim to understanding," since, after all, one can transmit only what one understands. But this makes transmission itself, the movement from event to event (sjuzet), also a consequence of death's ending. Thus narrativity proper, which resides in "connective processes," depends upon death as the end-perspective.

The concept of death as necessary end that creates the movement, the driving force of narrative, allows Brooks to bring in Freud's idea of a death-instinct, creating a further refinement: "We emerge from reading *Beyond the Pleasure Principle* with a dynamic model that structures ends (deaths, quiescence, nonnarratability) against beginnings (Eros, stimulation into tension, the desire of narrative) in a manner that necessitates the middle as detour, as struggle toward the end under the compulsion of imposed delay, as arabesque in the dilatory space of the text" (Peter Brooks, 107–108). In Benjamin, death creates the possibility of narrative. But it also spells the end of narrative. Since narrative, like a number of other things, does not occur in death, death is "nonnarratability." Freud's explanatory force here resides in its placement of a death-instinct against a pleasure-instinct, the first functioning as the necessary closure toward which narrative moves, thus articulating narrative drive and direction, the second functioning as the drive itself, the movement toward beginning, the tension and stimulation that create movement. This relationship also spells out a narrative paradox. The force moving within a narrative moves toward death. But each event within the narrative enacts a desire to delay that end, making the events of a narrative a "dilatory space." Taken to its logical conclusion, this relationship between the pleasure-instinct, which stimulates, and the event, which delays the end, involves a resistance against the forward movement, the connective process between event and event that creates narrativity. The space of the text becomes an attempt to turn from its closure, death, which creates the shape of that space as one of temporal connection moving inevitably forward to a necessary end. This resistance to an ending transforms temporal connection into the endless tension and stimulation of event.

The reason for my discussion of Brooks's theory should by now be clear. Brooks need hardly have gone to Freud for this model of narrative. Pater's intense fear of death as the motivating force behind his desire for intense sensation, indeed that fear's role in creating the intensity and tension within the language with which he describes sensation, has been noticed before.[6] And the inevitability and finality of death lead in the "Conclusion" to a desire to "expand the interval" of our existence. This desire leads to a paradox whereby an attention toward abstract principles (in narrative terms, thematic explanations) involves a turning away from sensations, the only content to life. But an indulgence in sensations leads to an immersion in the flux of sensations (in narrative terms, the forward movement, the connective processes of narrative). And that flux drives us forward without allowing us to fix on any given sensation, robbing us of awareness as it moves us toward death. This paradox creates Pater's form of sensation that is also a sensation—in the first instance, the grounding sensation of self-dissolution. In effect, the abstract formalization that both enables sensation and threatens a loss of awareness acts in Pater as the death-instinct, which is both the end of narrative and its motivating force. The Eros of stimulation and tension occurs in his fixing upon friction as the driving force between sensation and sensation within life. The paradox of narrative as a moving forward and a delaying tactic occurs in his definition of an abstract form of perception based on flux, and yet seeing it from without.

Pater's philosophy in the "Conclusion" can be read in Brooks's terms as virtually a description of narrativity and its conflicting forces. Further, his description of and espousal of a particular form of sensation now make sense as a refinement upon Brooks's theory, an espousal of a form of narrative engagement that explicitly resists the forward movement of temporal flux, through an engagement in that flux that allows us to fix on it as an atemporal form. Pater's "Conclusion" thematizes the ambivalent value of sjuzet or arrangement, which both allows fabula's events to emerge to perception and at the same time diverts our attention from them as events. In response to this ambiguity, both philosophic and narrative, the "Conclusion" outlines a definition of sensation that also instructs us how to engage in narrative event for its own sake so that the event contains the form of the arranging force, just as sensation contains flux as the form of sensation. Thus the "Conclusion" functions both as theme, in its philosophy, and as sjuzet, in its direction for organizing the events of art criticism by seeing how each contains within it the connective flux that holds all together.

Pater's "Conclusion" poses an argument that may be taken as an explanation of sjuzet and offers a justification for attending to narrative event over organizing theme. It does this by construing and experiencing theme as narrative event and by learning to see narrative event as theme. This argument occurs implicitly in Pater's discussion of philosophy and experience. In a famous passage, Pater seems, at first glance, to dismiss philosophy completely:

> Not to discriminate every moment some passionate attitude in those about us, and in the very brilliance of their gifts some tragic dividing of forces on their ways, is, on this short day of frost and sun, to sleep before evening. With this sense of the splendour of our experience and of its awful brevity, gathering all we are into one desperate effort to see and touch, we shall hardly have time to make theories about the things we see and touch. What we have to do is to be for ever curiously testing opinion and courting new impressions, never acquiescing in a facile orthodoxy, of Comte, or of Hegel, or of our own. Theories, religious or philosophical ideas, as points of view, instruments of criticism, may help us to gather up what might otherwise pass unregarded by us. *La philosophie c'est la* [sic] *microscope de la pensée*. (*Renaissance*, 189, 174)

This passage starts by again tying the importance of experiencing, of standing at the focus of forces, to the imminence of death and the threat of a loss of awareness, a simulated death in life, a "sleep before evening." Pater almost dismisses abstraction entirely as a form of early death. He then draws back slightly from this dismissal, giving abstraction the value of helping us to gain experiences we might not have had if we did not entertain it. In this sense, more than an instrument of criticism or a microscope of thought, abstraction is an instrument for experiencing, a microscope allowing us to detect a sensation that might otherwise have escaped our notice. Even this somewhat more positive evaluation of abstraction, however, reverses the normal relationship between philosophy and the experiences it sometimes appeals to as examples of its accuracy. Rather than the experience being valuable as evidence in an argument, abstract argument becomes valuable by drawing our attention to new experience as it searches to embody its position. This relationship between philosophy and experience extends fairly easily to a consideration of the relationship between theme and narrative content. In this formulation, theme becomes the organizing principle of narrative, that which allows the narrative experience by raising mere event (an element of fabula) to narrative attention (as an event within a sjuzet, which we can focus on as a result of the meaning-creating potential of theme).

Critics have frequently faulted Pater's position. First of all, to the extent that a philosophy's ability to act as an instrument of refined perception takes precedence over its particular content, Pater seems to relegate philosophic thinking to lesser minds, the results of which he will sometimes find useful (see Eliot, 388). Moreover, surely the "Conclusion" is nothing if not a theory about the things we see and touch (as Meisel, 115, claims). But this misses some of the shadings of meaning in the passage. The argument for philosophy's subordination takes on a slightly different color when we notice here the examples of philosophers whose facile orthodoxy we should avoid. Pater had sympathy for Comte's "Religion of Humanity," since it bore some resemblance to the humanism he admired in figures *The Renaissance* addresses (Hill, *Renaissance*, 457), though he was certainly far from an acolyte. And he used Hegel extensively, as we will see, in his essay on Winckelmann, citing him profusely in the essay's first journal appearance, and still with some frequency in the first edition of *The Renaissance*. Although he uses Hegel in a distinctly idiosyncratic way, one that exemplifies his use of philosophy for narrative ends, he still refers to him with marked respect.[7] In other words, if he distances himself here from the very philosophies he respects and finds amenable, at the same time he must be finding their subordinate position more than negligible.

We have already seen in the analysis of the previous chapter the resolution to the seeming contradiction between Pater's manifest fascination with philosophy—often precisely with theories of seeing and with Hegelian absolutes—and his suspicion of it. The danger of philosophy lies in its tendency to abstract us from sensation and the demand abstract propositions make that, in assenting to one, we refuse to entertain some other idea or even experience (and the thinking of any idea is for Pater an experience). On the other hand, philosophy has the ability to create the friction that ordains sensation by providing the service to the human spirit of rousing and startling it "to a life of constant and eager observation" (*Renaissance*, 188). We need the presence of philosophy in order to keep from losing ourselves in the flux of sensation. We need to entertain its abstractions as sensations and to employ the abstractions to enable sensations, however, without allowing exclusiveness and ideality to occlude sensation. Thus, if the service of theme, like the service of philosophy, is to startle us to the awareness of narrative event, narrative event needs theme (functioning as the arrangement of sjuzet) in just the way that sensation needs philosophy. From this perspective, the importance of narrative event lies in its ability to enact experientially the philosophy, its theme, that is its reason for being, even as the importance of philosophy is (merely) to allow experience, narrative event. As philosophy provides the first version of the form of sensation that is also a sensation, narrative event provides, along with the aesthetic experience it recounts, the experience of philosophy that is the only meaningful form of philosophy.

Within the narrative structure of *The Renaissance*, having identified the discrete acts of art criticism and historical commentary as a seemingly unnarrativized fabula, I have argued that the philosophy of the "Conclusion" functions as the narrative's theme and that that philosophy's dual definition of flux as both necessary to event and destructive of it describes the ambiguous role of narrative arrangement. Here one might object that the philosophic difficulty inherent in the concept of sjuzet is not in itself a sjuzet. But the "Conclusion," identifying an awareness of flux as a dissolution of sensation with an awareness of flux as form, also identifies the conceptual difficulty of sjuzet, as a category of narrative, with its formal functioning. Both a philosophy and an organizing principle, both a theme and a sjuzet, the "Conclusion" thus holds the events of *The Renaissance* together in a narrative structure. The identification of philosophical abstraction with the form of flux, of a narrative's theme with the formal process of narrative arrangement, thus gives further extension to the identification within the "Conclusion" of philosophy with sensation. Showing us how to perceive philosophical abstraction as sensation, thus capturing its formalizing abilities within discrete sensational events, the "Conclusion" also shows us how to capture each of its essays, and the separate moments in those essays, within a sjuzet by showing us how to see each event as containing within it philosophical abstraction and the flux that that abstraction transforms into a narrative arrangement. But, at this level, sjuzet, theme, and structure may still seem too abstracted from the content of the art criticism to connect the essays meaningfully. Here, however, the extension of Pater's aestheticism into a paradoxical historicism gives the narrative its final shape. We have seen how Pater's aesthetic philosophy demands the interpretation of historic specificity as its own material embodiment. If the aesthetic philosophy of the "Conclusion" can function clearly as a theme, it functions as a sjuzet most clearly in the form of historical analysis, the explanation of an event's meaning in terms of a larger historical arrangement.

The critic who accused Pater of ripping artworks from their historical context and treating them like air-plants (Seiler, *Walter Pater, The Critical Heritage*, 72) may have been responding to the absence of an explicit attribution of art to historical causation in *The Renaissance*. All of its historical commentary appears in the language of aesthetic evaluation, and Pater never offers historic cause as a final ground or explanation of the evaluations, nor does he posit a specific historical arrangement as their organizing principle. But such explanations would have been, either in structure or content, transhistorical. Instead, he offers historical commentary as a part of aesthetic evaluation and aesthetic perception as a form of historic interpretation. In so doing, he informs each of his aesthetic evaluations and perceptions with the frictions within and between historic moments. Like Derrida and de Man, as we will see in Chapter 4, Pater suspects that attributing problems to historical contexts is itself a philosophic abstraction rather than an analysis of historic particularity. He connects aesthetics with history by making aesthetic perception a mode of reading history and making historical particularity a necessary aspect of that mode. Because all these issues—Pater's epistemology, his historicism, and his art criticism—become manifest in all their complexity in the narrative structure of *The Renaissance*, narrative operates as the medium through which Pater's aestheticism takes its most comprehensive form. To see how Pater's philosophic aestheticism functions as a way of reading history, then, we will look at the workings of narrative in the two most historically and philosophically expansive critical essays in the book, "Leonardo da Vinci" and "Winckelmann." The first addresses a Gothicism within the Renaissance, the last a Renaissance within the Enlightenment. Taken together, they make of the Renaissance a form of aesthetic perception constructed of historical placement and philosophic understanding.

II

Within both "Leonardo" and "Winckelmann," the problem of making sense of historical change without either formulating a transhistorical evaluation or falling into pure historicist relativism operates as a more or less explicit common theme. The narrative movement from one essay to the other takes the form of that issue becoming constantly more explicit. In "Leonardo," Pater raises the problem of periodization by showing, in response to Ruskin, that Leonardo represents Renaissance qualities by embodying an example of Gothicism within the Renaissance. Here, though, Pater questions the status of two historical periods. In "Winckelmann," he offers a dual definition of the Renaissance as both a historical period and a perceptual stance, thus making *the situation behind the theme of the first essay his explicit theme in the second*. Behind that theme, however, hovers the issue of how one can define a period either historically or perceptually without losing either the stance from which one perceives or the historical specificity that creates that stance's value. This theme becomes more explicit in the process by which Pater rereads Hegel's *Aesthetics* in "Winckelmann." As Pater makes an earlier essay's implicit conflict the explicit theme of the later essay, he also allows the later essay to contain the earlier within its own aesthetic moment. But one can also find the act of containment completed at each earlier point in the movement. Thus, as I will show in this section, "Leonardo" contains the same theme of conflicting historic and epistemological interpretation held within an aesthetic contrast that reads both ways. At the historic level, the essay describes a friction between Leonardo's Gothic and his Renaissance qualities. At the epistemological level, this friction may be read as a conflict between Leonardo's scientific curiosity and his desire to create artistic perfection. Because the historic periods bear labels that have psychological significance, however, both the historic and the perceptual analyses are inextricably mixed. They are mixed even further when Pater, in his interpretation of Leonardo's art, understands the art in terms of the essay's prior historical and epistemological issues. The containment of the philosophic and epistemological issues that occurs between essays also occurs within each essay. The sjuzet of the work entails, at every level, precisely this movement to contain all issues within each moment, to make of every aesthetic sensation a philosophy and a history, even as Pater reads philosophy and history through moments of aesthetic perception and sensation. In this structure, the "Conclusion" does not leap to a different order of discourse but simply enacts the arranging process in the most explicit thematic terms.

Since Pater lauds the Renaissance in implicit and antagonistic response to Ruskin's denigration of it in favor of the Gothic, critics usually assume Pater's consequent antagonism to the Gothic.[8] In the same way that Pater revised Ruskin's aesthetic theory by encompassing it (showing that it was an *aesthetic* theory), however, he revises Ruskin's history by encompassing the Gothic within the Renaissance. Among other things Ruskin found wanting in the Renaissance were a demand for perfection and a pride in science. To Ruskin, these features defined Leonardo, though his genius protected him from the failings that normally result from these flaws. Pater agrees in attributing to Leonardo precisely these features. But he then shows them as elements of what Ruskin would call Gothicism.

Ruskin claims that the "main mistake" of the early Renaissance "was the unwholesome demand for *perfection*, at any cost" (*Works*, 11: 17). Pater describes Leonardo's search for perfection as a turning away from Renaissance perfection of form: "And because [Florentine miniature-painting] was the perfection of that style, it awoke in Leonardo some seed of discontent which lay in the secret places of his nature. For the way to perfection is through a series of disgusts; and this picture—all that he had done so far in his life at Florence—was after all in the old slight manner. His art, if it was to be something in the world, must be weighted with more of the meaning of nature and the purpose of humanity" (*Renaissance*, 81). As we saw in the previous chapter, Ruskin criticizes a perfection of finish achieved at the expense of emotional fire. But Leonardo looks for a deeper perfection, signaled by his disgust with each past achievement. In a sense, Leonardo shares Ruskin's attitude to perfection of form, but, as a natural consequence, he seeks perfection of fire, "the meaning of nature and the purpose of humanity." In effect, he even reproduces the Gothic belief that perfection is not humanly possible here: since the way to perfection is through a series of disgusts, evidently with prior, insufficient perfections, we must presume that each perfection becomes a sign of its own inadequacy. The disgust, rather than the pride of perfection, replaces the Gothic belief in man's inherent flaw, but that replacement does not deny the flaw.

Pater addresses Ruskin's critique of Renaissance science and his combined inclusion and exemption of Leonardo in precisely the same way. Ruskin distinguishes between the natural sciences, which teach human beings humility before the grandeur of creation, and all other human sciences, which instill pride in human achievement. He then admits that Michelangelo and Leonardo were fascinated by these proud sciences, but attributes their artistic successes to their genius, which overcame that fascination (*Works*, 11: 68–70). Pater, by contrast, stresses not Leonardo's interest in engineering, but his natural philosophy: "To him philosophy was to be something giving strange swiftness and double sight, divining the sources of springs beneath the earth or of expression beneath the human countenance, clairvoyant of occult gifts in common or uncommon things, in the reed at the brookside, or the star which draws near to us but once in a century" (*Renaissance*, 84). This passage more naturally applies to the science that investigates the external world, the science that *Modern Painters* linked with the best art, and that *The Stones of Venice* refused to unlink from it even in the midst of its general attack upon Renaissance and modern science. Thus when Pater concludes that, through this fascination, Leonardo's "clear purpose was overclouded," and "he had almost ceased to be an artist" (*Renaissance*, 84), his agreement with Ruskin's belief that Leonardo's desire for perfection and his engagement in science led him frequently to leave pictures incomplete (*Works*, 10: 203; 11: 70–71) has a certain irony. Ruskin sees Leonardo's failure as a matter of his Renaissance pride, Pater as resulting from his Gothic curiosities. But the irony does not end here, because Pater does not see Leonardo as a failure.

First Pater insists that the diversions and exoticisms of Leonardo's science did not indicate a Renaissance degradation of the Gothic but rather the effect of a Gothic sensibility in a Renaissance context. He generalizes from Leonardo's situation to that of fifteenth-century Milan and then restores Leonardo to his surroundings: "The *Duomo*, work of artists from beyond the Alps, so fantastic to a Florentine used to the mellow, unbroken surfaces of Giotto and Arnolfo, was then in all its freshness; and below, in the streets of Milan, moved a people as fantastic, changeful, and dreamlike. To Leonardo least of all men could there be anything poisonous in the exotic flowers of sentiment which grew there. It was a life of exquisite amusements—Leonardo became a celebrated designer of pageants—and brilliant sins" (*Renaissance*, 85–86, 230). The *Duomo* is not, in fact, a Milanese, Renaissance novelty, but a Gothic cathedral, built in part by German architects (Hill, *The Renaissance*, 367–368). Its fantastic quality owes solely to its placement in a context of Italian Renaissance architecture. If the Milanese are "as fantastic," their exoticism must be read in the same way. And, indeed, Pater attributes to them the Ruskinian Gothic quality of changefulness and, it almost seems by implication, grotesqueness (*Works*, 10: 184) as part of what makes them fantastic. One may even connect "the exotic flowers of sentiment" and the "exquisite amusements" to the Gothic decorative intricacy and profusion, which Ruskin often praises. Their decadence and that of Leonardo's pageants and sins Pater attributes directly to their Gothicism. And indeed, intricacy and profusion may be as easily connected with these qualities as with those Ruskin prefers. The whole scene, indeed, of Leonardo in Milan is a Gothic grotesque, and described for that aesthetic effect.

The workings of this scene move us closer to the way Pater uses Ruskinian history in order to produce his own aestheticized, historical moment. Although Ruskin saw moral paradigms and lessons in history,[9] his descriptions of historical periods and his identification of artistic forms with the qualities of the historical periods that produced them, particularly in *The Stones of Venice*, partook of the mid-Victorian tendency toward historicist cultural analysis.[10] By connecting Gothic qualities with the Renaissance moral decadence that Ruskin railed against, Pater undoes the sharp boundary definitions Ruskin imposes between historical periods while using those definitions for his own description of this moment. Identifying a Renaissance moment in terms of Ruskin's definition of the Gothic both uses and undercuts his periodic distinctions, while the general aesthetic effect of the passage depends on the same melting together of methods. On the one hand, this passage describes the intrinsic and special qualities of a historical moment, Milan at the turn of the fifteenth and sixteenth centuries. But there is more to this passage than simple historical curiosity, that

Burckhardtean desire to let historical facts inform us of their own special quality. By melding Gothic naturalness and changefulness into Renaissance refinement and sensuality, by making pageants and sins respond to a Gothic grotesque, Pater embeds in the historical scene the friction between contrasting qualities that, in his own theory, creates aesthetic power. By reading this historic moment in terms of his aesthetic interpretation, however, Pater comprehends rather than expels historic relevance. Ruskin explained Leonardo by referring him to the weaknesses of his period, those weaknesses being determined by Ruskin's ahistorical moral and aesthetic evaluations. Showing the evaluations to be ahistoric by finding the ostensibly Gothic qualities in the Renaissance, Pater analyzes the Renaissance, and particularly the moment of da Vinci's life in Milan, to understand the complexities of its own specific historic working. And only from that more intrinsic, and thus paradoxically more deeply historic, understanding can the passage assume its aesthetic effect in Pater's narrative as a moment that contains within it the conflicting interpretations that produced it.

The next stage of the essay's narrative analysis reinscribes this historical moment within a discussion of Leonardo's life and art. Leonardo's meshing with the fantastic scene in Milan is an atypical moment in an essay that constantly sees Leonardo in terms of his differences from his world. By translating the conflict between Gothic and Renaissance into one between two motive forces, Pater transforms the historical conflict into an epistemological one that determines Leonardo's actions:

> Curiosity and the desire of beauty—these are the two elementary forces in Leonardo's genius; curiosity often in conflict with the desire of beauty, but generating, in union with it, a type of subtle and curious grace. The movement of the fifteenth century was two-fold; partly the Renaissance, partly also the coming of what is called the "modern spirit," with its realism, its appeal to experience; it comprehended a return to antiquity, and a return to nature. Raphael represents the return to antiquity and Leonardo the return to nature. (*Renaissance*, 86, 230)

The conflict between curiosity and the desire of beauty at first obstructs Leonardo's art, but ultimately becomes the friction that defines it. Here that conflict in desires first partakes of its age, then exists in conflict with it, then represents a part of it. In the next paragraph, the fifteenth century contains both the Renaissance and a prediction of the modern spirit in its move toward realism. If Leonardo's return to nature connects him with the modern, Pater, as much as Ruskin, also identifies realism with the Gothic (in his discussion of the medieval quality of Morris's realism, for instance, in "The Poems of William Morris"). Although Leonardo's curiosity is a facet of his age, that facet also exists in contrast to the Renaissance. Thus Pater also implies that Raphael represents Renaissance art, Leonardo the beginning of modern science. And thus a paucity of artistic production marks Leonardo's stay in Milan: "this struggle between the reason and its ideas, and the senses, the desire of beauty, is the key to Leonardo's life at Milan—his restlessness, his endless retouchings, his odd experiments with colour. How much must he leave unfinished, how much recommence!" (*Renaissance*, 88). To precisely the extent that Leonardo meshes with Milan, he exists in conflict with himself and his art.

Up to this point, I have been describing the essay in terms of two conflicts: a historical one between refined Renaissance beauty and a realism described as modern but often producing a Gothic grotesque; and a psychological one between Leonardo's curiosity and his desire for beauty. But of course these two conflicts match up, since his desire for beauty makes him one of the primary artists of the Renaissance even as his curiosity connects him with Gothic naturalism and modern science. Thus when his conflict leads to an art of "curious beauty" and of "strange blossoms and fruits hitherto unknown," the historical conflicts and the psychological ones combine in one object. Leonardo's art, as an apex of Renaissance achievement, includes within it various historical and psychological conflicts, allowing the Renaissance, which is neither a return to nature nor a return to antiquity but an artistic and perceptual mode, to contain those conflicts within an aesthetic moment.

Pater will even take the flaws and unfinished aspects of Leonardo's art, resulting from his obsession with scientific experimentation, and connect them with a significance to his art that is both historical and aesthetic. Thus, analyzing the fading figure of Jesus' head in the *Last Supper*, Pater concludes:

> Vasari pretends that the central head was never finished. But finished or unfinished, or owing part of its effect to a mellowing decay, the central head does but consummate the sentiment of the whole company—ghosts through which you see the wall, faint as the shadows of the leaves upon the wall on autumn afternoons; this figure is but the faintest, most spectral of them all. It is the image of what the history it symbolises has been more and more ever since. Criticism came with its appeal from mystical unrealities to originals, and restored no life-like reality but these transparent shadows—spirits which have not flesh and bones. (*Renaissance*, 95, 223)

Leonardo painted the *Last Supper* not in fresco but in "the new method" of oil, according to Pater, because oil "allowed of so many afterthoughts, so refined a working-out of perfection" (*Renaissance*, 94).

Whether Leonardo left the central head unfinished or it has faded from premature decay, its ghostliness results from the series of disgusts that sets Leonardo off on his search for perfection, from both his curiosity and his desire for beauty. This fading effect, though, far from being a flaw, turns into an allegory of how modern historical research vitiates Christianity. Leonardo's art and his science, in this Renaissance moment, lead to an artistic manifestation of a scientific development, at least from the perspective of the modern critic.

Here, at first, Pater seems to be treating art as an air-plant in precisely the way he does in his more notorious reading of the Mona Lisa. His reading of the painting cannot conceivably refer to any meaning Leonardo intended. Neither Leonardo's technical failure nor his artistic impatience could intend an effect in the fading head. And Pater describes what that fading symbolizes as a function of subsequent history, what the head has symbolized ever since. Instead of looking for the historic cause of the artwork, however, Pater reads the work itself as a way of attaining historic understanding. And his aesthetic impressions describe precisely the historic conflicts the essay has been discussing. Leonardo's flaws, both his desire for artistic perfection leading to disgust and his scientific curiosity leading to technical failure, embody a historic conflict, as we have seen, between Renaissance perfection and changeful, Gothic curiosity. Indeed the flaws embody that conflict both separately and together in their working within Leonardo. Even the modern impression of Christianity's fading responds to a process that our subsequent history understands to have started in the Renaissance, a process of which Leonardo was part, and for which this book values both him and his period. Pater's reading may not reveal the painting's historically valid meaning nor its historic cause. But, through his interpretation, Pater discusses precisely the painting's historic situation. We understand that situation only through Pater's aesthetic interpretation. And that aesthetic interpretation takes on its full resonance only in the narrative context, the various historical and psychological conflicts Pater encompasses in his reading. By themselves, Pater's aesthetic impressions, philosophically informed as they are, can seem merely impressionistic, thus merely concerned "with the suggestive power of the picture" he interprets (Hill, *The Renaissance*, 361). And, of course, this intrinsic quality, we saw in the first chapter, is part of the philosophic power of aesthetic sensation. Seen as part of the narrative by which historic issues are contained within the aesthetic moments that explain them, however, these aesthetic readings become ways of interpreting historical moments, and, as we will see in the next section, ways of discussing the problem of historical interpretation itself.

III

"Leonardo da Vinci" establishes the possibility of understanding the Renaissance as a mode of perception rather than merely as a historical period. It contains historical change and friction within aesthetic perception by progressively reducing the scope of its focus until it culminates in readings of Leonardo's paintings. Yet these readings cannot be dismissed as impressionism, nor yet understood in what we normally think of as purely aesthetic terms. To comprehend the highly wrought descriptive prose as analysis, we must see within it all the historical and psychological reference it contains. "Winckelmann," the last, and longest, critical essay in *The Renaissance*, extends Pater's comprehensive aesthetic perception in every direction.

This extension occurs in two ways. First, the historical content "Leonardo" finds necessary to aesthetic perception and understanding becomes far more inescapably explicit. "Winckelmann" deals not with one Renaissance critic or artist but with an art critic who re-creates the Renaissance experience of rediscovering Greek art, but in the context of the German Enlightenment. The essay further insists on the relevance of that eighteenth-century location by making not Winckelmann but Goethe's comprehension of Winckelmann the focus of the biographical section of the essay. And the essay comprehends not just Goethe's use of Winckelmann but the availability of that relationship to modern perception for its own renaissance and enlightenment.[11] Thus "Winckelmann" holds before us constantly four historical periods: Classical, Renaissance, Enlightenment, and Contemporary. The tensions between these periods create the aesthetic possibilities inherent in their comprehension. Second, the essay moves on to discuss aesthetic experience directly in terms of historical transformation. In the process, it transforms Hegel's *Aesthetics* from a philosophic comprehension of aesthetic experience as the product of a specific historical moment into a comprehension of history and philosophy within an aesthetic process. It thus reproduces Hegel's philosophic realization of the absolute spirit in an aesthetic apotheosis that has exactly the same effects as Hegel's philosophic culmination. So, reversing the direction of "Leonardo," "Winckelmann" extends from aesthetic experience pointedly back out into historical and philosophic contexts, while finally, in the mode of Paterian narrative, containing all those extensions in a final event of aesthetic perception.

By making explicit a concern with the meaning of the term Renaissance—the more general issue implied by "Leonardo" and its narrative concern with the contrast between Gothic curiosity and Renaissance beauty—"Winckelmann" thematizes the earlier essay's arranging concept. It thus enacts the book's more comprehensive sjuzet of relating to earlier events by encompassing their significance within a later terminology while preserving the crucial specificity of the earlier events. This process generally informs the movement of "Winckelmann" as a whole, moreover. Having stated in abstract terms the conflict between a perceptual and a historical Renaissance, the essay redescribes that conflict in its narrative of Winckelmann's life and Goethe's consideration of it. This narrative functions aesthetically to transform a set of historical events into a resolution of the conflict between historically specific analysis and comprehensive perception. Accordingly, the essay finally treats this general problem explicitly in its rereading of Hegel. But, on this most philosophic topic within the essay, "Winckelmann" articulates its historicist aestheticism crucially through its own narrative transitions rather than through any explicit critique of Hegel. In this manner, narrative arrangement finally expresses in aesthetic form the book's linking of philosophical abstraction with historic particularity. Linking implicit sjuzet with explicit theme in its treatment of specific narrative event, the narrative structure of the entire book functions as a constant intersection of aesthetic perception and historical interpretation. In this narrative, the statement of philosophic theme in the "Conclusion" becomes both a final word and just one more aspect of a narrative conflict previously construed in perceptual and in historical terms.

Pater's broadening conception of the Renaissance actually starts with the first essay in the book. His extension, there, of the Renaissance backwards into the Middle Ages, while widely criticized by contemporary reviewers of his book (Hill, *The Renaissance*, 244–245), has since become a long-held commonplace in Anglo-American history, indeed was, as Pater notes, a common idea in French histories of his own time.[12] But Pater did not want merely to shift our understanding of the twelfth century in his first essay; he wanted to change our notion of the Renaissance:

> For us the Renaissance is the name of a many-sided but yet united movement, in which the love of the things of the intellect and the imagination for their own sake, the desire for a more liberal and comely way of conceiving life, make themselves felt, prompting those who experience this desire to seek first one and then another means of intellectual or imaginative enjoyment, and directing them not merely to the discovery of old and forgotten sources of this enjoyment, but to divine new sources of it, new experiences, new subjects of poetry, new forms of art. (*Renaissance*, 1–2, 209)

Rather than justifying a redefinition of the twelfth century by reseeing the events of its history, this passage redefines the Renaissance by seeing it as a "movement" identified solely in perceptual terms. Those terms reflect the argument of the "Conclusion," all of them involving a broadening of experience and thought as an inherent value. If we think of "Renaissance" in this way, the connection between the essays and the "Conclusion" becomes clear. The essays articulate through specific representative figures and events the general form of experience and perception that the "Conclusion" then defines; thus, perceiving in terms of the "Conclusion," one engages not only in a personal renaissance but in the Renaissance.

Redefining the Renaissance in this way, however, removes all historical specificity from it and threatens to reduce it to a generalization about the value of novel experience in which active experience itself would be lost. Consequently, when in "Winckelmann" Pater again suggests "that it may be said that the Renaissance was an uninterrupted effort of the middle age, that it was ever taking place," he immediately follows this generalization of the term with a historical specification:

> When the actual relics of the antique were restored to the world, it was to Christian eyes as if an ancient plague-pit had been opened; all the world took the contagion of the life of nature and of the senses. Christian art allying itself with that restored antiquity which it had ever emulated, soon ceased to exist. For a time art dealt with Christian subjects as its patrons required; but its true freedom was in the life of the senses and the blood—blood no longer dropping from the hands in sacrifice, as with Angelico, but, as with Titian, burning in the face for desire and love. And now it was seen that the medieval spirit too had done something for the destiny of the antique. By hastening the decline of art, by withdrawing interest from it and keeping the thread of its traditions, it had suffered the human mind to repose, that it might awake when day came with eyes refreshed to those antique forms. (*Renaissance*, 180–181, 267–268)

The oppositions of sensuality and Christian asceticism (or abstract spirituality), oppositions that in different terms exist everywhere in Pater, define the Renaissance and its alternative here. But the historical location of those oppositions gives them their distinctive force. Only because the Middle Ages had repressed the antique does its restoration come with the force of contagion. Renaissance art derives not merely from the life of the senses but from a prior repression of that life in which blood was both abstracted and given outlet in violent symbol (Pater elsewhere describes Angelico's art in terms of "overcharged symbols," and blood "dropping from the hands in sacrifice" certainly qualifies as such a symbol). The blood burning in the Titian faces has been liberated, but one still feels the force behind the liberation in the intensity with which it burns; and that force and its consequent intensity are the gifts of the earlier repression. Thus the intensity in the Renaissance re-creation of the antique needs the repose given to the mind by the Middle Ages. To the extent that an intense sensual experience, whose intensity is something more than merely sensation, also creates value in the "Conclusion," then we must say that somehow even its aesthetic reawakening draws its specific force from its attachment to a description of Renaissance art.

For Pater, then, the Renaissance embodies a philosophically central perceptual stance because its liberation from medieval abstract spirituality achieves its significant intensity from the historical context in which it occurs. Renaissance intensity arises from the historically specific conditions of that period's liberation from medieval asceticism. But the values that liberation provides, the broader and freer experience of life, the comprehensiveness Pater also insists on, not only transcend that historical specificity but are threatened by it. This contrast between historical specificity and epistemological generality, of course, produces another version of the various frictions that construct Pater's narrative, his philosophy, his underlying version of sensation. The problem of the book, in this context, becomes one of making the epistemological Renaissance broadly available without losing the vital distinctiveness of the historical Renaissance. To this problem, the narrative depiction of "Winckelmann" and its comprehension of his intensity and Goethe's larger view directly respond:

> Filled as our culture is with the classical spirit, we can hardly imagine how deeply the human mind was moved, when, at the Renaissance, in the midst of a frozen world, the buried fire of ancient art rose up from under the soil. Winckelmann here reproduces for us the earlier sentiment of the Renaissance. On a sudden the imagination feels itself free. How facile and direct, it seems to say, is this life of the senses and the understanding, when once we have apprehended it! That is the more liberal life we have been seeking so long, so near to us all the while. How mistaken and round-about have been our efforts to reach it by mystic passion, and religious reverie. (*Renaissance*, 146, 249)

Our culture cannot, at first, either share Renaissance intensity or even imagine it. Our very fortune in having the classical spirit readily available, already a part of us, denies us that experience. In Winckelmann's rediscovery, Pater suggests, we can see the earlier rediscovery more clearly. At this point, the syntax of the passage becomes distinctly odd: whose inner voice does the free, indirect style of the next sentences express? Their direct reference seems to be to "the earlier sentiment of the Renaissance," and its shedding of "mystic passion, and religious reverie" seems to enforce this connection. The voice here does not speak in the language of the Renaissance, though, but in the tones of Pater's Arnoldian aesthete, searching for "the more liberal life," classifying the Middle Ages in terms of its mysticism and reverie. In effect, as a result of Winckelmann, we experience in the language of the modern the emotional force with which the Renaissance rediscovered the classical.

But Winckelmann's intense rediscovery of the pagan only partially reproduces the Renaissance for us. To complete the Renaissance offered by his example, we must first recognize the limitation of that example. Its narrowness derives from the very quality in Winckelmann that creates his greatness as an aesthetic critic, an artistic engagement that supersedes all the various moral shortcomings that Pater describes—for instance, his dubiously motivated conversion to Catholicism. This merging of all other considerations in the artistic is, of course, the usual description of the aestheticist stance. Pater, however, while finding it a success, clearly indicates its partial nature in his analogy: "Savonarola is one type of success; Winckelmann is another; criticism can reject neither, because each is true to itself" (*Renaissance*, 150). Pater's aestheticism appreciates Savonarola, with all the intensity of his moral engagement, in the same way it appreciates Winckelmann. It therefore places that engagement within an aesthetic view while also placing Winckelmann in the same way, recognizing both his value and his partiality.

Thus, if Winckelmann gives us the intensity of the Renaissance, he does not give us its comprehensiveness. Accordingly, despite the essay's title, its biographical section concerns more centrally Goethe's interpretation of Winckelmann than it does Winckelmann per se. It opens with Goethe and, immediately after it establishes Winckelmann's importance in his reproduction of the Renaissance, describes Goethe's comprehension of him:

> Through the tumultuous richness of Goethe's culture, the influence of Winckelmann is always discernible, as the strong, regulative under-current of a clear, antique motive. . . . If we ask what the secret of this influence was, Goethe himself will tell us—elasticity, wholeness, intellectual integrity. And yet these expressions, because they fit Goethe, with his universal culture, so well, seem hardly to describe the narrow, exclusive interest of Winckelmann. . . . But what affected Goethe, what instructed him and ministered to his culture, was the integrity, the truth to its type, of the given force. (*Renaissance*, 147, 250)

Goethe contains the comprehensive values of wholeness and elasticity. Winckelmann gave him in addition a model of artistic integrity, though a narrow one.

Goethe's containment of Winckelmann's narrow integrity within a cultural wholeness clearly exemplifies the essay's vision of a comprehensive Renaissance stance. Thus Goethe's artistic vision, in the closing paragraphs, as we have seen, becomes an example of what aesthetic perception ultimately has to offer. And Pater's analysis of Winckelmann occurs fittingly—but also dangerously—almost entirely through Goethe. The danger is that while Goethe has confronted Winckelmann and encompassed his intensity within a vision of wholeness, we have confronted only Goethe's comprehensive interpretation. To experience Winckelmann's intensity ourselves, we must look, at least momentarily, around Goethe. That moment occurs when Pater laments that a proposed meeting between Goethe and Winckelmann never took place: "German literary history seems to have lost the chance of one of those famous friendships, the very tradition of which becomes a stimulus to culture, and exercises an imperishable influence" (*Renaissance*, 157). In effect, Pater creates that meeting in this text through his concentration upon Goethe's interpretation of Winckelmann. But he also creates it through his sense of poignancy at the lost possibility of that meeting, not poignancy for Goethe but for us who lament what German literary history might have had. This joining of Winckelmann's intensity, Goethe's comprehensiveness, and our sense of loss finally completes the expansion of Renaissance experience through the German Enlightenment and Goethe's summation of it to our experience of Goethe's achievement. Thus an essay on Winckelmann and Greek art, in a book on the Renaissance, ends with a vision of a moment from Goethe's fiction.

In linking Goethe and Winckelmann's Renaissance-like rediscovery of Greek art within his own aesthetic view, Pater effectively combines both the epistemological and the historical elements of the Renaissance experience within one of those narrative moments that enact his philosophy. But, to insist that the aesthetic perception afforded by this narrative moment has the most extensive philosophic and historical significance, Pater also uses his history of the Renaissance to interrogate Hegel's historicist theory of art. Reinterpreting the ideal, transhistorical elements of Hegel's theory in historicist terms, Pater places at the center of historical interpretation an aestheticism that gives it its real coherence. Although, in philosophic terms, that aestheticism serves a transhistorical function, Pater explains it through narrative accounts of historical transitions. Thus the aestheticism of the "Conclusion," which functioned as a philosophical analysis, becomes a historical analysis as well—both a way of analyzing history and a way of analyzing that accepts its own historical specificity in the most profound way. Hegel's *Aesthetics* provided Pater with an art history whose central moment was classical art as the embodiment of the aesthetic ideal. Hegel's history moved into and out of Greek art, however, by virtue of an extra-aesthetic, philosophical concept that placed aesthetics as only a moment in a larger historical process. Staying as close to Hegel as possible, Pater made calculated revisions that replaced Hegel's philosophical concept with an extra-philosophical, aesthetic concept.[13]

The clearest mark of Pater's divergence from Hegel occurs paradoxically with an explicit citation of his *Aesthetics*, one of many that Pater later suppressed. Those suppressions generally seem to serve the purpose of de-emphasizing the explicit philosophy of the essay in favor of its embodiment in an aesthetic history, a transformation that accords with Pater's general use of Hegel. But Pater may have suppressed this particular passage because of the inaccuracy that distinguishes it from his other, more careful citations. Having stated that Greek religion transformed itself into an artistic ideal, Pater then goes on to define his terms:

> "Ideal" is one of those terms which through a pretended culture have become tarnished and edgeless. How great, then, is the charm when in Hegel's writings we find it attached to a fresh, clear-cut conception! With him the ideal is a *Versinnlichen* of the idea—the idea turned into an object of sense. By the idea, stripped of its technical phraseology, he means man's knowledge about himself and his relation to the world, in its most rectified and concentrated form. This, then, is what we have to ask about a work of art—Did it at the age in which it was produced express in terms of sense, did it present to the eye or ear, man's knowledge about himself and his relation to the world in its most rectified and concentrated form? (*Renaissance*, 257–258)

Pater cites in a footnote part 1, chapter 3, of Hegel's *Aesthetics*, which concerns the Ideal, but he does not cite any passage for his definition of the Idea. Nor could he accurately cite Hegel for this definition because Pater's conception is thoroughly his own, both historicist and relative. Since "man's knowledge about himself and his relation to the world" changes from age to age, the Idea here signifies only the fullest and most coherent expression of an age's state of knowledge. One hears in this notion Arnold's concept of the minds of an age entering into "possession of the general ideas which are the law of this vast multitude of facts [which complex ages present to individual contemplation]" (Arnold, 1: 20). But Arnold presumes that these ideas will change with the age.

The Idea for Hegel, however, occurs beyond the limit of his historicism and indeed gives history a transhistorical teleology. Hegel starts with Plato's definition of the Idea as the essential truth behind intellectual concepts and material entities, but then insists on the partiality of this distinction: "It was Plato, as we mentioned in the Introduction, who emphasized the Idea as alone the truth and the universal and indeed as the inherently concrete universal. Yet the Platonic Idea is itself not yet the genuinely concrete; for, although apprehended in its Concept and universality, it does count as the truth, still, taken in this universality, it is not yet actualized and, in its actuality, the truth explicit to itself. . . . the Idea is not genuinely Idea without and outside its actuality" (*Aesthetics*, 143). The Platonic Idea exists in distinction to any actuality by virtue of its universality. It is an articulated truth, thus for Hegel a Concept, but not an actually embodied truth. The embodiment of an essence in actuality, that totality alone, is thus an Idea. Different Ideas will be embodied in different ways, of course, but Hegel also posits an Idea of truth in its totality, which he calls the absolute Idea. The actuality of this Idea occurs only in the "*absolute* spirit which out of itself determines what is genuinely the true." The absolute spirit exists as spirit in complete knowledge of itself. Since such knowledge can exist only in concrete actuality, the absolute spirit creates finite spirit, individual minds (the German word for spirit is also the word for mind), within which it may become an object of itself (*Aesthetics*, 92–94). This moment of knowledge is the absolute Idea. That Idea is the goal of history, since it can occur only when finite mind, having gone through various stages, has achieved for itself in thought the knowledge of the absolute Idea. Then, that Idea has its embodiment and the absolute spirit has achieved itself. Hegel identifies three realms of absolute spirit, which differ only as forms "in which they bring home as consciousness their object, the Absolute." But his definition of these forms fairly quickly becomes a hierarchy: art "is *sensuous* knowing, a knowing, in the form and shape of the sensuous and objective itself"; religion is "*pictorial* thinking"; and philosophy "is the *free* thinking of the absolute spirit" (*Aesthetics*, 101). Since absolute spirit occurs only in free thinking, philosophy represents the highest form of the Absolute. Here we can clearly see how Pater has drained from the definition of the Idea all universality and totality so that its artistic embodiment may not be transcended.

To see the implications of Pater's reduction here, we must realize the importance of this transcendent activity of the absolute spirit to Hegel's history. Since the *Aesthetics* does not present Hegel's philosophy of history explicitly, we do not see how these three forms relate to each other as historical stages. We can extrapolate that relationship, however, from Hegel's discussion of the stages of art. The first stage, the symbolic, "begins when the Idea, still in its indeterminacy and obscurity, or in bad and untrue determinacy, is made the content of artistic shapes" (*Aesthetics*, 76). Since the Idea is known either indeterminately or in untrue determinacy, the shapes in which it will be embodied will be inaccurate as embodiments, only abstractions of the Idea. The second stage, classical art, at first sounds like an achievement of the absolute spirit. Classical art "is the free and adequate embodiment of the Idea in the shape peculiarly appropriate to the Idea itself in its essential nature" (*Aesthetics*, 77). Classical art is thus the Ideal of art, the embodiment of the Idea, as Pater said, in accurate sensuous form. We see the limitation of this stage, however, in its falling away into the third stage, romantic art, which, as art, breaks the ideal, but which Hegel nevertheless labels a higher stage.

In romantic art, the idea once again does not find embodiment adequately in sensuous form, but this is because in the romantic stage the spirit begins to grasp the Idea in a more accurate form:

> The classical form of art has attained the pinnacle of what illustration by art could achieve, and if there is something defective in it, the defect is just art itself and the restrictedness of the sphere of art. This restrictedness lies in the fact that art in general takes as its subject-matter the spirit (i.e. the *universal*, infinite and concrete in its nature) in a *sensuously* concrete form, and classical art presents the complete unification of spiritual and sensuous existence as the *correspondence* of the two. But in this blending of the two, spirit is not in fact represented in its *true nature*. For spirit is the infinite subjectivity of the Idea, which as absolute inwardness cannot freely and truly shape itself outwardly on condition of remaining moulded into a bodily existence as the one appropriate to it. (*Aesthetics*, 79)

Because spirit is actually inward, thought embodies it most accurately. Consequently, the Idea of beauty, the defining idea of art, by its own nature cannot embody spirit adequately, and its most adequate embodiment is less accurate than an artistically less satisfactory work whose flaw owes to the superiority of the knowledge it tries to convey. Thus the romantic stage of art, because its conception of spirit is too inward to be fully embodied sensuously, coincides with the religious realm of the absolute spirit, in which spirit may be merely pictorially thought about rather than sensuously embodied. When the spirit reaches the philosophical stage, art will evidently cease to exist. In that philosophical stage, we have the philosophy of art instead of art itself (*Aesthetics*, 11). One can thus easily see the three forms of absolute spirit, the artistic, the religious, and the philosophic, as operating in the same temporal relationship as the stages of art, the symbolic, the classical, and the romantic, with the third stage of each form bringing on the first stage of the next. The absolute spirit's quest for its own self-knowledge and embodiment in absolute Idea thus becomes the mechanism that moves Hegel's history, as well as his history of art.

The drama in which the absolute spirit, working through various stages of the finite mind's understanding of itself and its world, arrives at a comprehensive awareness of itself in philosophical thought creates the teleology that makes the complex of Hegelian history operate. Since Hegelian teleology can be construed as an attempt to exit history by offering a final—and thus a transhistorical—explanation of it, Pater's replacement of the Idea within a historical context would be a fuller acceptance of a relativist historicism, an acceptance so full that history would lack coherent pattern and the only consistent attitude toward it would be a satiric undercutting of historical explanation and an irony toward one's own stance as a historian.[14] From such a stance, his notion of an artistic ideal achieved within history has no coherence, and for this reason, among others, a comprehensive historicism, with its submergence in historical flux, had only limited appeal for Pater. But if he wanted for his aestheticism a concept of a Greek artistic ideal, why did he go to Hegel for it? Hegel's definition of that ideal, as we have seen, depended upon its being transcended. And versions of a Greek ideal were so commonplace in Romantic and Victorian thought that he had any number of other possible sources for it.[15] But Pater wanted an aesthetic concept that contained within it a historical explanation, so that one could experience historical change with aesthetic intensity while still comprehending history adequately. To do this, he places the Hegelian Idea within the boundaries of history, and replaces its working with a recurring aesthetic drama that he does not label here but that accords with his description of Renaissance. In this way he inscribes the Hegelian historical narrative within certain aesthetic descriptions and evaluations.

We see this replacement most clearly in moments when Pater must account for historical transition, particularly in his description of the passing of the Greek ideal. For Hegel, the end of Greek art comes from the inherent limit to the Artistic form of spirit. It marks a progress. Without a teleology, however, and with no reason to prefer philosophy over art, Pater must explain why one would fall away from an achieved ideal. Hegel, indeed, shows the decline of Greek art and religion occurring in its very apex, as a result of a rigorous logic developing from the deficiency in its own ideal:

> The germ of their decline the classical gods have in themselves, and when the deficiency implicit in them is revealed to our minds through the development of art itself they therefore bring in their train the dissolution of the classical Ideal. The principle of this Ideal, as it appears here, we have laid down as the spiritual individuality which finds its wholly adequate expression in an immediate corporeal and external existent. But this individuality

broke up into a group of divine individuals whose determinate character is not absolutely necessary and therefore from the start is surrendered to the contingency in which the eternally powerful gods acquire alike for the Greek mind and for artistic representation the source of their dissolution. (*Aesthetics*, 502)

Because the artistic manifestation of spirit could conceive its own distinctness, but had not yet arrived at a sense of complete inwardness, it could be embodied in distinct and individuated forms, but it did not demand that those forms represent individuals with separate inward lives. Thus the various Greek gods were distinct from each other without at first being individuals. But individuation leads to individuals, and so the individuality of the classical ideal broke up into separate divinities. But their separateness, since it does not derive from the classical Idea, is arbitrary, contingent, thus not divine, certainly not an embodiment of a universal Idea. Thus as soon as the individuation necessary for the Greek ideal occurs, it brings with it the seeds of its own recognition of inadequacy.

By bringing to bear the higher standard implicit in the Idea's advance to a higher stage of spirit, this explanation marks the deficiency of the Greek ideal without calling its ideality into question. Since a shift in Ideas does not operate against any higher standard in Pater but merely marks a shift in historical period, he faces the problem of explaining the end of his Greek ideal without denying its ideality. This difficulty is made more acute by Pater's lack of sympathy for the medieval asceticism that followed. His explanation serves as a key confirmation of the contrasts I have been claiming operate in his thought: between individual sensation and abstract form in his aestheticism and between historicism and transhistorical explanation in his narrative. The implicit revision of Hegel also demonstrates the working of philosophy upon the moments of experience on which he concentrates:

> The longer we contemplate that Hellenic ideal, in which man is at unity with himself, with his physical nature, with the outward world, the more we may be inclined to regret that he should ever have passed beyond it, to contend for a perfection that makes the blood turbid, and frets the flesh, and discredits the actual world about us. But if he was to be saved from the *ennui* which ever attaches itself to realisation, even the realisation of perfection, it was necessary that a conflict should come, that some sharper note should grieve the perfect harmony, in order that the spirit, chafed by it, might beat out at last a broader and profounder music. (*Renaissance*, 177–178, 265)

One could hardly ask for a clearer statement of Pater's dissatisfaction with an enclosed, protective, stable aestheticism. The Greek ideal at least encountered the outside world. But unity, any realization of perfection, creates unrest, ennui. Thus ideality itself creates the problem. The broadest and profoundest music must contain unresolved conflict within it, and thus cannot achieve unity of form and content. From this perspective, Pater, with Hegel, can claim that "a sort of preparation for the romantic temper is noticeable even within the limits of the Greek ideal itself," a perception he attributes to Hegel in the first published version of the essay (*Renaissance*, 265). Where Hegel found a limitation to the Artistic Idea and thus to the ideal that embodied it, Pater finds a limit to ideality itself. A Paterian ideal must contain conflict within it. As soon as that conflict is stabilized into ideational form, it ceases to be an ideal.

We also see why Pater uses Hegel and what replaces the apotheosis of philosophy here. The Hegelian notion of a spirit moving to a higher state by its recognition of a limitation inherent in its present condition occurs in Pater's end of the Greek ideal, but that spirit is not an Absolute, not even an Absolute comprised of the human mind's thoughts upon it, but the human spirit, working in history in the Arnoldian cultural terms of Pater's original revision of Hegel's Idea. And its higher state Pater measures in aesthetic terms: it learns a broader and profounder music. In effect, Pater replaces Hegel's absolute spirit with an aesthetic perspective. That perspective can effectively replace the Hegelian spirit because it accepts flux as a necessary part of itself and thus can look upon its own history in an attitude structurally similar to that of the Hegelian spirit, and make its ideal out of the conflicts and developments in that history it encompasses. Pater's aesthetic overview once again discovers the conflicts that his book labels Renaissance. Its final achievement we have seen in my earlier discussion of the closing pages of "Winckelmann." The claims of those pages we can now see as growing directly out of the essay's prior analysis both of the perspective created by connecting the classic, the Renaissance, Winckelmann, Goethe, and Pater's narrator, and by the expansion of that perspective into a historicist force and a historical explanation. Pater's aesthetic perspective, looking upon Goethe's transformation of historical necessity into tragic denouement, experiencing a sense of freedom in a recognition of itself, exactly coincides with the Hegelian freedom in the absolute spirit's self-understanding. Far from trying to escape history, this aesthetic version of Hegelian freedom, we can now see, is constructed by historical analysis and engages even more fully than Hegel in historical flux.

This passage constitutes an experience enabled by the use of, but not the superimposition of, a philosophical explanation. Its interpretation contains the narrative that has led up to it: aesthetic perspective enables historical change and then results from it as its apotheosis. At the end of the previous chapter, I attributed some of the attacks upon Pater to his inclusion of his attackers' positions. We have seen that Pater's claim to be writing a history also faced early attack, and I think for the same reason. More versed in the possibilities of historicism than his reviewers, he extended that historicism to a point at which it could be contained by its opposite. In that sense, of course, his reviewers were correct in arguing that his ultimate context was not a historical one but an aesthetic one. And perhaps for that reason he retitled *The Renaissance* in subsequent editions. His critics did not explain, though, how any historical context that genuinely accepted historical relativism and flux could claim to be ultimate without becoming some other kind of context. Pater, in his aestheticism, does create a transhistorical context, but one that uses the duality of aesthetic perception to immerse itself more deeply in the historicism it contains than did Hegelian historiography. Although it eschewed a conventional historical context as the explanation for artwork, it was thus far more historicist in the very aestheticism it used to transcend history than were his positivist critics. Once again, and this time through the working of his narrative, Pater has transformed by including.

My introduction specified two challenges to aestheticism: the first connects it to a relativism that reduces all philosophy to "mere" fiction; the second assumes that lauding the aesthetic must mean placing it in contrast to the Real and finding in it an escape from the forces of history and ideology. Pater's "art for art's sake" has always been a primary item in the list of particulars such polemics draw up against aestheticism. In these two chapters, I have argued that Pater saw his aestheticism, in fact, as a form of both philosophical and historical analysis. Skeptical of both empirical foundations of logic upon sensation and of positivist treatments of history as an explanatory context or ground, he retreats neither from the reality of sensations nor from the reality of historical change but uses the duality of aesthetic perception to investigate those realities. The interest of these chapters might be solely historic were not aestheticism a current issue in literary theory. And yet, perhaps the element of historic distance may aid in this project as much as Winckelmann and Goethe aided Pater. The literary historical interest that makes reinterpreting Pater safely a matter of Victorian concern may also allow an easier hearing for the reformulations in this chapter. If so, their extensions in the next two will have more effectiveness. In any case, my next two chapters, following the model of these, analyze the same charges of aestheticism as they apply to deconstruction in Derrida and de Man. And their discussion will follow a similar itinerary: my first chapter's discussion of Pater's analysis of empiricist, foundational sensations and his placement of aesthetic perception at the center of that analysis leads to a discussion of Derrida's analysis of foundational reflection in Continental philosophy and the consequent role that literary language plays in his and de Man's theories. Discussing the way, through his narrative, Pater defines his aesthetic interpretation as a form of historical analysis leads to my interpretation in Chapter 4 of the conflict between historicism and philosophical abstraction in Derrida, and of the way de Man transforms that conflict into historical and rhetorical analysis.

Three

Deconstruction: Foundations and Literary Language

WALTER PATER appears in works of contemporary literary theory mostly in footnotes and asides, where he plays the role of ghostly indicator of troubles to come. Earlier I compared the criticism of Pater with a certain strand of attack upon deconstruction. But I could make that comparison because the attacks themselves identify deconstruction with Pater's aestheticism. Essentially, these critiques argue that Pater's work privileges art and literature by making them irrelevant to any social, political, philosophical, or intellectual concerns (this irrelevance is what critics seem normally to have in mind when they use the phrase "art for art's sake") and then charge deconstruction with the same set of beliefs or assumptions.[1] This charge has larger resonance because when critics accuse deconstruction of being reconstructed New Criticism, they frequently have in mind the same accusation of espousing a special terrain of hermetically enclosed textuality.[2] More recent defenders of Derrida, on the other hand, have sought to distinguish his thought from such positions by also distinguishing it from what we now separate out as Yale deconstruction, or deconstruction in America.[3] Disagreeing over the status of Derrida's thought, these critics all contend that deconstruction as literary theory amounts to a new aestheticism, a new New Criticism. In offering a rereading of Pater as a focus for a discussion of deconstruction, I want to dispute precisely that contention: I will connect Derrida's questioning of the foundational claims of philosophy with Paul de Man's extension of that system, from the perspective of literary language, into a discussion of the common ground between philosophy and literature. The deconstruction that emerges from this linking will, I hope, renew our sense of how a certain perspective on philosophic problems may have consequences for our understanding of literature and its social, intellectual, and political implications.

In the previous two chapters, I discussed first the epistemological and then the historicist implications of Pater's aestheticism. The first chapter argued that the art Pater envisioned, far from being an escape from social, scientific, or philosophic discourse, was self-justifying only insofar as it embodied a central philosophic concept: the paradoxical formulation of experiencing as abstraction the very flux of sensation. The second chapter argued the workings of an intense historicism within an aestheticism usually conceived as ahistorical. My discussion of deconstruction will fall into the same two rough categories. We hardly need Pater to see Derrida's project as centrally philosophic. The charges of nihilism leveled at Derrida by his American critics, however, and of arguing that there is no meaning or there is no truth, will start to seem less telling, and his philosophic import may become clearer, in the context of Pater's barely discussed philosophic project. Pater fixed his analysis on sensation, a foundational concept in nineteenth-century scientific empiricism, not to make science, philosophy, or their truths disappear but to show how the difficulties within the notion of sensation included the discourses science was thought to undercut, centralized the art it was supposed to make irrelevant. Derrida's philosophic argument also questions the foundational ambitions of philosophy, not in order to make truth or meaning disappear but precisely to call into question the validity of the arbitrary exclusionary maneuvers that moments of foundational definition seem to necessitate. Literary language, as we will see both in Derrida's discussion of that concept and in de Man's consequent articulation of a literary-critical deconstruction, operates as aesthetic perception did in Pater's definition of sensation. As the mode of language that allows the problems of foundational philosophy to emerge, literary language hardly proves that all philosophy is really just literature, nor does it show that literature disproves the referentiality of philosophy, proof and disproof being after all concepts within the foundational philosophy ostensibly being called into question. Rather, literary language, even as it constitutes the literariness of the literary, also embodies an excluded but logically necessary aspect of foundational philosophy, just as aesthetic perception, in its ability to be self-justifying, embodies for Pater the exemplary form of sensation. Thus literary discourse becomes central to the understanding of a certain philosophic perspective, just as art in Pater offers most clearly the sensation on which empirical philosophy and science grounded themselves. That, in any case, will be the argument of this chapter. The next chapter will extend Derrida's and de Man's philosophic and literary positions to an analysis of their treatment of aesthetics. Again, as in Pater, we will see that their aesthetics includes within itself and intensifies historicism and ideological debate, rather than transcending either.

Before directly addressing Derrida's analysis of philosophical foundation, however, I want to note a comment in one of the philosophers he discusses most frequently, Edmund Husserl, in order to clarify a difference between the Continental philosophy Derrida takes for granted and the empiricism Pater and Derrida's Anglo-American critics share. This distinction in philosophical traditions causes many of the problems troubling readers of Derrida from an empirical perspective. An application of Derrida's themes in the literary-critical "deconstruction" of Pater and other nineteenth-century writers with little attention to this distinction has also created the arbitrariness many critics complain about in that reading method. In his *Origins of Geometry*, Husserl begins by defining his goal as the articulation of an ideal meaning of geometry that necessarily preceded any actual geometry used by any actual, historical geometer. He further claims that only by knowing this meaning can we know the truth of geometry:

> without the actually developed capacity for reactivating the original activities contained within its fundamental concepts, i.e., without the "what" and the "how" of its prescientific materials, geometry would be a tradition empty of meaning; and if we ourselves did not have this capacity, we could never even know whether geometry had or ever did have a genuine meaning, one that could really be "cashed in."
>
> Unfortunately, however, this is our situation, and that of the whole modern age.
>
> The "presupposition" mentioned above has in fact never been fulfilled. How the living tradition of the meaning-formation of elementary concepts is actually carried on can be seen in elementary geometrical instruction and its textbooks; what we actually learn there is how to deal with *ready-made* concepts and sentences in a rigorously methodical way. Rendering the concepts sensibly intuitable by means of drawn figures is substituted for the actual production of the primal idealities. (Derrida, *Edmund Husserl's "Origin,"* 169)

Husserl's claim here may be so counterintuitive to those accustomed to an Anglo-American discourse about meaning that they may not even realize how different it is. The textbooks he complains about explain the meanings of separate geometrical concepts and sentences—we might call them propositions—by matching them up with drawn figures, in other words by showing the pictures to which they correspond. That correspondence we would take to be precisely the meaning of a formal proposition. Husserl, however, complains that that correspondence artificially replaces the primal idealities that actually ground the concepts. Those idealities, the bulk of the essay makes clear, are not the intention of any specific geometer in uttering a geometrical proposition,[4] but an original cognition of geometrical principles at the moment in which their universality is understood, but prior to their externalization in language. In effect, and to simplify, Husserl follows Kant and Hegel in grounding the meaning and the truth of a concept in the moment of its original appearance in an internalized reflection untainted by phenomenality and language. In contrast, Anglo-American correspondence would find such a procedure to smack of the genetic fallacy and would ground the meaning of a concept in its ability to match up with what the early Wittgenstein would call a logical simple, a sensation or some other irreducible phenomenal reality.

The philosophy Derrida discusses, then, he can rightly posit, founds itself upon a moment of pure reflection within a subject's unmediated consciousness in just the way that empirical philosophy founds itself upon the objective source of the sensations that constitute our experiences. This distinction between the founding concepts of empirical philosophy and its development into Anglo-American analytic philosophy and the founding concepts of Continental philosophy and its development into phenomenology and structuralism creates some rather odd effects when Anglo-American critics address Derridean themes. For instance, Derrida, particularly in his discussion of Rousseau in *Of Grammatology*, shows with considerable care how the concept of an unmediated presence of the subject to itself grounds Continental philosophy and even certain seemingly commonsense beliefs about truth and meaning. When he then shows the logical fissures in this concept, the destabilizing consequences seem, in precisely the way Derrida wants, both necessary and unthinkable. As we have seen in the discussion of Pater's image of a dispersed self, literary critics have been quick to apply this theme of a disseminated self to British literature—with less telling results. Since Hume, the solidity of the self, far from being a founding concept in empiricism, has been dispersed across the various sensations felt by that self. Thus British writers and philosophers have entertained the image of a disintegrated self more calmly, whether they finally believed in it or not, because that disintegration challenged no foundations.

A reverse problem occurs when Derrida says rather off-handedly, "I don't believe that anything like perception exists. Perception is precisely a concept" ("Discussion," 272), or "there never was any 'perception'" (*Speech and Phenomena*, 103). Such remarks may seem willfully paradoxical to an audience for whom the foundational quality of at least the identity one gives to one's sensations, if not of the sensations themselves, is a philosophical commonplace. Richard Rorty, after all, spends nearly sixty pages analyzing the problems with the idea that one's identification of "raw feels" is incorrigible, but he never simply throws the concept away (*Philosophy*, 70–127). And Pater places conceptuality at the center of sensation, as we have seen, without ever denying sensation's primacy. But, since Kant's attempt to define the a priori conditions of perception in *The Critique of Pure Reason*, far from being foundational givens, perception and experience have always designated concepts needing further grounding in Continental philosophy. The "perception" that Derrida denies refers not to perceptions of empirical phenomena but to Husserl's transcendental acts of pure perception in the absence of outside objects perceived, a concept Husserl thinks necessary to ground the empirical perceptions Pater and Mill, and Hume and Locke before them, saw as necessary grounds.

This may seem an elementary distinction and its rigid formulation simplifies to the point of falsehood if it is taken to imply that no argument in one tradition has any validity for another. Certainly, when Derrida analyzes problems in the concept of meaning (in "Signature Event Context," for instance) his arguments are hardly irrelevant to American literary theory. Nevertheless, the unfamiliarity with the foundational discourse he presumes often causes mistakes in the reactions of both critics and literary disciples. Since his target is the internal purity of reflection within the subject, Derrida frequently shows the incoherence of that ostensibly founding moment without really contesting—or indeed wanting to contest—the status of consequent particular, phenomenal moments. Thus critics will take his questioning of certain foundational definitions of meaning for a claim that we never understand each other or ought not to try.[5] Similarly, explicators and followers of deconstruction frequently take the nonconcept of differance to refer to the old empirical problem that abstract nouns must group together an infinite number of separate items, as the word "tree" imposes a grouping upon all the different objects we call "trees." Or they take Derrida's argument in "White Mythology" that the concept of metaphor is necessary for defining literal language to show that all language is empirically metaphorical.[6] I will discuss some of these problems in detail below. I raise them now to reiterate the value of Pater in restaging Derrida for us. Pater represents for us more than someone operating in an empirical tradition that we take for granted. The problems he addresses concerning the value of art in a world increasingly founded on science are quite familiar to literary critics. His placement of artistic experience at the center of the scientific foundation that sought to exclude art and his definition of artistic sensation as constitutive of science's foundational sensation offer us a model for seeing how Derrida analyzes the workings of philosophic foundation. More specifically, just as Pater's shaking of sensational foundations neither questions science nor excludes the cultural beliefs thought to be unsettled by science, but redefines each by ungrounding all, Derrida's unsettling of the foundational structure of reflection intends both to operate from within philosophy and to include in it various moments and concepts that it must exclude before its foundations can operate. While the theme of multiplying sensation in Pater may appear hedonist, when we understand his expanded concept of sensation, we know that hedonism is not the case. In the same way, while one of Derrida's recurrent themes is the problematic definition of meaning and signification that occurs at key philosophic moments, his sense of the significance of these problems makes the charge that he is nihilistic or tries to prove that we never know the meaning of anything simply irrelevant to his project. Finally, as Pater's definition of the special role of art clearly entails something that all art does rather than something specific artists do or do not intend, Derrida's—and finally de Man's—understanding of the relevance of literary language to the philosophic problems they address also entails a constitutive element of all literature. It does not interpret the meaning of particular texts or their ability in specific empirical instances to mean or not to mean what their authors intended.

II

Derrida states clearly enough his philosophical project in the introduction to *Margins of Philosophy*, which addresses the coherence of philosophy as its central theme. Near the end of that introduction, he justifies the marginal concerns of the essays collected in the book with a familiar twist: "if they appear to remain marginal to some of the great texts in the history of philosophy, these ten writings *in fact* ask the question of the margin.... They interrogate philosophy beyond its meaning, treating it not only as a discourse but as a determined text, enclosed in the representation of its own margin" (*Margins*, xxiii). Derrida's gesture of claiming to question explicitly in an essay the label by which the essay might be classed and possibly condemned has by now become a familiar way of turning a question. In order to see its specific power here, however, we must first make some distinctions. Logically, questioning the general problem of a category by which an essay is criticized does not necessarily undercut the validity of criticizing that specific essay. An essay that addressed marginally scientific texts, say popularized essays on biology, in order to question where biology places its margin, would not by that questioning automatically become more properly biological. Biology might effectively draw its margin in such a place as to exclude those texts, whatever the conceptual problems of that placement were, because the conceptual problem of placing margins is not in itself a biological question. Moving somewhat closer to home, an essay in literary criticism that attempted to answer criticisms of its logic by contending that the margin between literary criticism and literature was an uncertain one would not have offered a complete answer for

DECONSTRUCTION 81

two reasons. First, neither literature nor literary criticism, at least at the outset, determines the definition of logic, so that being or not being logical does not necessarily have anything to do with being literary or critical but may be another kind of value judgment entirely. Second, and consequently, an uncertain margin between literature and literary criticism by itself would not show that some literary criticism might not follow canons of logic—the question of whether those canons are valid is not at issue at least at this stage of our argument—and therefore, for reasons that are quite properly extra-literary, might not be better literary criticism for doing so. In each case, the regionality of the field protects it from being unsettled by the question of margins and makes that question quite comfortably marginal to its own concerns, though possibly central to the concerns of some other field. The situation changes, however, when we question the margins around the field of philosophy, since, at least according to philosophy itself, it is the field that properly sets both its own margins and those of other disciplines. Nor is this ambition itself a marginal bit of overreaching:

> Does philosophy answer a need? How is it to be understood? Philosophy? The need?
>
> Ample to the point of believing itself interminable, a discourse that has *called itself philosophy*—doubtless the only discourse that has ever intended to receive its name only from itself, and has never ceased murmuring its initial letter to itself from as close as possible—has always, including its own, meant to say its limit. (*Margins*, x)

The contorted language stretches a standard historical observation back into a philosophical question. Let us for the moment follow Rorty's version of this history: prior to Kant, philosophy was simply the field that considered the most universal of questions, and writers like Descartes did not aim to define the preconditions of knowledge but to justify the discoveries of the new science by justifying its methods (*Philosophy*, 131). Kant, however, did claim to define a theory of knowledge, thus to offer a foundation for all other forms of knowledge and to determine the proper divisions between the disciplines. And that ambition has defined modern philosophy (*Philosophy*, 132, 163). For our purposes, it does not matter whether or not Rorty's attempt to specify a historical beginning of foundationalism is accurate. Derrida's point remains the same: philosophy responds to the need to explain what constitutes knowledge. That need must include defining what is proper to its own knowledge. Thus, it gives itself a name. The defining moment of philosophy, the moment in which it finds the need that justifies its existence, occurs when it names itself and defines its own margins. An ostensibly marginal essay that questions philosophical margins would no longer be marginal by the definition of what counts as central and defining in philosophy.

Nor does Derrida simply play word games here. The fact that defining the contours of knowledge means also defining the limits of one's own field of knowledge creates a fundamental problem that challenges not only philosophy's own self-definition but also the position of any critique of that definition. Thus Derrida asks a question with two sharp edges:

> If philosophy has always intended, from its point of view, to maintain its relation with the nonphilosophical, that is the antiphilosophical, with the practices and knowledge, empirical or not, that constitute its other, if it has constituted itself according to this purposive *entente* with its outside, if it has always intended to hear itself speak, in the same language, of itself and of something else, can one, strictly speaking, determine a nonphilosophical place, a place of exteriority or alterity from which one might still treat *of philosophy*? (*Margins*, xii)

On the one hand, to the extent to which philosophy's foundational goal entails remaining connected to what it defines as exterior to itself, either as improper or as simply beyond its margins, that exterior remains in some sense within its purview, part of itself. And philosophy must retain that connection or it could not properly define the nonphilosophical as exterior. Something entirely exterior would be beyond its capability to define either as exterior or not. A foundational definition of knowledge must stand outside knowledge in order to set its boundaries. But not standing within the proper bounds of knowledge, the definition cannot be knowledge, or at least cannot be only knowledge. On the other hand, if this comprehensiveness creates trouble for philosophy, it makes a critique of philosophy equally problematic. One can critique a field comprehensively only from its outside. Thus philosophy sets the bounds of other disciplines from outside those disciplines. But if there is no outside to philosophy, then its critique lacks a coherent standpoint just as much as its establishment does.[7] In short, foundationalism, as a concept, must contain its own logical fissures within it. If that situation questions its ultimate coherence, it also questions the stance from which to ask questions, at least as that stance implies another establishing foundational concept. Derrida's task then involves constructing an analysis that includes these contradictory but mutually entailed critiques within it.

We can see both the difficulties and the workings of this analysis in Derrida's extended discussion of one of his key terms, "differance." This term has caused considerable problems in Derridean discussion, not least because its status as a term is one of its problems. Derrida asserts near the beginning of the essay bearing the term for its title, "*Differance* is neither a *word* nor a *concept*" (*Speech*, 130),[8] to which Richard Rorty replies with a certain evident logic: "This is, however, not true. The first time Derrida used that collocation of letters, it was, indeed, not a word, but only misspelling. But around the third or fourth time he used it, it had *become* a word" ("Deconstruction," 18). To understand how both Derrida's and Rorty's statements can be true, we must describe what the term designates, why the nature of what it designates questions the aptness of designation as a description of what it does, and why that question nevertheless allows for Rorty's empirical intervention without being made irrelevant in the process. This explication will lead us finally to an understanding of what Derrida's questioning of foundationalism does and does not do.

To start this process, I want to look fairly closely at a moment in which Derrida tells us what differance is rather than what it is not or what it does. He starts with a fairly straightforward definition of an aspect of a sign:

> The sign is usually said to be put in the place of the thing itself, the present thing, "thing" here standing equally for meaning or referent . . . the sign, in this sense, is deferred presence. . . . And this structure presupposes that the sign, which defers presence, is conceivable only on the *basis* of the presence that it defers and *moving toward* the deferred presence that it aims to reappropriate. According to this classical semiology, the substitution of the sign for the thing itself is both *secondary* and *provisional*. (*Margins*, 9)

So far, Derrida does not mean to be controversial. The difficulty he wants to designate with the term "differance" does not involve simply the difference between a sign and its referent. That difference is part of the definition of the sign and its secondariness, not an indication that signs have no referents. If, as some deconstructionists have argued, some form of infinite material difference between sign and referent resulted in there being only signs without referents, the sign would simply become a referent, and the basic situation would remain unchanged. All the passage argues at this point is the nearly self-evident contention that signs have as part of their definition two kinds of difference that are mutually dependent upon each other. First, a sign declares that it comes after what it designates. Thus it differs in time from the presence of its referent, which is deferred. Second, in that deferral, the sign points to where the presence is as part of a promised reappropriation, thus establishing a spatial difference between itself and its referent. Differance stands for the temporal deferral and the spatial difference. But if differance is necessary to a definition of sign-systems, where in the system could we place it? It cannot be part of the sign, since if it were the sign would not be self-identical and would cease to function as a sign. This is, of course, not a problem with distinctions between different versions of the same sign in actual discourse. We can tolerate many phonological and typographical differences without losing sight of an ideational identity. But we tolerate these differences precisely by declaring them not part of the sign but extraneous. Equally obvious, the differance cannot be part of the referent, since if that is not univocal nothing determinate would be referred to and there would be no meaning. Normally, if we determined an entity that stood outside any part of a structure to which it was nevertheless necessary, we would be talking about some form of originary cause. But differance, as designating only what is not there, cannot by definition designate something originary: "in attempting to put into question these traits of the provisional secondariness of the substitute, one would come to see something like an originary *differance*; but one could no longer call it originary or final in the extent to which the values of origin ... have always denoted presence" (*Margins*, 9).

To understand the workings of this term, we have to distinguish between the operation of any particular act of signification and the formal working of the concept "sign." No doubt we use signs to refer successfully to things and meanings with fair frequency. If "differance" stopped us from doing that, it would not designate something not there but a material obstruction of some kind. Rather it designates a necessary gap in the *concept* of the sign, a flaw in the concept that it cannot work either with or without as a concept. "Differance" questions not the meaning of any specific sign but the working of the formal structure of the sign-system. As in Derrida's questioning of philosophy's self-founding, this specific term works only because of the sign-system's necessary ambition to be able to designate anything, even that which is outside itself.

"Differance" is not a word, because while words can refer to voids and absences, they cannot, by definition, not refer, but differance refers to that which in reference does not refer. In other words, it refers not to an absence but to a negation, a nonreference, an alterity to any reference. But a sign that does not refer is not a sign. For similar reasons, "differance" is not a concept. Designating something necessarily external to the sign-system, it cannot coherently function within that system as word or concept. But, of course, Rorty is right that once Derrida does designate that exterior nonreference, we have precisely a word designating a concept. Indeed the strangeness of the denial of its status inheres in our awareness that we can understand the assertion that differance is not a word or concept only if we understand what concept has been designated by the word.[9] Derrida exploits precisely this capacity of language to designate anything, to make any word, to create any concept, toward his end of creating contradiction within its foundation. Here, again, it may help to see "differance" working in a way analogous to Pater's form of sensation that is also a sensation. Pater showed how that empirical foundation, sensation, needed its excluded opposite, abstract form, in order to be apprehended as a sensation. In a way, he claimed that sensation is precisely a word and a concept. Derrida determined that a foundational abstraction, the structure of reference, depended on a material entity that it also excluded. In each case, the necessity of being comprehensive leads the foundational system to include something it defines as external. Like Pater, Derrida does not exclude meaning but includes its other.

We are now ready for a first fleshed-out justification of linking Pater and Derrida. From a certain perspective, they seem opposite rather than analogous. Pater showed some taste for a style of philosophy similar to Derrida's in his writing on Plato and Hegel, so he might well have had a like interest in Derrida. But, finally, Derrida's thought would surely represent for him the kind of abstraction that constantly sacrifices experienced perception to its fanaticism for its own philosophical ends. Equally, Derrida has written with sympathy on figures sufficiently similar to Pater in their dual roles as critics and artists to indicate that he might find some aspects of Pater congenial. But, finally, Pater exemplifies, from a Derridean perspective, a nearly unanalyzed belief in the primacy of perception—regardless of the contradictions Pater sees within that perception—and his mechanism of differance questions that belief. Moreover, Pater always subordinates his concern with what Derrida might call the classical topoi of philosophy to his final goal of opening a space in the battle between science and religion for an aesthetic that includes the freedom to experience both. In contrast, although literary language becomes an important deconstructive concern, at least in his early work Derrida subordinates it to his goal of destabilizing philosophy from within. At precisely this point, the linking becomes instructive, however. The parallels in the above contradictions I hope are evident. Essentially Pater works upon empiricism's grounding in sensation an analysis similar to Derrida's interrogation of Continental philosophy's search for a founding moment of originating self-identity. Pater needed such an analysis precisely because he wanted his defense of aesthetic sensation to be not a banal relativism but an inclusive form of both the science and the religion that ostensibly excluded art. Similarly, by determining a necessary exterior to philosophy's moment of self-identification, Derrida does not intend to provide an easy freedom from rationality in a simple alternative that philosophy would have always named in advance in any case. Rather, he provides a questioning of hierarchy and authority whose very strength lies in an inclusion of the philosophy that attempted to exclude it as improper or exterior.

One further, somewhat looser analogy: the roles played in Pater by religion and science, and more particularly by Arnold's sacralized Culture and by Ruskin's scientized art, recur in Derrida's persistent concerns with phenomenology and structuralism. Critics frequently contrast phenomenology and structuralism in terms of the former's concern with genesis, punctual events, and acts of consciousness and the latter's concern with structural coherence, synchronic continuity, and common codes or conventions. In this contrast, Husserl's search for a founding moment of pure, reflexive self-identity behind material signs and events operates in a way similar to religion's claim in Pater's time to ground a value that science could not reach. Similarly, structuralism's claim to ground a study of the human sciences as sciences on an analysis of common codes underlying individual intentions plays for Derrida the role that science played for Pater.[10] Like Pater, Derrida interrogates that opposition by showing the necessity of each system to the other, thus extending his definition of a paradoxical inclusiveness within philosophic foundations to an inclusion within his theory of opposed philosophic systems in terms of their own foundational contradictions.

Both phenomenology and structuralism claimed a decisive break with past philosophy, while, consciously or not, making the traditional philosophical claim of refounding knowledge, and each did that through an itinerary that both exactly opposed the other's and reproduced exactly that aspect of its opposite that it had tried to expel. Husserl's phenomenology begins by denying provisionally what he thought philosophy tried constantly and unsuccessfully to establish: the presence of a world external to the subject. By defining an absolutely pure subjectivity through a transcendental reduction that eliminated any traces of a presumed externality, eliminating even a psychological subject as empirical externality, he sought to rebuild a ground for knowledge by showing what the transcendental subject presupposed through its acts of perception.[11] In contrast, structuralism tried to define codes that, by definition, operated in the absence of any given subject. This was also a reduction of a kind, since it gave up claims to understand the individuality of events or meanings in favor of defining the externally necessary codes that were the preconditions for the occurrence of those events or meanings. In contrast, Derrida argues that what each tries to eliminate or reduce constitutes precisely one of its preconditions, so that each foundation contains—though incoherently—precisely that which it had tried to expel as unscientific or unprovable.

DECONSTRUCTION 87

Since Husserl primarily concerned himself with defining a transcendental consciousness, Derrida must begin his analysis of that philosophy with a justification of his own concern with the themes of language and sign theory, particularly since, as Derrida readily admits, Husserl rigorously subordinated the problem of language and signs to the problem of transcendental logic (*Speech*, 7-8). Derrida argues, in contrast, that the subject's ostensibly pure apprehension of itself within consciousness is always at least partly linguistic: "since self-consciousness appears only in its relation to an object, whose presence it can keep and repeat, it is never perfectly foreign or anterior to language" (*Speech*, 15). But the conventionality of language, the externality of structure that explicitly concerns structuralism, must obviously be expelled from phenomenological consciousness if it is to function with the pure internality that the transcendental reduction demands. The logic by which *Speech and Phenomena* operates involves constantly showing that each division Husserl proposes to expel language's externality from transcendental consciousness nevertheless smuggles that externality back in. First Husserl distinguishes between an indicative sign and an expressive sign: an expressive sign has a meaning, while an indicative sign, though it has signification, has no meaning, no extra-linguistic sense. Thus "tree" would be expressive, "which" would be indicative. Obviously the point of language is to express, and so expressiveness should be the prior form. Nevertheless, in order to express, every word in some sense depends on its linguistic form; thus every word has an element of indication within it. So far, Derrida merely explicates a problem Husserl describes openly. But, for the transcendental consciousness to operate without any presumption of an outside object, Husserl must find an internal language without indication, without any external form.

To escape language's externality, Husserl first expels communication from the language of the transcendental consciousness. He proposes an inward speech that enacts a pure, imaginative representation. Since one is representing to one-self, one does not need to communicate, and one does not therefore need the material, indicative aspect of language. Since the act is imaginary, it in fact makes no use of that aspect. In a maneuver that he will repeat frequently, Derrida insists in contrast on an irreducibly indicative aspect to any sign, any representation: "When in fact I *effectively* use words, and whether or not I do it for communicative ends (let us consider signs in general, prior to this distinction), I must from the outset operate (within) a structure of repetition whose basic element can only be representative. A sign is never an event, if by event we mean an irreplaceable and irreversible empirical particular. A sign which would take place but 'once' would not be a sign" (*Speech*, 50). Any representation, even a purely imaginary one, must be in principle repeatable or it could not re-present. The very form of a sign opposes it to a purely phenomenological event and necessitates that even the most rigorous internal soliloquy, with no communicative end, with no use of material language, in fact carry within it the indicativeness that would prevent it from being entirely an act of transcendental consciousness.

Husserl cannot expel language entirely, since the presentation of even the ideational image of an object to consciousness already creates the problem Derrida has identified here. But he can make one more radical reduction of indicativeness by claiming that internal language is not merely an imaginary soliloquy but an atemporal act of purely internal speech or voice: "the ideality of the object . . . can only be expressed in an element whose phenomenality does not have worldly form. *The name of this element is the voice*" (*Speech*, 76). The unworldliness of speech's phenomenality consists in its being a completely internal voice. The Derridean theme of phonologism, which seems such an arbitrary claim to American literary critics at times, takes its persuasiveness from Derrida's analysis of its connection to the concept of pure consciousness here. The voice is the medium of pure consciousness because: "when I speak, it belongs to the phenomenological essence of this operation that *I hear myself . . . at the same time* that I speak. The signifier, animated by my breath and by the meaning-intention . . . is in absolute proximity to me" (*Speech*, 77). The relationship between speaking and hearing, even when they are internalized within the same subject, allows Derrida to describe this situation, however, not as self-presence but as auto-affection, the self sensing itself. Hearing oneself speak is a pure auto-affection, unlike touching oneself or seeing one's own reflection, because it occurs entirely within the body, without any intervention from an outside (*Speech*, 78–79). But even this pure auto-affection cannot be identical to simple self-presence since it entails relationship, a relationship created by the medium of the voiced speech. At this point, Derrida can conclude that the transcendental subject always carries within it the exterior structures it constantly tries to reduce away: "this movement of differance is not something that happens to a transcendental subject; it produces a subject. Auto-affection is not a modality of experience that characterizes a being that would already be itself. . . . It produces sameness as self-relation within self-difference" (*Speech*, 82).

The central themes and deconstructive techniques made so notorious by *Of Grammatology* all occur in this discussion of Husserl. The specific value of *Speech and Phenomena*, though, arises from the very aspect of the work that has made it relatively less interesting to deconstructive literary critics and critics of deconstruction, its very technicality. The intervention of differance in Husserl's transcendental subject seems less melodramatically threatening than some fictive destruction of meaning with which critics usually credit Derrida. The example of Husserl specifies the general analysis of philosophical foundation discussed above: the foundational, reflective moment of philosophy naming itself occurs with the voicing of the transcendental subject, and in response Derrida identifies the entrance of otherness and externality into that voicing. This argument, again, does not question any specific forms of knowledge, meaning, or truth. It connects the ambition to construct a system for grounding knowledge with a contradictory exclusion of some form of nonknowledge. As Arnold's best self excludes science from his grounding of culture, Husserl's transcendental subject excludes any form of intervening materiality or externality. But as in the case of Pater's movement between Ruskin and Arnold, Derrida's method does not limit itself to the content of any specific exclusion but concerns the act of exclusion in general. We can see this in his frequently misread essay on Lévi-Strauss and structuralism, "Structure, Sign, and Play."

The frequent commentary on this essay, particularly on its constantly quoted penultimate paragraph, enables me to focus my discussion on one aspect of it, precisely the substitution of center with play in structuralism's sense of structure. The essay starts by explaining "center" as that which defines a structure and thus contains its totality. A center is thus, in a sense, both a structure's essence and that which is outside it. The relationship of center to structure here pretty clearly equals the founding relationship that exists between the transcendental subject and the world that Husserl thought to rebuild from his reduction to that subject. Thus phenomenology may claim to be prior to structuralism as a center is a prior necessity for any structure. The essay proceeds to explain the intervention of structuralism as its replacement of that center first with the concept of signs and then with the play of substitution among signs. Indeed, Derrida makes clear that this escape from the idea of center is so important to Lévi-Strauss's ethnographic structuralism at least—one might even say central to it—that its very claim to being a science rests on it: "one can assume that ethnology could have been born as a science only at the moment when a decentering had come about: at the moment when European culture—and in consequence, the history of metaphysics and of its concepts—had been *dislocated*, driven from its locus, and forced to stop considering itself as the culture of reference" (*Writing*, 282). This indeed sounds like a freeing alternative to Husserl's attempt to solve the crisis of European sciences; it identifies science as the moment when one realizes that the center is a cultural construct. And structuralism replaces this center with play. Already this replacement should make play suspect, though, given what we have seen about Derrida's insistence on the impossibility of finding a pure outside to philosophy. The suspicion pays off when we look at what play does and what forms it takes.

At first, analyzing a passage from Lévi-Strauss, Derrida identifies play in terms of supplementarity (*Writing*, 289), one of those intentionally oxymoronic terms that implies both originariness and its determined negation, thus providing neither an alternative nor a substitute for concepts of center and origin even as it occupies precisely the place of those concepts. Derrida defines "supplement" most precisely in *Of Grammatology*, where he marks its two significations. First, a "supplement adds itself, it is a surplus, a plenitude enriching another plenitude, the *fullest measure* of presence" (144). But the supplement also replaces a lack in the original structure: "as substitute, it is not simply added to the positivity of a presence, it produces no relief, its place is assigned in the structure by the mark of an emptiness" (145). As differance both constitutes the sign-referent system and yet cannot exist within it, supplement defines itself as a replenishing exterior even as its definition implies an emptiness within that it replaces. In the position of the structure's center, in "Structure, Sign, and Play," Derrida places the supplement in the form of the sign. But since supplements work by substituting, the sign does not replace the center as a positive alternative but as an activity of substitution. This activity of substitution Derrida identifies as play. Usually one finds critics either praising or condemning "play" here as an alternative to logic and traditional, rational discourse, an activity freed from reason by the fact that signs have no meanings or are infinitely distant from meanings. But, in fact, to the extent that "play" operates in a manner similar to "differance," we must specify two things about it. First, the substitution of center with play will not justify a claim that all writing is, in some sense, just language, a movement from word to word or sign to sign. Substitution occurs within the concept of sign as it is attached to the concept of referent. A positing of a movement from sign to sign as replacing the movement from sign to referent would in fact replace the center with another stable concept, another form of center, that of the sign, since a sign without a referent would have no more necessity of a difference embedded within it than does the traditional concept of a meaning. Second, one cannot really imagine this play either as a loss of center or as a freeing into a new form of interpretation, no longer constrained by the rules of center. Either of these alternatives again gives play a ruling meaning.

Derrida does almost close the essay with the usual reading of play as a positive alternative. At first, he seems to offer this alternative play as

DECONSTRUCTION 91

the one that will free us from the fallacies of center and of metaphysics: "Turned towards the lost or impossible presence of the absent origin, this structuralist thematic of broken immediacy is therefore the saddened, *negative*, nostalgic, guilty, Rousseauistic side of the thinking of play whose other side would be the Nietzschean *affirmation*, that is the joyous affirmation of the play of the world and of the innocence of becoming, the affirmation of a world of signs without fault, without truth, and without origin which is offered to an active interpretation" (*Writing*, 292). Comment on this passage, both by proponents and by critics of deconstruction, almost universally assumes that Derrida espouses Nietzschean affirmation.[12] And certainly, as a matter of choice, most of us would rather be joyful than saddened, I expect. If we place the passage back in context, however, the situation does not look this simple. Neither of these alternatives constitutes a traditional interpretive attitude exactly. Derrida identifies both of them in this passage as forms of the play that was supposed to replace centering. They differ only in terms of attitude, either the joy or the sadness of the interpreting subject. But structuralism at least designed the elimination of the center to expel an unscientific and philosophical subjectivity from its system. Play as alternative, either as joyful or as saddened alternative, merely reimports the Husserlian project of founding knowledge and choice upon some form of consciousness. In attempting to replace a center with play, either joyful or saddened, we succeed only in crafting play into a new center. Thus, in his last paragraph, Derrida denies the possibility of choice—the category of choice, after all, entails an acceptance of a founding subject—proposing instead that we learn both the common ground and the differance between these different attitudes. When he discusses Husserl's attempt to found science upon a philosophy of the subject, Derrida shows the necessity of assuming an externality that Husserl tries to rule out of bounds in his founding, originary moment. Then, discussing structuralism's attempt to found the human sciences by eliminating unscientific concepts of the subject and subjective, ethnocentric attitudes, he shows the necessary subjective moment in that founding of structural play. In each case, Derrida embeds within the foundational moment of one discipline the founding principle of the other, using this excess of inclusiveness to call foundational exclusion into question.

Against critiques of Derrida either as a nihilist or as a defender of subjective interpretation, I have opposed a reading of his argument as a questioning of foundations that shows the necessary inclusion within foundational systems of elements they need to exclude in order to remain internally coherent. I will end this section with a brief consideration of the consequences of such a theory. Only in this chapter's subsequent discussion of the significance of literary language to the theory, the next chapter's analysis of Derrida's and de Man's redefinition of aesthetics, and the final chapter's explicit broaching of the subject of political implications can those consequences be worked out in real detail. Here, however, since most of the charges of relativism or nihilism leveled at deconstruction derive from its transformation into a method of literary interpretation, I want to differentiate it from that method. Recognizing the flaws in that methodological extension will also lead to a sharper sense of Derrida's mode of analysis and thus clear the way for the next section's attempt to delineate what I take to be the telling pertinence of deconstruction for the study of literature.[13]

I am not primarily interested in the particular methods of reading proposed by deconstructive literary criticism nor in the extent to which they accord with Derrida's theory. Rather I want to address two related problems, the problem of conceiving of a method different from the theory but in some determinable relationship to it and the problem of the knowledge that would both ground and derive from this method. J. Hillis Miller's formulations exemplify both of these problems because he so clearly conceives of what he does as a method justified by results. Thus he gives instructions for what a critic should do: "the deconstructive critic seeks to find, by [the] process of retracing, the element in the system studied which is alogical, the thread in the text in question which will unravel it all, or the loose stone which will pull down the whole building" ("Stevens' Rock," 341). Moreover, he tells us where to look for this thread or loose stone: "Attention to the play of figure is necessary . . . because the heterogeneity of any text expresses itself in the fluctuations of figure. An example is a figure which functions simultaneously as a metaphor, therefore as mimesis, and as metonymy, therefore as the assertion of a discontinuity or contingency which destroys mimesis" ("Deconstructing," 31). Finally, in a response to an essay that discusses his methods, he complains not of the idea that he was articulating a set of procedures but only of the effect of divorcing these abstract directions from the particular readings of literary works in which they originally appeared. He insists on the value of what he does as deriving from the results of the method: "the primary value of 'deconstruction' is not its coherence as a theory but the fact that it has made possible new insights into what is going on in particular works, even where that has been insight into the necessary blindness of the work to its own incoherence or heterogeneity" ("Theory," 610). Although Miller's version of deconstruction has been much criticized, in this discussion as well, if only by implication, one can see at least a family resemblance between the destabilizing analysis of foundational concepts practiced by Derrida, the discovery of self-contradictory inclusions and exclusions, and this search for figures that, by simultaneously enacting contradictory modes of signification, unravel a structure of which they partake. The problem is less the content of Miller's method than that his very concept of method rests on certain presumptions that run counter to Derrida's claim that his reading of philosophy cannot justify or be justified by any particular method.

First, as I said, Miller clearly sees his readings as separable from the theory, which might or might not have its own coherence, and sees the value of the theory as resting on the insights produced by its method. This is, of course, a schema common to theories of knowledge arising from empiricism. The problem is that questioning the project of formulating a theory of knowledge will be radically separated from that schema, since it depends on one of those theories, empiricism, already being correct. Imagine, for instance, that Miller or some other deconstructive critic established that a particular text or all the canonic texts actually did self-deconstruct in the way Miller posits that they will. To the extent that the content of these readings demonstrated the value of the theory, the fact of the demonstration would imply the reverse, since such a demonstration can be effective only in the situation of a foundational theory grounding a method whose resultant readings have the status of evidence. In the absence of such a situation, this set of deconstructive readings would show only that a certain set of works happened to contain a common meaning or nonmeaning. Now imagine the reverse case, that one could show that a deconstructive reading of a particular work was wrong or, according to some criterion other than correctness or incorrectness, less than satisfactory. That demonstration would not show the incorrectness of Derrida's argument. Foundational systems do not articulate items of knowledge but only determine the preconditions of some proposition being knowledge. Undermining the possibility of there being coherent foundational systems, consequently, does not undermine the truth or falsehood of some particular statement. Thus, proving that some text had some determinate meaning would not prove that a coherent foundational system existed for deciding whether we had arrived at the determinate meaning of any text. The problem here is not that Miller's system of reading or Derrida's theory is unfalsifiable.[14] The falsifiability of Miller's system has no relevance to Derrida's theory. And Derrida's theory is no less falsifiable than any foundational theory. Falsifiability is a criterion for measuring the truth of particular propositions established by a certain theory of knowledge. Thus it cannot measure the status of that theory itself or one opposed to it.

These objections to the literary method Miller proposes finally depend on a larger objection. Methods depend for their validity upon being at once outside of the particular knowledge statements they produce and inside a foundational system that grounds their procedures.[15] In other words, if readings deriving from a method produce its value, the readings must be separable from the method. They must also be available to estimations independent of them and the method. Thus behind both must be some ground of knowledge justifying both. In the case of theories questioning foundations, the knowledge that grounds methods or readings usually entails some version of knowing one's own entrapment in a situation of groundlessness. Thus Gayatri Spivak asks, "when Derrida claims for himself that he is within yet without the cloture of metaphysics, is the difference not precisely that he *knows* it at least?" and answers, "in the long run, what sets 'Derrida' apart is that he *knows* that he is always already surrendered to writing as he writes" ("Translator's Preface," *Of Grammatology*, xxxviii, xlv). Assuming that the obvious internal contradiction of this position does not render it invalid,[16] such a position would ground Miller's method for showing an inevitable reduction of meaning to writing. And the readings specifying how that reduction works, in their elucidation of the particular texts they read, would give value to the method. And Miller knows the location of this knowledge at least in the case of literary criticism: "great works of literature are likely to be ahead of their critics. They are there already. They have anticipated explicitly any deconstruction the critic can achieve" ("Deconstructing," 31). Even if one ignores the status of the larger, general contradiction entailed in claiming knowledge of the impossibility of founding knowledge, however, Miller's schema radically undercuts the content of its own contentions: he sets up a situation in which critics, albeit with great effort, by using his method, accurately repeat a knowledge already articulated by the great works of literature. This is in fact so faithful a depiction of traditional interpretation that one wonders how one may specify as "knowledge" that ostensible critique of tradition, which we interpret the great works of literature as showing.

Nor, if one solves the general contradiction in the way I have been arguing for—by separating foundational systems from the knowledge for which they might or might not serve as preconditions and contending that Derrida's argument pertains only to the former—does one's position with regard to Miller's method improve, since, unlike specific statements of knowledge, methods do necessarily rest upon the foundations that outline their validity. The problem, in other words, is not with Derrida's theory but with a method of literary reading grounded on that theory. Derrida's own discussion of method in *Of Grammatology*, rather than grounding that literary method, despite the family resemblances I mentioned, precisely analyzes the problem of method as another version of the problem of foundation. That analysis specifies further how to think about the consequences of his analysis of philosophy's project of self-founding.

Derrida breaks his reading of Rousseau at the strategic moment after he has articulated the concept of the supplement but before he deploys that concept to produce a more specific reading of Rousseau's *Essay on the Origin of Languages*. In this break he addresses versions of the questions posed above. First he asks what particular status his reading has among other possible readings of Rousseau: "following the appearances of the word 'supplement' and of the corresponding concept or concepts, we traverse a certain path within Rousseau's text.... But are other paths not possible: And as long as the totality of paths is not effectively exhausted, how shall we justify this one?" He then asks what larger significance his reading of Rousseau has: "In Rousseau's text, after having indicated ... the function of the sign 'supplement,' I now prepare myself to give special privilege, in a manner that some might consider exorbitant, to certain texts.... By what right?" In other words, Derrida knows that for his readings to produce their value, they must have a certain relation of exemplariness to his theory: to act as evidence, the reading must be distinctive, not merely one among others, and it must be sufficient to evidence the theory in question without evidencing more than that theory. And he knows further that rather than having this relation of adequacy, his reading of Rousseau precisely exceeds the explanatory capability of his theory: "in a certain measure and in spite of the theoretical precautions that I formulate, my choice is in fact *exorbitant*" (*Of Grammatology*, 161).

Rather than justifying his method by his reading, Derrida essentially admits that this reading, in particular, could not justify any method, is beyond the orbit of theory or method. He then uses precisely the contradiction of a method producing a reading that exceeds the logic of any method to justify the exemplary situation of this reading at both the general and the specific level. First, identifying his reading of Rousseau as "radically empiricist," in the sense of being so individual as to be beyond any relation to any theory, thus implying the inability of any foundational theory to contain that which the reading shows, he then doubles back on his own claim: "to *exceed* the metaphysical orb is an attempt to get out of the orbit ... to think the entirety of the classical conceptual oppositions, particularly the one within which the value of empiricism is held" (162). The claim to be beyond any foundational theory, he realizes, is itself one kind of foundational claim. This paradox, however, extends too far to hold within it the particular case of Rousseau. Raising again the question of Rousseau's exemplariness, then, Derrida admits "this avowal of empiricism can sustain itself only by the strength of the question" (162). And then he specifies further: "In certain respects, the theme of supplementarity is certainly no more than one theme among others. . . . *But it happens that this theme describes the chain itself, the being-chain of a textual chain, the structure of substitution, the articulation of desire and of language, the logic of all conceptual oppositions taken over by Rousseau.* . . . It tells us in a text what a text is" (163). On the one hand, the very questions he asks deny his ability to offer specific readings as examples of his theory (as he realizes and Miller does not). On the other hand, Rousseau thematizes the questions that create suspicions of fastening on merely one theme among others. In effect, the problems articulated by this reading delineate the problems of describing a method whose logic cannot be assured by any foundation, a method that, to make a case for its own validity, must produce a reading so radically specific that it could not serve to exemplify any case. As he embeds the problem of foundation within foundational philosophy, and embeds the problem of the sign and referent within the relation between the two, he also embeds the problem his reading will show within the relation among foundation, method, and reading. The case is at once absolutely specific and—because only one case like this creates all of the problems he needs—absolutely general in its significance.

The problem of deconstruction as a literary-critical practice, thus, may be less its specific fidelity or lack of fidelity to Derrida's philosophy—and fidelity to theory should be a critique that this theory in particular makes us wary of—than the inability of such a theory to ground any method more general than the specific interpretation that produced it. In particular, a literary practice based on a philosophical theory about foundational definitions of meaning reproduces precisely the traditional relationship among theory, method, and resulting reading that one would think Derrida's theory would lead us to want to question rather than to enact. But if Derrida's theory has no consequences beyond itself, what value does it have? I will argue, in the balance of this chapter on literary language and in subsequent chapters on aesthetics and ideology, for the implications of Derrida's theory based on a process of expanding significance. In other words, I will contend that the mode of theorizing that characterizes his thinking about philosophical foundations contains within it a mode of thinking about literary language and a mode of thinking about aesthetics and ideology. This process of expanding the boundary of the original theory in fact forms the only methodological justification offered by Derrida's chapter on method. One does not seek specific readings but seeks to enact a certain process of reading in different contexts. One demonstrates the excess of event to foundational ground by explicating the theme of excess in a specific case whose significance exceeds the model of exemplary adequacy by which we connect specific cases with general theories.[17] This process also follows the way Derrida questions all foundational moments of reflection by showing that for the reflection to be foundational it must exceed the boundaries it sets up to guard its own integrity.

With regard to the specific relevance of Derrida's theory to literary criticism, however, the way I detail his theory's inclusive significance derives from my earlier reading of Pater, and the only surprise about this situation is that no one would question this relationship between philosophy and art in Pater's case. In other words, Pater's attempt to formulate a mode of concentrating on sensation by embedding abstraction within it as a *form* of sensation obviously does not entail any particular method of interpreting art nor does it entail any specific readings of artworks or exclude any other readings. Rather, by interpreting art, regardless of the content of that interpretation, one enacts in the most exemplary way the mode of sensation Pater defines. The next section will argue that Derrida's theory of literary language extends from and has its place within his analysis of foundational philosophy in precisely this way and that, further, Paul de Man extends this theory of literary language not into specific critical practices but into a theory of critical practice and its relation to literature. In other words, Pater argues not for a mode of interpreting art but for the inclusion of artistic interpretation within the science that attempts to exclude it. Equally, neither Derrida nor de Man argues for a specific literary method but for the inclusion of literary interpretation within the philosophy that expels it as less scientific.

III

Derrida has insisted on the importance of the literary to his interests: "for I have to remind you, somewhat bluntly and simply, that my most constant interest, coming even before my philosophical interest I should say, if this is possible, has been directed towards literature, toward that act of writing which is called literary" ("Time of a Thesis," 37). So one could hardly deny some relevance of his philosophical project to the study of literature. Yet, when he specifies his interest in literature, he gives little indication that his interest lies either in breaking down the distinction between the literary and the philosophical (Rorty, "Deconstruction," 2) or in posing those categories as foundational ones that need deconstructing (Culler, *On Deconstruction*, 149–150). Derrida's interest in the literary has been as a way of addressing philosophy, of writing about philosophy: "in literature, for example, philosophical language is still present in some sense; but it produces and presents itself as alienated from itself, at a remove, at a distance. This distance provides the necessary space from which to interrogate philosophy anew" (Kearney, 109). If Derrida wants to use literature to interrogate philosophy anew, one can hardly say that he wants to deconstruct an opposition between literature and philosophy. It would be more accurate to say that he wants to use literature to deconstruct other oppositions within philosophy. Neither can one say that he wants to get rid of the distinction between philosophy and literature, since the distinction provides him with the distance he needs for his interrogation.

Much of this problem clears up if we distinguish between an interest in literary works and an interest in a form of language classed as literary language. In the first quotation above, for instance, Derrida specifies that he has been concerned with an act of writing, which has been called literary. And, although the second statement seems to identify the occurrence of philosophical statements within works of literature, Derrida quickly adds, "and it was my preoccupation with literary texts which enabled me to discern the problematic of *writing*." Defined variously, the concept of a specifically literary language has played a more or less important role in thinking about literature since at least the Russian Formalists. They defined the role of literature as one of defamiliarization, of making us see the familiar in an uncustomary way. Literature might defamiliarize anything, of course, but the most literary thing it might defamiliarize would be literature itself, and it did this by focusing on literary devices and strategies normally backgrounded as part of form; thus Victor Shklovsky could label *Tristram Shandy* "the most typical novel in world literature" because it focused on modes of narrative organization common to all literature (57). Obviously, the next step would be to define a form of language that, instead of referring to something extra-linguistic, would refer to its own linguistic quality and call that literary language (Jakobson, 18–51). American New Criticism could then specify that such language would be figurative rather than scientific or straightforwardly referential and thus delineate the particular way that literature communicated (Cleanth Brooks, 1–21). Without denying the possibility of distinguishing between forms of language in this way, many critics have denied that that which we label literary language is in any sense some quality essential or exclusive to literature, arguing that so-called normal speech uses so-called literary language pervasively and centrally (see particularly Pratt, 3–38). Thus literary language may or may not be coextensive with the category of literature but is, in any case, separable from it.

We have then a form of language identified with a disciplinary category, literature, but which may not in any sense be proper to it. One could go further and note that if literary language were in fact proper only to literature, and Shklovsky were then correct in identifying literary works about literary language as the most essentially literary, the model of propriety operating would be classically philosophical rather than literary, since it would denominate essential features directly. And the model through which the literary work that referred more directly to its own literariness would be labeled as more literary would in fact be one of nonliterary, straightforward reference. As a concept, then, literary language would seem to undercut its own definitive mode of reference to the precise extent that it can operate with a propriety special to itself. The embedded contradictions of this situation would have obvious attractions to Derrida, and, indeed, at precisely the moments that he specifies his interest in the literary, with a simultaneous gesture, he questions the category of the literary:

> Yes, it is incontestable that certain texts classed as "literary" have seemed to me to operate breaches or infractions at the most advanced points. . . . Why? At least for the reason that induces us to suspect the denomination "literature," and which subjects the concept to belles-lettres, to the arts, to poetry, to rhetoric, and to philosophy. These texts operate, in their very movement, the demonstration and practical deconstruction of the *representation* of what was done with literature, it being well understood that long before these "modern" texts a certain "literary" practice was able to operate against this model, against this representation. (*Positions*, 69)

Although this passage does not specify the concept of "literary language," it does identify the activity of representation as that around which the distinction "literary" revolves. Moreover, those "literary" texts that question philosophy also question the category of literature, not because literature actually contains philosophical discourse and philosophy actually contains literary discourse, but because the categories themselves, as representations, belong to the activity of representation at issue.

This problematic category of literary language, then, helps Derrida articulate the problems in philosophy's moment of self-founding in two ways. First, literary language, rather than merely referring directly to objects or ideas, either because it is figural or because it is explicitly self-reflective, focuses on its own acts of reference. It thus foregrounds an element of reference that a foundational system has both to explain and exclude in a single self-contradictory gesture. To put the case too simply, literary language is obviously secondary, a special use to which language can be put because of its expansive powers of reference, but not the primary use to which we put it: denominating things in the world. But, on the other hand, linguistic self-denomination, which has a foundational and logical if not chronological priority over any subsequent denomination, automatically enacts an instance of literary language's special case. Like the terms "differance" and "supplement," literary language thus becomes an ideally problematic category—a margin or a boundary to philosophy that also carries within it central philosophical acts—through which Derrida may question the continual problems with self-founding. But second, literary language is not merely a site from which such problems may be formulated. It offers primary versions of the very problems that it helps to define. As a category, it reenacts, even as it represents in an essential way, the foundational problems it works to analyze. It does not then provide any alternative to foundational discourse through which we might exit from those problems. If, having discovered literary language's "real" centrality to philosophical discourse, we pose it as enacting a central truth—the truth of polysemy or omnipresent figurality—that posing will have enacted a type of denomination that contradicts its own process. The problem with thinking of literary language as the essence of literature, discussed above, becomes the problem with thinking that literary language could be the essence of anything, even if it were the only thing that could be that essence.

Literary language, for Derrida, has the role that art had for Pater, and the difference in the categories derives from the different foundational conceptions they questioned and at the same time indicates the essential similarity of their projects. Art enacts for its own sake the sensations Pater seeks to identify and thus, in its very refusal to have any other purpose than its own, assumes a central philosophic and cultural value. Likewise, literary language operates in Derrida as a crucial philosophical and, we will see, ideological category—crucial precisely in its ostensible marginality, reflecting denomination and denominating reflection with a paradoxical simultaneity that Derrida places at a then paradoxical center, the philosophical act of self-naming and self-reflection. The value of coupling Pater and Derrida occurs precisely at this moment in its indication of the connection between the two sides of deconstruction that are rapidly becoming fissured in battles between philosophical and literary interpretations. If the original reception of deconstruction as a literary method distorted Derrida, new attention to his philosophical significance, at the expense of marginalizing the literary, will distort equally. Refixing on the centrality of the literary will not make Derrida seem "aestheticist" in the usual sense that accusation carries of being deliberately irrelevant or without other than artistic significance, because that centrality occurs, as in the original aestheticism, only as a result of a philosophical project. It will, however, prepare for a reformulated understanding of the connection between Derrida's work and Paul de Man's, whose central theoretical concern was also with literary language, rather than with transforming Derrida into a method of practical criticism. Thus after working through Derrida's definition of the subject in "The Double Session," this section will focus on de Man's struggles with the concept of literary language and the effect of his deconstructive turn on those struggles, thus the theoretical connection between Derrida's deconstruction and literary concerns.

The difficulty of taking literature as one's subject if one defines it as that which exceeds the denomination of a subject pervades Derrida's most central consideration of literature, "The Double Session." Thus his opening announcement of subject matter circles around the subject rather than announcing it:

> The double session ... about which I don't quite have the gall to say plumb straight out that it is reserved for the question *what is literature*, this question being henceforth properly considered a quotation already, in which the place of the *what is* ought to lend itself to careful scrutiny, along with the presumed authority under which one submits anything whatever, and particularly literature, to the form of its inquisition—this double session, about which I will never have the militant innocence to announce that it is concerned with the question *what is literature*, will find its corner BETWEEN ... literature and truth, between literature and that by which the question *what is? wants* answering. (*Dissemination*, 177)

If Derrida believed in the priority of philosophic language over literary language, of direct reference over figural reference or self-reference, then he could start a philosophical analysis of literary language with a straightforward announcement of his topic. Since his philosophic interest, however, is in the prior necessity of marginal and indirect modes of reference to definitions of reference, such a straightforward announcement would be deceptive in its implications. Using literary language to outline the difficulties of defining reference, he lists them by describing the difficulties of referring to his topic directly. First, a completely direct reference to the question of literary language is *literally* impossible since the question "what is literature?" is always a citation: because the question of literature immediately raises the question of accurate denomination as prior to it—"the place of *what is* ought to lend itself to careful scrutiny"—in the moment of its being asked, the question immediately cites itself in order to ask the prior question embedded within its own citation. In effect, if literature, straightforwardly defined with both gall and militant innocence, is language about its own particular mode of using language, then it always cites language in its references. We could remove those quotation marks only by asking the question of what it is from outside literature, from a straightforward philosophy, and, the essay will argue, literature will always proceed to put quotation marks around that philosophical asking at the moment philosophy defines its own truth of denomination, thus cites itself in a literary mode. If one can address neither the question of what literature is directly nor the foreshortened question "what is?" an essay moving between the philosophic categories of literature and truth, the in-between where that essay will locate literature, may manage to indicate what it will, at least formally, refuse to address directly. Being concerned with the philosophic status of the in-between that literary language embodies, the essay demonstrates what in its own terms it cannot label: the interdependence of direction and indirection in the activity of reference, whether literary or philosophical. Thus to analyze Mallarmé's embodiment and definition of literature in *Mimique*, Derrida first analyzes a passage from Plato that uses images of the arts to define how we know the truth. In the course of that analysis, he may then analyze what literature does.

Derrida opens his analysis with a passage from Plato's *Philebus*, which he claims tells "true history, the history of meaning" (*Dissemination*, 184). Explaining how we come to our knowledge of our experiences, Socrates proposes a threefold process whereby first we have the feelings, then we describe them to ourselves in an internalized discourse, thus inscribing the feelings on our souls as assertions, after which, finally, an internal painter paints pictures of the assertions also in our souls. Although Socrates images the second stage of the process as writing, a category *Of Grammatology* has taught us to be wary of, the stranger aspect is the final stage. As Derrida asks, "what, in fact, is the painter doing here?" His answer to that question opens the topic of mimesis, which structures the essay: "The painting that shapes the images is a portrait of the discourse; it is worth only as much as the discourse it fixes and freezes along its surface. . . . But painting, that degenerate and somewhat superfluous expression, that supplementary frill of discursive thought, that ornament of *dianoia* and *logos*, also plays a role that seems to be just the opposite of this. It functions as a pure indicator of the essence of a thought or discourse defined as image, representation, repetition" (189). Within the terms of Socrates' own definition, the internal writing that creates assertions about memories, feelings, and sensations comes after those experiences and constitutes the possibility of truth or falsehood: only the assertions about the feelings may be true or false. But how would we decide whether the assertions are true or false? The standard definition involves accurate or inaccurate depictions of what assertions represent. But we cannot see accuracy directly, since that concept assumes two entities in a relationship that may or may not be correspondent. Nor can we measure the relationship between the assertion and the feeling, since the feeling emerges into an evaluable entity only at the moment we make assertions regarding it. Thus Socrates posits an internal image, which would be of the essence of the feeling, and to which the assertion might correspond. But this image of essence comes only after the original representation in writing. The image then serves as both a purification of that representation back to essence and as a supplementary and ornamental act. This image of the painter Derrida then connects to the activity of mimesis and its relationship to truth.

In order to see the problematic working of mimesis, we must first understand Derrida's claim that truth "has always meant two different things": "the process of truth is *on the one hand* the unveiling of what lies concealed in oblivion (*aletheia*), the veil lifted or raised {releve} from the thing itself, from that which *is* insofar as it is, presents itself, produces itself, and can even exist in the form of a determinable hole in Being; *on the other hand* . . . truth is agreement (*homoiosis* or *adaequatio*), a relation of resemblance or equality between a re-presentation and a thing (unveiled, present)" (192–193). By itself, neither definition is controversial. The first entails capturing the essence of a thing rather than its accidents. The second involves the familiar notion of correspondence: truth describes an accurate correspondence, "a relation of resemblance or equality" between an assertion or a proposition and the aspect of reality it describes. The problem occurs when we think of one definition in the context of the other. Truth as unveiling also pretty clearly involves a correspondence occurring between the essence and its own image; what we unveil, separating essence from its appearance and its accidents, is a purified image of essence. But also truth as correspondence contains an act of unveiling, since the correspondence occurs when the imitative statement "effaces itself of its own accord in the process of restoring freely, and hence in a living manner, the freedom of true presence" (193), or when a statement does not call attention to its own status as linguistic imitation but points directly to its referent, allowing that referent to be handled without the concerns of linguistic intervention, through the veil of language. As the internal but tertiary painter haunts Plato's internalized system of truth, mimesis forms the common ground between these two definitions of truth. Prior to its meaning of imitation, "*mimesis* signifies the presentation of the thing itself, of nature, of the physis that produces itself, engenders itself, and appears (to itself) as it really is, in the presence of its image, its visible aspect, its face" (193). In truth as unveiling, in which no imitation occurs, nevertheless the image of essence produced by unveiling exists in a relation of mimesis to the essence being imaged. And of course mimesis describes precisely the standard situation of correspondence in which a statement mimes or imitates that to which it corresponds. But since mimesis creates the possibility of correspondence, it reimports unveiling into this second definition: before mimetic correspondence, we have no truth, because truth is that correspondence; thus the correspondence mimesis imports into the process unveils that truth. In other words, mimesis as the process of truth in each case, importing correspondence into one definition and unveiling into another, is necessary to both definitions of truth but is itself not part of the truth of either. We have then two definitions of truth, each of which contains the other definition as a secondary mimetic effect: truth as unveiling creates the necessary side effect of an imitation; truth as correspondence unveils essence as a mimetic effect of its successful imaging. Logically, by looking at the workings of the secondary category that keeps getting in the way, mimesis, we might be able to determine the hierarchies in the definitions of truth. What then would be a truth of mimesis? How would one unveil it without imitating it or imitate it without unveiling it?

To find the truth of mimesis, we will look for its most comprehensive representation, a miming of mimesis. Such a representation will be literary, since mimesis defines the activity of literature—and, under certain theories, the activity of all art—and the most literary of works would be precisely one that represents its constitutive activity, thus miming mimesis. This, as we might expect, is the defining activity of Mallarmé's *Mimique*: "The Mime mimes reference. He is not an imitator; he mimes imitation" (219). This situation is basically linguistic. If referring to its own quality as language constitutes the defining feature of literary language, then miming mimesis would be the most generalized version of this "essential" literariness. But here we need a slight clarification. Derrida does not actually say that the Mime mimes mimesis. Rather he mimes reference; he mimes imitation. Mimesis cannot precisely mime only mimesis in the sense of imitating a pure act of imitation or referring to a pure act of reference. By their very definitions, neither imitation nor reference has an aspect that one might imitate or to which one might refer: these are purely relational qualities. But mimesis itself is a dually significant process, entailing both the process of truth as unveiling and the process of truth as corresponding. Thus one mimesis can mime the other. One can imitate reference, copy or correspond to it; one can refer to imitation, identify or unveil it. These differences allow the infinite mirroring of this hyperliterature to occur without ever introducing a referent or an original behind the imitation: "in this speculum with no reality, in this mirror of a mirror, a difference or dyad does exist, since there are mimes and phantoms. But it is a difference without reference, or rather a reference without a referent, without any first or last unit, a ghost that is a phantom of no flesh" (206).

One can immediately say two things about this mimesis that finally becomes a topic as well as a process in Mallarmé. First, as deconstructive literary critics are fond of discovering, it places literariness, if not precisely literature, at the center of the philosophical process of determining truth. After all, truth needs mimesis to occur, and so, in a purely logical sense, the process of mimesis is prior to truth: "What is marked [in the text of *Mimique*] is the fact that, this imitator having in the last instance no imitated, this signifier having in the last instance no signified, this sign having in the last instance no referent, their operation is no longer comprehended within the process of truth but on the contrary comprehends *it*, the motif of the last instance being inseparable from metaphysics as the search for the *arkhe*, the *eskhaton*, and the *telos*" (207–208). I want to stress the logic of this statement rather than its melodrama. To the extent that *Mimique* indeed succeeds in having no imitated object and no referent, then it follows that, while there cannot be truth without mimesis, there can be mimesis without truth. Mimesis is thus the logically prior category. But the second thing one can say about this situation is its reverse. The analysis of Mallarmé simply could not have occurred without the prior analysis of Plato. Mimesis has meaning only in its connection with the process of truth. Mallarmé can mime mimesis only because its two different forms allow the act of reference to occur. Thus, it needs the structure of straightforward, truthful reference to refer to its own literariness. Like the term "differance," mimesis both must have priority and cannot have it. Its priority says nothing about itself but both refers to and imitates a problem within the process of truth.

One can now specify the value of the concept of literary language to Derrida's project. The battle over whether Derrida's primary significance is philosophical or literary is precisely as Pyrrhic as a battle over whether Pater cared about art for what it allowed him to understand about a philosophy of perception or whether he cared about a philosophy of perception for its artistic qualities. As an eccentric center to Derrida's thinking, literary language allows his philosophical analysis to occur in two ways. First it forms a provisional outside to philosophy's attempt to found itself as the precondition of all knowledge, an outside from which that attempt may be extended to include all within it at the cost of its own working. Literary language also allows that analysis precisely by enacting the version of it that is so outside as to be absolutely exemplary. Thus having used the doubly literary act of miming mimesis to place that differential process at an impossible center of the process of truth, Derrida then concludes by denying any possible existence to literature: "if this handbook of literature [*Mimique*] meant to *say* something, which we now have some reason to doubt, it would proclaim first of all that there is no—or hardly any, ever so little—literature; that in any event there is no essence of literature, no truth of literature, no literary-being or being-literary of literature" (223). By claiming that there is hardly any literature, Derrida does not mean that only a very few literary texts, such as Mallarmé, embody some pure form of literature, and that other literary texts are simply more or less mystified and degraded forms of philosophical reference. Rather, he argues that, since purely literary language, pure mimesis, is an impossibility, in that it designates a concept dependent upon something outside itself, there can be no essence of literature, no purely literary texts. But it cannot be true to say that there is no literature, since mimesis exists always within the process of truth. It has that bare existence of differance and supplementarity, both logically impossible and logically necessary.

Because Derrida embeds his analysis of literary language within his analysis of foundational philosophy, it has as little relevance to the interpretation of actual literary works as his philosophical discussion has to the status of particular propositions. Derrida's theory can no more prove that philosophy is really literary than it can prove that literature is really philosophical. First, its analysis of the workings of mimesis within the definitions of what it calls the process of truth is so much logically prior to the integrity of the generic categories philosophy and literature that whether or not these categories have empirical integrity would have no effect on the status of his argument. Second, if the claim that literature deconstructs philosophy means that philosophy is necessarily fictive in some way that significantly undercuts its claim to be at least potentially truthful, Derrida's argument again has no relevance to an empirical claim about a specific work's fictiveness and simply contradicts a formal claim about philosophy in general. The fact that the process of truth might depend on the differential workings of mimesis would not undercut the possibility that specific statements would function as true. At the more formal level, as we have already seen, claims about the ultimate fictiveness of truth rest on the forms of direct reference and correspondence that they supposedly call into question.

In these terms, the centrality, eccentric or not, of literariness to Derrida's thinking may seem only thinly connected to the activity of literary studies, and one might easily argue that Derrida's significance is primarily philosophical rather than literary. The problem may be less a lack of significance, though, than an insistence on finding a methodological significance in a system that questions every aspect of system-making upon which methodologies rest. Obviously one can construct techniques and methods from aspects of Derrida's analysis, as one can from aspects of any analysis, and no analysis doubtful of the integrity of foundations can declare a priori the invalidity of those techniques. That validity, though, will have to rest completely on what the techniques achieve rather than on any prior theoretical connection.[18] But not every literary significance entails a method of interpretation.[19] If the workings of literary language, vexed and problematic as they are, enact a model case of the workings of any system-building, then the experience of reading that language becomes, not an isolated aestheticism, but a central mode of understanding philosophy, ideology, and various other cultural constructs. In particular, Paul de Man's centering on the problem of literary language, rather than trivializing Derrida, reenacts Pater's attempt to make aesthetic experience culturally comprehensive even as it ties that aesthetic to a philosophical analysis that would seemingly make its own aestheticism problematic. We saw in the discussion of Pater's "Conclusion" the role aesthetic perception played in his analysis of empirical, founding sensations. Related to the centrality of aesthetic perception, Pater proposed in his "Preface" a detailing of the causes and make-up of that perception. This delineation led to no directed method of interpreting art and certainly to no preference for one thematic meaning over another. But Pater's central concern with understanding the workings of art is hardly, for those reasons, in question. De Man's concern with literary language, particularly as it was shaped by his encounter with deconstruction, reenacts Pater's paradoxical attempt to define the philosophic centrality of aesthetics in terms of its reflexive self-sufficiency.

De Man remains an extremely controversial figure; his significance has hardly been addressed from anything like a critical distance.[20] The philosophic contradictions with which he is often accused generally derive either from the attempt to transform his concern with literary language into a method of interpretation or from an imposition of his own earlier phenomenological epistemology on his later work. While his response to Derrida became the framework for the deconstructive literary criticism that I have been addressing skeptically here, his own work from the time of *Blindness and Insight* on has included almost nothing that one would usually call literary criticism in the sense of an argument that aims at providing a reading of a literary work. Even the essays that discuss closely Shelley's "Triumph of Life" or a passage from Proust's *Recherche* do not really have as their target a reading of these works, deconstructive or otherwise, but rather use the works to delineate a theoretical, philosophical, or ideological problem of reading.[21] Thus the transformation of his extended thinking on the status of literary language into a methodology of interpreting literature has created a misapprehension whereby his arguments are read according to the presumption that his point will be to provide a reading that shows a work's expression of some deconstructive truth, the death of the subject, perhaps, or the omnipresence of figural language. More seriously, as some critics have noticed,[22] de Man's early work had a phenomenological epistemology and conception of literary language that structured his encounter with Derrida in *Blindness and Insight*, giving way to a consistent rereading of these issues only in *Allegories of Reading* and his later essays.[23] Connecting de Man's deconstructive sense of literary language with his earlier phenomenological epistemology may partially account for the formulation in American literary criticism of deconstruction as a kind of ultimate insight, despite the obvious logical problems with this position. Only that connection allows the transformation of Derrida's thought through de Man's into a reading method. And yet, in de Man, the insistent concern with literary language, combined with the exigency of accepting a deconstructive formulation of it, resulted in his abandoning the stance of insight that enabled that method.

Despite the changes I am about to discuss, de Man remains fixed throughout his career on the epistemological difficulty of defining a position for knowing that coincides with the act of knowing,[24] and on the role of literary language in defining such a position. Prior to *Blindness and Insight*, though, his position, which shared more with Harold Bloom's theories from *Anxiety of Influence* onwards than with Derrida, entailed defining poetic language as constituted by its contradistinction from the processes of nature and positing the absolute ontological priority of consciousness. Thus "The Intentional Structure of the Romantic Image" begins by using the form of a simile to the effect that words originate like flowers to deny the content of its comparison: flowers originate like nothing but themselves, whereas words originate like other things, such as flowers (*Rhetoric*, 4). Instead of then moving on to analyze the intrinsic significance of the disjunction between rhetoric and grammar, as he later does, de Man proceeds to detail the search for a poetic language that might accept its radical separation from natural objects, concluding by positing an imagination that "has little in common with the faculty that produces natural images born 'as flowers originate.' It marks instead a possibility for consciousness to exist entirely by and for itself, without being moved by an intent aimed at a part of this world" (*Rhetoric*, 16). In another essay, describing Rousseau, he affirms the truth of that possibility, the priority of a pure, antinatural consciousness: "There was a man who, in reaffirming the ontological priority of consciousness over the sensuous object, put the thought and the destiny of the West back onto its authentic path; the same man had the wisdom and the patience to remain faithful to the limits that this knowledge, in accordance with its own laws, imposes upon the human spirit. He was thus able to safeguard the future of mankind. His name: Rousseau. His act: to re-collect oneself" (*Rhetoric*, 45). That this passage poses itself as an analysis of Hölderlin's attitude toward Rousseau does not really change de Man's clear endorsement of the position, particularly since the rhetoric occurs in the essay's concluding paragraph, with no distance taken from its implications. If we put these two positions together, we get a poetic language that, in the very fissures of its imagery, states its own separation from the natural world, a separation that is the founding truth of the ontologically prior consciousness, even if it knows its priority only in fissures of poetic imagery.

The title *Blindness and Insight: Essays in the Rhetoric of Contemporary Criticism* labels two of the three presiding concerns of that book. First, it describes an epistemological situation, one in which knowledge depends on some concomitant error.[25] Second, it discusses criticism in terms of its "rhetoric," which, in context, labels the stance of a critic toward the literary text and the cultural significance of his situation. But "rhetoric" also identifies the third concern of the book: delineating the philosophic significance of literary language in terms of the critic's stance. That significance indeed is the central theme, binding the titled issues together, since literary language embodies the presiding insight that determines the cultural context in which critics enact their dramas of blindness and insight. To an extent, then, de Man continues the phenomenological stance of his earlier essays in which consciousness obtains a privileged position by occupying and accepting a contradictory situation defined by the language of poetry. Nevertheless, *Blindness and Insight* revises and extends the concept of literary language. De Man there moves closer to Derrida's formulation of an enacted, eccentric, philosophic center, and away from his earlier definition that assumed a knowledge gained by accepting metaphoricity.[26] Moreover, this new literary language does not define a state of knowledge that primarily entails a state of consciousness. It embodies the insight with which consciousness, as represented by the critical project, connects in an always imperfect relationship. This relationship then describes both the cultural situation and the cultural significance of criticism. But the connection between the more extensive, and more nearly deconstructive, concept of literary language and the remnants of the earlier, phenomenological epistemology creates problems within the book's own theories, particularly in its explicit discussion of deconstruction, ironically the least deconstructive aspect of the book. *Allegories of Reading* reformulates these issues in a way that moves de Man even closer to Derrida's project. From that perspective, we can see that de Man's point, even in *Blindness and Insight*, was never to formulate a new method of literary criticism, but to use literary criticism to define its own cultural and historical role.

We may see the shift in de Man's theory of literary language in a passage from *Blindness and Insight* whose notoriety results at least partially from the persistence with which critics misread it. Having labeled the most current mode of demystification as structuralism's attempt to do away with the Romantic subject by asserting "the discrepancy between sign and meaning" (*Blindness*, 12), de Man introduces the thematic turn in the book by arguing that this mystification is the critic's and not the literature's because literature is defined by knowledge of this discrepancy:

> For the statement about language, that sign and meaning can never coincide, is what is precisely taken for granted in the kind of language we call literary. Literature, unlike everyday language, begins on the far side of this knowledge; it is the only form of language free from the fallacy of unmediated expression. All of us know this, although we know it in the misleading way of a wishful assertion of the opposite. Yet the truth emerges in the foreknowledge we possess of the true nature of literature when we refer to it as *fiction*. All literatures, including the literature of Greece, have always designated themselves as existing in the mode of fiction; in the *Iliad*, when we first encounter Helen, it is as the emblem of the narrator weaving the actual war into the tapestry of a fictional object. Her beauty prefigures the beauty of all future narratives as entities that point to their own fictional nature. The self-reflecting mirror-effect by means of which a work of fiction asserts, by its very existence, its separation from empirical reality, its divergence as a sign from a meaning that depends for its existence on the constitutive activity of this sign, characterizes the work of literature in its essence. (*Blindness*, 17)

The way in which this passage has been misinterpreted indicates the polemical value of Derrida's more nuanced and ellipitical mode of addressing the issue of literariness. Like Derrida, de Man does not address the intended meaning of a specific work here but the philosophic significance of the form literary statements take. Because, unlike Derrida, he addresses the meaning of that form in the phenomenological terms of delineating directly a transcendental reduction in a literary work, though, critics have thought that he argues for the actual thematic meaning of all literary works rather than the philosophic significance of literariness. Gerald Graff, for instance, takes de Man to be arguing that all literature, even the most ancient like the *Iliad*, shares the modern meta-fictional play with its own fictional status, and responds first that it is highly unlikely that Homer shared this attitude and second that, even if de Man is correct, he does not evidence the claim in any way (*Literature Against Itself*, 174–175). But de Man does not make any claim here about Homer's thematic intents. He is arguing about the formal status of literary language: the label "literary" carries with it the assumption that the language in question does not correspond to empirical event directly. Labeling literature as mystified because various authors may assert thematically the coincidence of sign with meaning in the concept of the symbol thus ignores the denial of that coincidence in our most obvious definition of literary representation as noncoincidental with empirical event. Thus de Man's assertion that we all know what we wishfully deny seems obscure and unevidenced only if we take the knowledge to mean anything more than the obvious meaning of identifying fiction as fictive. Homer's weaving Helen designates narrative representation itself, not the Trojan War, as fiction. De Man does not evidence his interpretation because he does not interpret the *Iliad* but generalizes from what labeling something literature means to a conclusion about an assumption built into literary language.

What then, Graff might ask, is the great discovery of this passage? Indeed, no one ever thought that the truth of fiction rested on a correspondence between the events its sentences describe and actual empirical events (Graff, *Literature Against Itself*, 154). But why make theoretical heavy going out of that? It hardly supports the ostensible deconstructive contention that "language is by definition incapable of referring to anything external to its own systems" (Graff, *Literature Against Itself*, 173). But the context in which this passage occurs suggests that that contention is hardly de Man's. A sign's lack of coincidence with its meaning hardly entails its having no meaning; indeed noncoincidence implies a meaning with which not to coincide. The nearest candidates for holders of this contention in the essay are the literary structuralists against whom de Man argues here. Assuming that lack of coincidence between sign and meaning must be a deconstructive theme, critics also assume de Man's sympathy with these critics.[27] But, like Derrida, de Man argues, in fact, for the mystification of precisely this belief. Without working out the philosophical logic as Derrida does when he discusses structuralist linguists and anthropologists, de Man poses the commonplace truth about our knowledge of what fiction means against the structuralist's ostensible philosophical discovery about the fallacy of the Romantic belief in the symbol. Out of this doubling, de Man reprivileges literature by pointing out that its definition assumes this ostensible truth. At first, then, de Man re-creates—or, more accurately, predicts—Derrida's definition of literary language as the marginalized foundation of foundational philosophy. And much of the affinity of these two writers, I will argue, derives from their shared project of articulating the consequences of such a self-contradictory proposition.

But proposing an alignment between this passage and Derrida's discussion of mimesis and literature in "The Double Session" presents two problems. First, Derrida would surely realize, but de Man seems not to, that the final sentence of the passage quoted above contradicts itself radically. If literature asserts in its existence—regardless of the statements of particular works of literature—the divergence of sign from meaning, how can its "self-reflecting mirror-effect"—the declarative statement the existence of a work as fiction makes with regard to any specific content it might have—"characterize the work of literature in its essence" (*Blindness*, 17)? If the statement of the form characterizes the essence of literature, then clearly the form as sign coincides with its own essence. Derrida, as we have seen, very carefully works out the contradictions of his own position on the founding aspect of mimesis, indeed makes it part of his critique of the concept of founding. His constant theme is the necessary but contradictory inclusiveness built into the foundational gesture. Thus, in Derrida, one can never achieve direct reference or direct knowledge, even by referring directly to the necessity of a divergence between sign and meaning. His opposition is not between knowledge and ignorance but between direction and indirection. De Man, here, however, seems to assume that foundation upon essence may be restored by an adequate reflection of a constitutive divergence.[28] Second, de Man in fact extends an aspect of the definition of fiction to a definition of literary language, but that extension seems less self-evident than the implications of fictiveness upon which the passage bases its claims. Fiction indeed does not claim that its sentences correspond to empirical reality. But that narrative noncorrespondence does not necessarily extend to poetic language itself: the statements in a lyric poem might without any formal contradiction, at least on the face of it, be posed as indirectly correspondent, even though they are figural. The first problem derives, I will argue, from the contradictory remnant of de Man's epistemology in his argument here. The logic that leads him to make the second connection, worked out in *Allegories of Reading*, carries him away from that epistemology and completes the alignment of his project with Derrida's.

The contradictions in de Man's epistemology have been discussed frequently. If all insights derive from some concomitant blindness, why does literature have a privileged unblindedness? If it has privileged insight into the exigencies of signification, it becomes a founding insight in a classically contradictory manner too obvious even to demand deconstruction. In fact, de Man has constructed a phenomenological foundation, a moment of consciousness with logical if not temporal priority. He differs from Husserl only in that he builds from the workings of language rather than from its exclusion. The dialectic between blindness and insight as constitutive of criticism works as long as the blindnesses and insights at issue are local: specific insights could derive from specific errors or blindnesses without any contradiction. But if one posits an ultimate insightfulness to literature, then all blindnesses become local in relation to that insight and therefore accidental in relation to their own insights. Critics could have had those same insights by having reached the ultimate insight of literature. Although de Man defines the role of the critic rather than a method of literary criticism (and this distinction, we will see, is significant), my criticism above of Miller's contention that the great literary works are ahead of their critics surely applies equally to de Man's contention that Derrida's analysis of Rousseau is blinded because Rousseau has an unblinded literary knowledge of Derrida's philosophical insight and thus deconstructs himself (*Blindness*, 139).

De Man's critique of Derrida's blindness of course raises the problem of self-deconstruction, its ties to Derrida's deconstruction, and its redefinition of that as a state of knowledge and the basis of a method. First, the problem with the concept is not one of Rousseau's actual knowledge of deconstructive truths. De Man once asked Derrida why he denied to Rousseau "the value of radicality which you attribute to Mallarmé" (Derrida, *Mémoires*, 129). Derrida does not tell us what he answered, but his answer in his reading of Mallarmé involved the irrelevance of whether or not Mallarmé intended the reading of mimesis that Derrida articulates: "whatever might have been going on in Mallarmé's head, in his consciousness or unconscious, does not matter to us here" (*Dissemination*, 225). Rousseau might have intended the meanings Derrida comes to through deconstruction. Derrida thinks that Mallarmé did intend the reading he offers. But since he uses the textual situations thematized in these authors to define a situation common to all literary language, their intentions with regard to their own specific textual situations do not affect the validity of his position in one way or the other. Nor would authors somehow escape the general problem they define by their mere awareness of it. Second, neither does the problem with self-deconstruction involve de Man's contesting Derrida's assertion of a deconstruction from the outside. As we have seen, Derrida's wariness of claiming to have gotten outside structures matches his attempt to do so. Thus, describing de Man's argument as stating "deconstruction cannot be applied, after the fact and from the outside, as a technical instrument of modernity" (*Mémoires*, 123), Derrida, with conditions one might predict,[29] assents to de Man's claim. Rather, de Man's problematic divergence from Derrida entails his combining these two reservations about Derrida's analysis—the necessary embeddedness of deconstructive analysis in literary texts with a claim about Rousseau's intentions—to move from the state of a literary text to a state of demystified consciousness: "Rousseau escapes from the logocentric fallacy precisely to the extent that his language *is literary*" (*Blindness*, 138). Although de Man's conception of literary language has changed from his earlier works, no longer delineating an ontologically prior, antinatural state of consciousness but enacting in its formal state the central problem for all other forms of thought, he still uses that literary language to open a privileged state of consciousness. Although de Man himself will not extend this vestigial definition of an ultimate insight tied to literary language into knowledge grounding a method, as Miller does, at this point one could argue that it forms a basis for such a method.

But the logic behind de Man's definition of literary language has a force of its own that will drive him away from this epistemology. The second problem I noted above in that definition involved its extension of a specific aspect of fictive statement—that the label "fictive" implies a lack of correspondence between statement and empirical event—to a definition of literary language in general. But that extension is not self-evident, since, as de Man himself notes in a footnote, "poetry abounds in general statements" (*Blindness*, 137), and the correspondence of those statements would not make them cease to be poetic. *Allegories of Reading*, in this context, becomes a detailed justification of this extension. In that book, he posits two significations within any statement: the meaning to which what for the moment we will call its literal or grammatical reading refers, and the implication made by its mode of formal existence. These two significations he designates in terms of a statement's grammar and its rhetoric. And, as might be expected, the relationship between them is not entirely straightforward.

In his introduction (3–19), de Man notes that while grammatically a rhetorical question seems to demand an answer, rhetorically it states that it does not care what the answer to its question is. Nor can we always know which is the primary or naive reading and which is the secondary or more sophisticated reading, since taking a question rhetorically, though interpreting against its grammar, may be more straightforward than taking it grammatically. Thus, de Man proposes taking the rhetorical questions at the end of Yeats's "Among School Children" literally as a disruptive interpretation, and notes, after explaining the implications of such a reading, that "the clumsiness of [his] paraphrase reveals that it is not necessarily the literal reading which is simpler than the figurative one" (11). De Man concludes that whenever one has a "rhetorization of grammar" (16), as in questions whose primary meaning is rhetorical, one arrives at a disjunction between two significances. The same disjunction occurs in the reverse case, "the grammatization of rhetoric." We see this situation in Proust's *Recherche*, in which the narrator states the priority of metaphoric connection, which gets at the essences of things, over metonymical connections, which, because they are based on the empirical appearance of juxtaposition, find only accidental and not essential relations. An extended reading of the passage in question, however (59–67), shows that it makes its imagistic case through the use of linguistically veiled metonymies. Thus the assertion of essence reduces, rhetorically, to another form of accidental connection, and the contiguous, grammatical connections Proust scorns in the grammar of his passage reassert themselves in its rhetorical form. This grammatization of rhetoric de Man first describes as reaching a truth by the negative road of exposing the error of asserting essential connection (16). Thus the fictive disjuncture de Man characterized as definitive of literary language in *Blindness and Insight* he specifies as occurring not only between narrative statements and the imagined events they describe but also between the grammar and rhetoric of potentially any statement.

This further specification of his theory of literary language also forces de Man to abandon the epistemological claims that may in the first instance have produced that theory. More particularly, an embedded duality in the status of literary language, one directly resulting from a fuller definition of the fissured state that originally privileged it, leads as a logical consequence to the abandonment of its claim to even a negative truth. First, as might be expected, de Man assimilates the literary to the rhetorical and the philosophical to the grammatic. In the introduction, he writes that "grammar and logic stand to each other in a dyadic relationship of unsubverted support" (7), logic being, of course, constitutive of philosophical argument. And in a discussion of Nietzsche, he writes that "if one wants to conserve the term 'literature,' one should not hesitate to assimilate it with rhetoric" (131). But literary language also refers to the whole fissured relationship between rhetoric and grammar, to the various ways that one category undercuts the other. One could possibly privilege rhetoric and its undercutting of grammatic meaning over grammar, but the relationship as a whole describes a process, not a conclusion. Like Derrida's mimesis, this expanded notion of literary language would include a reified notion of literature as a subverting rhetoric within its process. As mimesis operated as a necessary part of the process of truth, de Man's literary language, as the relationship between grammar and rhetoric, exists as a larger whole that neither the positive truths of logic and grammar nor the negative truths of literary rhetoric would contain. Thus in *Allegories of Reading*, de Man quite regularly contests his own earlier privileging of literary language. Having noted that "the discovery of the literary, rhetorical nature of the philosophical claim to truth is genuine enough," de Man nevertheless specifies that literature "is not the less deceitful because it asserts its own deceitful properties" (115). And this deceit entails rather more than the paradox of the cretin liar. Not simply would the genuineness of the literary discovery mark it as philosophical and therefore not a literary discovery at all, but the truthful announcement of deceit protects one from deceit only if the value of truth remains integral. Since literary language refers to all the possible relationships among these categories, it can never ultimately or only convey a truth. In this context, the notorious sentence that concludes the paragraph, "Philosophy turns out to be an endless reflection on its own destruction at the hands of literature," looks similarly double-edged. Reflection is the founding philosophical activity with which Derrida starts his corrosive analysis and upon which he applies it. A philosophy that was an endless reflection might as nearly be an interminable philosophy as a triumphant literary deconstruction, and each possibility would be equally partial from the perspective of the literary language that is both the reflection and the fissure that makes reflection possible.[30]

De Man's theory of literary language will no more produce practical criticism than does Derrida's. The literary language he delineates, first, could be found about equally in texts we designate as literary and those we designate as philosophical (or critical), just as philosophical language might appear in either, indeed must appear wherever literary language appears and simultaneously with it. Consequently, specifying a particular text as literary or as philosophical tells us nothing about the distinctive workings of its language. Even specifying whether a sentence is grammatic or rhetorical does not get us much further. But that does not mean we cannot read texts or sentences. In specific cases, we might be able to distinguish quite effectively enough to read a sentence accurately, and de Man's analysis of the problematic relationships of the concepts at the theoretical level might still be accurate. And, in reverse, even if all empirical sentences demonstrated unresolvable ambiguity, that accident would not itself demonstrate the accuracy of de Man's conceptual analysis. Thus, although de Man does write essays that entail interpreting literary works, one would be hard put to find an essay by de Man that claims to offer a better or more adequate reading of a work and that thus evidences the value of his interpretive method. Even "Shelley Disfigured," an extended interpretation if ever there was one, announces its topic not as an interpretation of "The Triumph of Life" but as a discussion of the significance of the debate surrounding it: "the entire debate as to whether 'The Triumph of Life' represents or heralds a movement of growth or of degradation is part of the same genetic and historical metaphor. The unquestioned authority of this metaphor is much more important than the positive or negative valorization of the movement it generates" (*Rhetoric*, 96). And indeed the essay ends with a discussion of its themes of disfiguration and monumentalization as they apply to our understanding of Romanticism, explicitly stating that the interest of "The Triumph of Life" is its thematization of these issues. Shelley becomes, like Rousseau and Mallarmé, significant in that the literary process under consideration emerges as a theme of the work. If de Man were wrong about that, it would be awkward for, though not deadly to, his larger argument. In fact, the debate among critics over whether Shelley handled this theme deconstructively or affirmatively[31] assents to the existence of the theme de Man identifies. After that, to the extent that de Man's theoretical arguments about the theme are adequate to the problem, the question of Shelley's intentions become as irrelevant to the issues raised by the essay as are the intentions of Rousseau and Mallarmé to Derrida's analysis.

De Man's concepts of self-deconstructive texts, his insistence on the priority of the text over its critic in the deconstructive analysis, and his emphasis that that activity takes place in the transformations from ostensibly literal to ostensibly figural language have all been centrally influential in creating deconstructive literary criticism. If that extension into practical criticism falsifies his argument about literary language, though, then what do we make of the consequences of his theory and how are we to take its concepts? The presiding theme of de Man's work, even when he saw himself as revising the literary history of Romanticism, has been less the meaning of works than the role of the critic, and the way that role connects with the subjects a critic analyzes. The title *Allegories of Reading* itself indicates as the book's common subject all conflicts between a text's grammatical statement and the statement made by its formal status and practice: a text will allegorize in its formal element the problems of reading its grammatical content. And, at times, only the recognition of that allegory will make sense of some of a text's more resistant statements. Thus de Man, at crucial moments in his argument, persistently turns an interpretive problem within the text into a problem of its reading:

> Taken literally, Rousseau's assertion that he does not know whether he or his fictional characters wrote the letters that make up *Julie* makes little sense. The situation changes when we realize that R. [ostensibly the narrator or Rousseau, characterized in the second preface to the novel] is merely the metaphor for a textual property (readability). Further inferences then become apparent, for example that R. is similar to N. in his inability to read *Julie* and that it is impossible to distinguish between reader and author in terms of epistemological certainty. It follows that we can reverse the priority which makes us think of reading as the natural consequence of writing. It now appears that writing can just as well be considered the linguistic correlative of the inability to read. (203)

The logic here is that, though the historical Rousseau of course knows the fictive status of his characters, we as readers cannot. Rousseau, having been in that position as a reader, writes to master that knowledge, only reproducing the reading problem that led him to write. At this point, the problem becomes not the status of Rousseau's intentions but the emergence within the text of the difficulty in determining those intentions. Even if we achieved knowledge or agreement about the status of Rousseau's characters—as, indeed, we probably have at least to some extent—the prior problem of the grounds of our reading decisions would remain. If literary language describes the connections between various aspects of a text, then as literally as is possible, literary language is critical language, and texts present to critics the problem of their critical reading.[32]

De Man does not draw from this situation the implication either that critics are freed from the constraints of logic as poets are or that all readings are misreadings in the empirical sense of producing incorrect interpretations of specific texts. After a sentence that seems to state precisely that ostensibly freeing assertion, de Man follows with a refinement that identifies the connection between his project and Derrida's: "There can be no writing without reading, but all readings are in error because they assume their own readability. Everything written has to be read and every reading is susceptible of logical verification, but the logic that establishes the need for verification is itself unverifiable and therefore unfounded in its claim to truth" (202). The reading of any given text may be subjected to logical tests, and correct readings may be discriminated from incorrect readings. But the logic that grounds these tests cannot be verified because of the contradictions in any originary account of the reading process. Like Derrida's analysis of foundational philosophy, this claim has one fairly thin theoretical consequence: we may be able to produce correct as opposed to incorrect readings, but in cases in which we disagree as to what a correct reading is, we will not resolve our dispute by an appeal to foundational principles for determining accurate readings. But it has the more obvious extension that the ways we read texts and the problems we confront in their interpretation become ways of discussing the stance of the critic and problems confronting that stance. De Man does not construct this situation in an attempt to achieve critical mastery in an epistemological position of negative knowledge. By *Allegories of Reading*, such a position does not exist. But even in *Blindness and Insight*, that position existed in a literary text, possibly also for the author of that text, but never for the critic, even as he fixed his attention on his own position. Rather, de Man's point seems to be fairly constantly to turn literary matters into matters for social and historical comment.

The essay "Criticism and Crisis," placed as an introduction to *Blindness and Insight*, should have made the point of that book clear. De Man first posits that criticism can exist only as a result of crisis: "in periods that are not periods of crisis, or in individuals bent on avoiding crisis at all cost, there can be all kinds of approaches to literature: historical, philological, psychological, etc., but there can be no criticism. For such periods or individuals will never put the act of writing into question by relating it to its specific intent" (8). Crisis, necessitating troubled reflection, produces criticism because criticism results precisely from that act of questioning self-reflection. Turning, like Derrida, to Husserl for an example of a founding act of reflection that contains its own contradiction within itself in its founding act of exclusion, de Man then argues that such contradictory moments constitute the structure of "all crisis-determined statements" (16). Thus crisis produces criticism, whose problematic self-reflection embodies but also produces crisis, since crisis is first a perception of a problem rather than any objective aspect of that problem. De Man concludes his essay with his definition of literary language to posit its recognition of its own fictiveness as the most generalized form of this critical situation. The argument entails here not the conclusion that textual analysis is a privileged form of negative knowledge, separated from mystified social discourse, but that social and formal criticism are mutually inclusive forms of discourse. *Blindness and Insight* does, however, propose literary language as constructive of a privileged mode of consciousness. But the expansion of textual reading to historical reading recurs in *Allegories of Reading* without any possible way of establishing priorities. Thus, in his reading of the *Social Contract*, de Man, as critics might expect, refers the political problems within the text to the problem of making promises as a linguistic performance: the text argues the impossibility of promising even as it performs various promises. Instead of ending with this linguistic situation, de Man concludes by extending his claim back out. The problem he identifies about promising is not specific to the text of the *Social Contract* since even if Rousseau had not openly invoked it, "the *Social Contract* would still promise by inference," as would any text with a social theory. But since neither reader nor author creates this problem unilaterally, language creates the problem with its own structures. And de Man concludes, "to the extent that [it] is necessarily misleading, language just as necessarily conveys the promise of its own truth. This is also why textual allegories on this level of rhetorical complexity generate history" (277). In other words, a textual analysis of the *Social Contract* does not attempt to escape social significance; it responds precisely to what generates that significance. For de Man, the role of literary critics is implicitly and inescapably ideological, not because of some extra-literary political or institutional demand upon their work—though those may well exist—but because the content of what they analyze and the acts of analysis they perform are also the content of cultural crisis, historical event.

We can now see, I think, more clearly the coincidence of the intellectual projects of Derrida and de Man. Certainly de Man does not extend Derrida's philosophical analysis—either legitimately or illegitimately—into a mode of practical criticism. Nor does de Man seem particularly to want to use deconstruction to "prove" that all philosophy is "merely" literary, thus freeing critical discourse for play. Rather the coincidence is also the one that gives problems to readers of Pater: pure aesthetic experience mattered to Pater because of its paradoxical philosophical centrality. Literary language plays the same role in Derrida, but because he writes in the academically established discourse of philosophy, we cannot fail to see that some philosophical project, rather than some literary experience, is at issue. De Man, arriving at a similar definition of literary language, driven away by the consequences of that definition from the phenomenological epistemology that produced it, reproduces Derrida's analysis of philosophical foundations in his extended discussion of the role of criticism in its moment of self-definition. From a different philosophical tradition, and by a different logic, but out of the same elements, he thus reproduces Pater's cultural critic who was simultaneously an art critic in a literary critic who, in his literary criticism, enacts cultural criticism. Indeed, de Man's claim for criticism at the end of "Criticism and Crisis" recalls Pater's argument at the end of "Winckelmann" that art offers freedom through its aesthetic comprehension of necessity. If we do not assume that either author intended the aesthetic to be defined in terms of its separateness from reality, the obvious implication of both essays is that aesthetic perception and literary language are primary modes of interpreting cultural issues.

Too frequently, critics compare the theories of Derrida and de Man to an aestheticism that existed only in the way they have misread Pater. Taking Pater as isolating art from reality and attempting to live in it in a way alien to every aspect of the ways he defined his own project, critics then reread in terms of that misread aestheticism deconstructive themes drawn from philosophies concerned with founding acts of reflection, themes of self-dissolution, and linguistic opacity. Meanwhile, applying empirical definitions to Derrida's and de Man's statements about language and literature, and empirical expectations for a method that will produce measurable experiences in the shape of specific interpretations, they then dismiss their theories as aestheticist and solipsistic or relativistic. But to argue for the political, historical, or philosophical significance of art or literature, we need not suppose a way of drawing extra-artistic conclusions from our aesthetic analysis. In a sense, the claim that we must draw such conclusions or remain apolitical already admits the aesthetic separation about which political critics complain in the first place. It implicitly separates formal artistic experience as different from the political conclusions they criticize formalists for lacking. In their analysis of an element of art or literature, sensation or literary language, that already exists as the excluded center of other disciplines, Pater, Derrida, and de Man do not isolate the aesthetic or drain it of extra-aesthetic significance but strongly deny the existence of the category extra-aesthetic. None of this, I recognize, defines any specific political position for these writers. That definition will occur in my final chapter. It does claim that their discourse has intrinsic intellectual or philosophical comment. In Chapter 2, I argued the intrinsic historicism of Pater's aestheticism. By extending that parallel in the next chapter, and discussing Derrida's and de Man's analyses of aesthetics, I will try to amplify de Man's implication that if certain linguistic activities generate history then certain rhetorical analyses will serve as the most acute critiques of ideology and its foundations. That analysis will complete the comparison and prepare for a final discussion of the politics of both aestheticism and deconstruction.

Four

Deconstructive Aesthetics: Literary Language, History, Ideology

IF PATER meant to show how a fully articulated aestheticism worked to provide the forms of social, cultural, and philosophical explanations offered by Ruskin, Arnold, and Hegel, he was clearly not successful. Matthew Arnold's proposal that literature replaced religion by adequately conveying humanistic values while withstanding the attacks of science by declaring itself a separated discourse has had far greater institutional effect in the establishment of English and American literature departments.[1] And Pater's influence acted entirely within a strand of aesthetic theory that stressed artistic isolation and enclosure within its own world.[2] In effect, Pater's heirs and deconstruction's critics share a proposition that it has been the aim of this book to refute: forms of representation, most significantly literature and language, have an irrevocable inside to which there is an inescapable outside given various names, history, political activity, ideological hegemony, empirical or transcendental truth. This being the case, any position to the effect that literary language or aesthetic experience is constitutive and comprehensive must deny the reality of those alternatives. Derrida's and de Man's skeptical discussions of philosophic and literary theories of meaning may easily be construed as an espousal of language as a structure opposed to all external referents. But Pater never questioned meaning. He based his philosophy and aesthetics on a grounding in experience, however paradoxically he defined that experience. Yet his followers construed him to argue the alterity of artistic intensity, the desirability for an enclosure within art. Thus the problem is not the specific arguments deconstruction espouses but the attack it shares with Pater's aestheticism upon this foundational belief that the aesthetic always excludes an outside, that one must either break out of it into the real, or establish a sanctuary within it.

Without a preliminary belief that art and language stand in opposition to direct discourse and represented reality, a contention that our understanding of history, for instance, follows certain literary or linguistic structures could not logically produce the corollary that there is nothing but language. Rather, one would think that the consequence of that statement would be that historic comprehension, and extrication from the ideologies that obstruct that comprehension, would follow from a fully articulated understanding of the ways literary and linguistic structures have made history by making our understanding of it. As soon as one abandons the presumption of that opposition, even merely provisionally, deconstruction's ostensibly rarified textual analysis takes on a new edge. One can hardly read de Man's works, with their constant gestures to redefining the role of the critic, their addresses of major philosophical texts, their expansions from their readings to explaining states of critical, literary, and historical debate, without realizing his desire to act as a cultural critic rather than simply as a professional literary critic. Thus we saw at the end of the last chapter his expansion of a concept of literary language into an explanation of how the structure of literary language explains the role of the critic and his dependence upon a situation of crisis. Following the earlier extension of Pater's theory of artistic experience into an aestheticism that contained within it rather than denied a radical historicism, this chapter will expand Derrida's and de Man's philosophical and literary theories into a historical and ideological analysis that critics claim they—and particularly de Man—seek to avoid or negate. We saw in the last chapter that the impossibility within their theory of determining consequences through the articulation of a method entailed finding theoretical significance by expanding the reference of the theory's analytic mode. In this chapter, I want to detail how that expansion works, in a deconstructive mode of historical analysis suggested by both Derrida and de Man, and in the critique of ideology de Man deploys through his late analyses of aesthetic theory. In order to follow that analysis, one must challenge at least the presumption that finding a base of a structure within literary language reduces that structure to the "merely literary."

The proposition that modes of representation—art, literature, and language—must have an irreducible difference from their represented content, so that a claim that historical understanding rests on literary structures must reduce the historical to the "merely" literary, can no more be disproved than it can be proved, of course. To show that one can make one claim without making the other, however, was the burden of my chapters on Pater and will be the burden of this chapter as well. We can show the logical separateness of the claims by showing how one must confuse them in order to argue that de Man wants to reduce all historical change to the merely literary. Frank Lentricchia, whose vehement antagonism to de Man leads him to insights amid his accusations, identifies his own presumptions even as he also identifies the aims of de Man that one would think would call them into question:

> De Man writes easily within the claustrophobic space of the literary man, but that is a deception; his ambitions have never been those self-trivializing ones of the simple formalist. Let me quote [the] last sentence [of "Literary History and Literary Modernity"]: "If we extend this notion beyond literature, it merely confirms that the bases for historical knowledge are not empirical facts but written texts, even if these texts masquerade in the guise of wars or revolutions." Despite the caution of its phrasing this sentence does insert the literary into history at large—and such insertion has the effect of transforming history at large into the literary: de Man's own literary heritage, from Blake to Wilde, makes itself felt.... He is saying that history is not merely a text, that the text of history is not merely an imitation of literature. He is saying that history is an imitation of what he has defined as the literary.... What de Man's claim carries, given his definition of the literary as massive ("fatal") persistence, is the postulation of the most genuine meaning of political conservatism. This, I think, is what de Man is teaching; this is the effect of his theory; this is his social work. (*Criticism and Social Change*, 49–50)[3]

The claim of the last sentence necessitates the realization of the first. Simple formalism, an exclusive concern with the literary, might entail political inaction, in the rather narrow sense that it does not attempt to engage in politics or anything else while it practices literary analysis. But in order to teach political conservatism, one cannot quite be a simple formalist, since one has what Lentricchia would have to identify as ends that exceed formalism. And indeed, the sentence Lentricchia cites does not look like an attempt to keep literature pure of extra-literary significance, claiming as it does that a mode of interpretation extrapolated from literature's consideration of literary history—the "notion" of the quoted sentence—will also read historical texts, even when those texts are what we usually designate as historical events. That claim is extraordinary enough, and one could rightly complain that it pronounces more than argues, since nothing in the essay approaches a justification of it. But it says nothing about history imitating the literary. Yet only if de Man were claiming such an imitation could Lentricchia claim his definition of the persistence of literary language or the literary to imply a persistence of specific political institutions or structures against which one ought not to struggle. Even if de Man did intend such an absolute identification of the historical and the literary, the final quietist extension Lentricchia infers would still be doubtful since de Man would hardly argue that one should or even could stop struggling against the doublings of literary language. That struggling, as we will see, forms part of what constitutes the doublings. Finally,

Lentricchia can claim de Man to be conservative only if his claims for literature are more than formal. And yet he extrapolates the conservative political implications from a hyperformalism that he cannot find in the text that he rightly claims as more than formal.

Lentricchia's reference to an aestheticist tradition behind de Man stretching from Blake to Wilde once again establishes the common ground with which this book starts. Lentricchia later also establishes Pater's role as if it were a given that needed no explication: "Pater's 'House Beautiful,' like the traditions of Curtius and Eliot, is not really open: invitations to this open house are extended only to those whose cultural formation guarantees that, once within, their manners will be beyond reproach" (*Criticism and Social Change*, 129). I will, as I have said, contest Lentricchia's political claims in the next chapter. To establish that argument, however, I need to make suspect the implications behind the image of the House Beautiful. In the case of Pater, my reading in the past chapters challenged the claim that he desired to be enclosed within the beautiful: Pater's definition of the constitutive role of artistic experience—which, by being experience purely for art's sake, paradoxically took on its extra-artistic significance—extends his aesthetic theory to a historicist, cultural critique. In the second chapter, we saw how Pater's expansion of his paradoxical form of sensation into a narrative mode allowed him to construct an aesthetics built on history. Narrative best embodied his form of sensation within discourse because it reproduced the constitutive conflict within sensation between the moment in which it occurred and the abstraction of it within thought needed to give it duration. Narrative duration not only allowed but necessitated a historical version of the conflict within sensation. Because the aesthetic system expanded upon a moment of sensation given duration through philosophic abstraction, its history contained the same paradoxes, reproducing the artistic sensation across different periods and yet depending upon periodic difference for the conflict sensation needed. Pater's definition of artistic experience comes to depend at once on the absolute specificity of given historic periods understood from a historicist perspective and on an aesthetic comprehension of the differences between periods that replaces the transhistorical absoluteness of Hegel's metaphysics in his ostensibly historicist *Aesthetics*. From this artistic experience, both a moment of sensation and an aesthetic and philosophic analysis of history, comes Pater's definition of an act of freeing oneself from ideological or cultural constructs through a containment of all ideological elements in a "supreme artistic view of life." Regardless of what might be the specific political implications of this view, it clearly seems the opposite of an enclosed formalism. The same process of expansion marks Derrida's and more particularly de Man's handlings of the issues of history, ideology, and aesthetics. By challenging precisely the notion of an alterity between the literary and other forms of representation, they also challenge an alterity between philosophic abstraction and historic specificity. Finally, de Man challenges an alterity between aesthetics and ideology.

The literary language delineated by both Derrida and de Man did not evade representation or show its impossibility, as has often been claimed. Rather it mimed or represented a necessary aspect of mimesis and representation, the *acts* of representing or miming. A proposition turned upon its own acts of representation represents an implied but necessarily excluded aspect of any foundational system, not because it creates infinite reflection, but rather because it shows reflection's necessary but impossible background. One extension of this conflicted form of representation occurs, as it did in Pater, in the attempt to formulate a perspective on the conflict between historical specificity and philosophical or theoretical abstraction: is there a unifying philosophy behind history, or must every philosophical position have an explanatory historical specificity? Recognizing that any deconstruction depends on historically specific, indeed completely ungeneralizable, historical moments—recall Derrida's analysis of the status of Rousseau's example in his theory—neither Derrida nor de Man wants a philosophy that transcends history, despite the constancy of this charge against them. But, to the extent that the problems they raise constitute necessary aspects of foundational systems—are therefore foundational in a paradoxical way—they must claim that all historical specificity reduces to versions of the problem they address, at least at the moment of history's formulation within a discourse. They analyze this dual status of propositions as historical and philosophical in terms of the eccentric linguistic structure they centralize. But that analysis itself also enacts the structure determining a mixed status for their own claims as both philosophic and historical, literary and ideological. Critics often allow Derrida a political and historical concern that they charge de Man with draining from deconstruction,[4] perhaps because Derrida explicitly thematizes political issues in various essays. Yet, far more than Derrida, as we will see, de Man addresses the problem of history in the form of his essays, trying to define a mode of historicization that accords with the abstractly necessary embeddedness of literary language in any historicization, making his failure to write a history an explicit theme that finally leads to his consideration of aesthetics and ideology.

In the previous chapter, I discussed the centrality of the conflicted form of representation exemplified by literary language to the analysis in Derrida of philosophic foundations and in de Man of the epistemological groundings of literary criticism. In this chapter, we will first see how this analysis of conflicted representation also encompasses and explains Derrida's and de Man's positions on the relationships between explanations of philosophic ideas in terms of historical context and interpretations of history as necessarily philosophical and transhistorical. De Man, as we will see, worries this issue far more extensively than Derrida. And it leads him to extend his literary analysis, through his attempts to connect rhetorical and historical criticism, to a discussion of the conflict between aesthetics and ideology. The original aesthetic discussions of Kant and the early Romantics, we will see, used aesthetics to ground ideological claims. To connect ideology and aesthetics, then, it seems we must begin by separating them, as Lentricchia and others begin by presuming the alterity of literature to history in order to criticize formalism for being ahistorical. De Man questions the separation by questioning connection itself, showing the pervasiveness of a certain linguistic disjuncture both within aesthetics and within ideology. By showing aesthetic disjunctions in ideological analysis, he thus also shows the ideology embedded within aesthetic claims. This connection no more reduces the ideological to the aesthetic via the linguistic than it reproduces Kant's grounding of the ideological on the aesthetic through a repression of the linguistic. It argues for an opening of each discourse upon the other.

II

For both Derrida and de Man, the status of history as a discourse and as the challenge of specific event to philosophy's foundational ambitions recurs as a constant theme that seems something more than simply one theme among others. For Derrida, the fundamental challenge to a foundational system always involves detailing a specificity that both defines and exceeds that system. That specificity—if it is to be truly specific and not some new form of foundational abstraction—can occur only in history. But history as a discourse, he also claims, can exist only as a consequence of the foundational metaphysics that the specific intervention challenges. Thus the theme of history and, to some extent, the positing of a history to philosophy that is something more than merely a philosophy of history, I will argue here, preoccupy his delineation of deconstruction and reproduce its particular turns. One could extrapolate from Derrida's discussion of literary language to his analysis of history as well, but de Man's persistent attempt to connect his literary historical ambitions with his move toward rhetorical criticism makes explicit the connection between deconstruction's concern with literary language and its constant turns toward and away from history. In each case, far from trying to transcend history, deconstruction tries to preserve the historical attack upon foundation without acceding to the replacement of one transhistorical foundation with another. In Derrida, this project entails opening history and philosophy out upon each other, using each to challenge the priority of the other. Neither writer reduces history to philosophy or history to literature since their identifications relentlessly void the question of priority. Only a separation of history from philosophy that is finally philosophical, as Derrida argues in his critique of Foucault, or a distinction between historical event and literary language that is equally literary in its impulse, allows either a polemic in favor of historical over formal analysis or a polemic in favor of formal over historical analysis.

Critics generally turn for a discussion of the connection between Derrida's interpretive mode and his stance toward history to his review of Michel Foucault's *History of Madness* (translated in an abridged form into English as *Madness and Civilization* with the passage crucial to the ensuing debate as well as Foucault's appendix responding to Derrida left out). In that review, Derrida criticized Foucault for construing an alterity between madness and reason as historical, whereas Derrida interpreted the opposition as a central difficulty within the philosophical establishment of reason. Thus a cursory reading of the essay would take Derrida as establishing a philosophical difficulty that supersedes all historical difference. In support of his position, Derrida addresses a passage from Descartes in which Foucault sees Descartes, as a result of historically determined reasons, ruling madness out of bounds as completely other to all rational thought. Derrida reads the passage as using narrative sequence to comprehend the problems with madness under the larger rubric of dreaming. Foucault responds by deploying a number of historically generated genre differences to show that Descartes' text does not proceed sequentially from madness to dreaming but in fact sections out madness as an element of the text inexplicable by formal method, that inexplicability indicating precisely the historical constraints behind "the discursive practice of meditation" ("My Body," 18). Foucault concludes by charging Derrida with practicing "a historically well-determined little pedagogy. A pedagogy which teaches the pupil that there is nothing outside the text" (27). The issue seems custom-made for importation into literary-critical wars that revolve around claims of formal or historical priority in the interpretation of texts. Derrida's critique and Foucault's response contain practical examples of each type of interpretation.[5]

But Derrida does not in fact try to replace historical analysis with a transhistorical, philosophic skepticism. Although he certainly doubted

Foucault's empirical claim that reason excluded madness at a specific moment in history, his argument does not try to establish the priority of a philosophical over a historical reading but to show the problems each discourse presents to the other at the necessary moment of their coincidence. His criticism of Foucault does indeed start as a reassertion of philosophic generality over the issues Foucault identifies historically, but it ends with the claim that Foucault mars his reading, not with his historical claims, but with his reestablishment of reason in his own practice of a philosophical analysis. In response, Derrida suggests an extrapolation of historical discourse from the problems within the history of philosophy. He begins with a version of the classical objection of a foundational philosopher to one who attempts to define a historical circumscription to reason:

> The unsurpassable, unique, and imperial grandeur of the order of reason, that which makes it not just another actual order or structure (a determined historical structure, one structure among other possible ones), is that one cannot speak out against it except by being for it, that one can protest it only from within it; and within its domain, Reason leaves us only the recourse to stratagems and strategies.... Since the revolution against reason, from the moment it is articulated, can operate only *within* reason, it always has the limited scope of what is called, precisely in the language of *internal* affairs, a disturbance. A history, that is, an archaeology against reason doubtless cannot be written, for, despite all appearances to the contrary, the concept of history has always been a rational one. (*Writing*, 36)

We are used to thinking of Derrida's insistence that one cannot overturn reason, logic, or truth from without as a kind of alibi against the charge that his project's inconsistency lies precisely in the use of reason and logic against themselves. Passages like this one show that this argument is no alibi. However much he intends to define the limits of reason, he means those definitions to operate within reason because, even in response to projects such as Foucault's, with which we might suppose him to be sympathetic, he shares the traditional philosopher's sense of reason's constitutive universality. The attempt to define an alternative to reason from a historical perspective, he argues, shares the inescapable rationality of all history.

Quoting Foucault to the effect that the exclusion of madness and the detachment from it of meaningful language are "linked to the possibility of history" (*Writing*, 42), Derrida can conclude first that the moment of exclusion Foucault describes at the beginning of the classical period must therefore be only one among others since prior to the first there could have been no history to determine originality: Foucault's moment of exclusion "is an example as sample and not as model" (42).

Second, by writing a modern history, even an archaeological history, Foucault must in his discourse, regardless of his intents, reenact the internment of madness he condemns: "In this sense, I would be tempted to consider Foucault's book a powerful gesture of protection and internment. A Cartesian gesture for the twentieth century. A reappropriation of negativity. To all appearances, it is reason that he interns, but, like Descartes, he chooses the reason of yesterday as his target and the possibility of meaning in general" (55). If Foucault's history becomes a restructured reason, Derrida proposes in opposition a skeptical analysis that will delineate the necessary historicity of any reason, including its own. He ends the essay by insisting that he aims not to reground reason but to use it to interrogate itself more fully in a reproduction of a Cartesian gesture: "we have attempted not to extinguish the *other* light, a black and hardly natural light, the vigil of the 'powers of unreason' around the Cogito. We have attempted to *requite* ourselves toward the gesture which Descartes uses to requite himself as concerns the menacing powers of madness which are the adverse origin of philosophy" (61). But how will requital as recognition of the debt to reason also achieve requital as revenge? A purely philosophical interpretation would remain even more embedded within the constraints of reason, one would think, than a historical one.

Denying that he intends to distinguish valuable philosophic generality from historical accident in his argument against Foucault, Derrida makes a first gesture toward discussing the intersection of philosophy and history:

> I am not proposing the separation of the wheat from the tares in every philosophy in the name of some *philosophia perennis*. Indeed, it is exactly the contrary that I am proposing. In question is a way of accounting for the very historicity of philosophy. I believe that historicity in general would be impossible without a history of philosophy, and I believe that the latter would be impossible if we possessed only hyperbole, on the one hand, or, on the other, only determined historical structures, finite *Weltanschauungen*. The historicity proper to philosophy is located and constituted in the transition, the dialogue between hyperbole and the finite structure ... in the place where, or rather at the moment when, the Cogito and all that it symbolizes here (madness, derangement, hyperbole, etc.) pronounce and reassure themselves then to fall, necessarily forgetting themselves until their reactivation, their reawakening in another statement of the excess which also later will become another decline and another crisis. (60)

By hyperbole, as earlier passages make clear, Derrida means the founding moment of claiming through universal doubt to reestablish grounds for knowledge. The moment is hyperbolic because it exceeds any rational limitations in its very founding of reason. But hyperbole reduces to mere abstraction without its emergence in historical specificity. Indeed the one way to see the hyperbolic element in Descartes' claim is to see its overadequacy, thus its inadequacy, to the historical situation in which it occurs. Thus the historicity of philosophy inheres not in any one historical moment but in the interaction of philosophical ambition with finite historical structures, a historicity that would not be a series of events, precisely, but an intersection that can be described neither as history nor as philosophy but as the meeting place of both. Thus we can see the historicity of philosophy, its being determined by historical specificity, only in seeing its actual history—logically enough—and that history emerges in an intersection of event and abstraction that reduces neither to mere abstraction nor to just event. Derrida does not claim to master Foucault's argument within an essentially traditional philosophy disguised as infinite interpretation. Rather, praising Foucault for determining within a historical description the founding philosophical problem of the conflict between reason and its other, he also notes that Foucault's determination rests on the philosophy he attacks.

My formulation of Derrida's position may sound so close to my previous description of Pater's historicism—historical event both determining and being constructed by philosophical abstraction—as to be suspicious. And, indeed, I do want to suggest here that there is no more real conflict between Foucault's historicism and Derrida's deconstruction than there was between Pater's aesthetic criticism and the historicism of those who criticized him. But the formulation of Derrida's position here derives, I think, not from my construction but from the necessities of the deconstruction that Derrida was beginning to articulate. In effect, the relation described here between history and philosophy produces in advance Derrida's solution to the problem of Rousseau's exemplarity in *Of Grammatology*. Thus he accuses Foucault of providing an example as sample and not as model. But then he concludes that historical samples of the specific but unspecifiable act of philosophical excess, hyperbole, form the only possible models of that excess. In this way, we have seen, he justified his use of Rousseau as an event that was too exorbitant to serve as an example even as that exorbitance itself was the only example possible. Deconstruction, then, occurs with an intervention of an excluded possibility in the form of a specific empirical and historical event that a foundational system cannot coherently construe. As such, it depends precisely on the formulation of the connection between history and philosophy I have been delineating and, thus, that connection gets worked out in its paradoxically historical specificity in *Of Grammatology*.

At the moment that Derrida turns from Saussure to Lévi-Strauss and Rousseau, he begins with a brief "Introduction to the 'Age of Rousseau' "; there he justifies naming our age with that less than central figure first with an extremely cursory history of philosophy, then with a turning upon that history that both justifies its cursoriness and extends its historical claims to the book as a whole. The history is as follows:

> Between the overture and the philosophical accomplishment of phonologism (or logocentrism), the motif of presence was decisively articulated. It underwent an internal modification whose most conspicuous index was the moment of certitude in the Cartesian cogito. Before that, the identity of presence offered to the mastery of repetition was constituted under the "objective" form of the ideality of the *eidos* or the substantiality of *ousia*. Thereafter, this objectivity takes the form of *representation*, of the *idea* as the modification of a self-present substance, conscious and certain of itself at the moment of its relationship to itself. (*Of Grammatology*, 97)

In the context of this passage, Derrida's encounter with Foucault seems less one between the values of ahistorical interpretation and historical specification of texts and more a conflict between two different histories. Both Derrida and Foucault agree on the centrality of Descartes, but Foucault has committed the philosophic hyperbole of imagining him to be a moment of historical inauguration rather than a modification in philosophical attitudes. Prior to Descartes, presence grounded itself on the external existence of both the form—the ideality—and the substance of objects of perception, ideality and substance being the two traditional places for philosophy to locate essence.[6] After Descartes, a subject's awareness of its own presence, pure self-presence, founded certainty, even in the face of a universalized doubt of externality. Derrida marks the next great philosophical moment with the name Hegel: "Hegel reappropriates the sensible sign to the movement of the Idea" (98). Derrida works this brief comment out in detail in the essay "The Pit and the Pyramid" (*Margins*, 71–108), which explains the importance of the sign to the sublation that in Hegel connects matter with idea. All that is left is to justify the significance of the rather eccentric figure of Rousseau—eccentric at least in the context of Plato, Descartes, and Hegel: "within this age of metaphysics, between Descartes and Hegel, Rousseau is undoubtedly the only one or the first one to make a theme or a system of the reduction of writing profoundly implied by the entire age" (*Of Grammatology*, 98). Rousseau, in other words, concentrates on a theme that must remain marginalized for philosophy to maintain its coherence. His thematically specific marginality determines his historic centrality.

This is history all right, even narrative history, complete with punctual changes adding up to a coherent sequence that one determines according to the binding of "the importance of presence to philosophy." The only question is what such a traditional history is doing in Derrida's philosophy. And, as one might expect, Derrida immediately draws back from it:

> It would be frivolous to think that "Descartes," "Leibniz," "Rousseau," "Hegel," etc., are names of authors, of the authors of movements or displacements that we thus designate. The indicative value that I attribute to them is first the name of a problem.... But as I also do not think that these texts are the simple *effects* of structure, in any sense of the word; as I think that *all concepts hitherto proposed in order to think the articulation of a discourse and of a historical totality are caught within the metaphysical closure that I question here*, as we do not know of any other concepts and cannot produce any others, and indeed shall not produce so long as this closure limits our discourse; as the primordial and indispensable phase, in fact and in principle, of the development of this problematic, consists in questioning the internal structure of these texts as symptoms ... I draw my argument from them in order to isolate Rousseau, and, in Rousseauism, the theory of writing. (*Of Grammatology*, 99)

One may connect names to history either by determining that they authorize a historically significant change or, in reverse, by determining that their thoughts derive from a prior historical context or structure. Derrida immediately denies both of those intentions, thus calling into question the validity of the history he has just outlined. He must do that because both of these modes of construing the connection between events, as well as any other modes, derive from the metaphysical theme of presence that he both identifies and questions in this history. But, of course, he cannot identify this theme without making a history, because history is also an inevitable consequence of its appearance. Outside the metaphysical closure he identifies, history cannot be, but once that metaphysics occurs, history also occurs as its concomitant and the only mode by which it may be identified.

From these remarks, we may transform Derrida's writing in *Of Grammatology*—and, indeed, in many of his major philosophical texts, including *Speech and Phenomena, Margins of Philosophy,* and *Dissemination*—into a history. To an extent I have been doing that here, following the model of my articulation of Pater's *Renaissance* as a history perceived through and constructing an aesthetic. And in the sense that metaphysics generally works relentlessly to marginalize history, either by providing a transhistorical explanation to comprehend it or by claiming its irrelevance to the foundational issues with which it deals, one can see that instating historic variability within that foundation as central would be a primary deconstructive goal. Although this makes of Derrida's analysis a certain kind of history, one cannot deny it to be a history that resembles the transcendental metaphysics being criticized. Certainly it cannot do otherwise without falling into Foucault's metaphysical claim of having found in a specific history an outside from which reason and metaphysics may be comprehended firmly. Still it is odd that so many critics allow to Derrida a historical concern that they deny to de Man, who not only reproduces his confrontation, though within the explicit theme of literature and aesthetics, but directly thematizes it in the attempts and failures of his own works to articulate a history of Romanticism as a crucial shift in the understanding of literary language.

The difference between Derrida's and de Man's treatments of history stems largely from the different stresses the reversed itineraries of their projects create for them. Although centrally concerned with the problem of literary language, Derrida poses that concern always within the context of the philosophic analysis it allows. His treatment of history grows out of the same conflicting demands of deconstruction that lead to his treatment of literary language, but the two themes are coincident rather than mutually productive. Thus, perhaps, though Derrida does not in fact historicize his discourse to the extent that de Man does, one does not see any immediate "reduction" to the literary in his argument. For de Man, as we have seen, the status of literary language as a perception, more than as a technique, was a constant concern. That concern led to his various encounters with philosophers, both phenomenological and deconstructive, and, through an evident long-standing, or at least often-stated, desire to rewrite the literary history of Romanticism, to an increasingly explicit attempt to assimilate the writing of history to the analysis of literary language. The also explicit failure of that attempt led to his final focusing on the connections among aesthetics, language, history, and ideology. Because the structure of language always performs a central role in his essays, his arguments often seem to suggest that history "reduces" to linguistic contradiction. A careful look at those arguments, however, shows that the problem lies in the concept of reduction. His treatment of historical discourse and his analysis of literary language always share a mutual interdependence that structures his argument. That interdependence of history and literary language resists reduction of either to a claim for the priority of the other.

As with his ideas about literary language, to understand de Man's attitude toward history, we must see the change it underwent: de Man did not precisely change from a phenomenological literary historian into an ahistorical and formal deconstructive rhetorician,[7] but rather turned from a literary history he found forestalled by rhetoric toward a rhetoric that he found explicative of historical and ideological situations. One sees the problem his discovery of deconstruction caused him in his decision to eliminate "The Rhetoric of Temporality" from the first edition of *Blindness and Insight* and his redefinition of that problem in his inclusion of it in a second edition. In his second preface to *Blindness and Insight*, de Man classifies the original essays as having articulated, without his deliberate intention, a response to the conflict between theory and literary interpretation. He terms "Rhetoric of Temporality," which he wrote at the same time, "a slightly different case. With the deliberate emphasis on rhetorical terminology, it augurs what seemed to me to be a change, not only in terminology and in tone but in substance. This terminology is still uncomfortably intertwined with the thematic vocabulary of consciousness and of temporality that was current at the time, but it signals a turn that, at least for me, has proven to be productive" (*Blindness*, xii). De Man's retrospective comment does not really describe the difference of the case—the excluded essay tried to articulate a history that fit ill with the rhetorical theory developing in the other essays—and thus does not give an explicit reason for the original exclusion. Rather it suggests, in hindsight, the history of a turn from temporality to rhetoric, even though the turn itself seems to be away from history. If "Rhetoric of Temporality" is caught by this contradiction, "Literary History and Literary Modernity" is both about it and an attempt to extend it into a connection between the status of literary language and the writing of history.

Rather noticeably for an essay that states its concern as literary, "Literary History and Literary Modernity" begins with an extended discussion of the problem of writing history in general. Through one of those odd readings in de Man that identifies a genuine issue in a work through a distorted close reading of a passage that does not quite comprehend the issue,[8] de Man, in a discussion of Nietzsche's *Use and Abuse of History*, identifies the mutually inclusive problems of trying to escape history by instituting new origins and trying to accept one's own historical entailment: "As soon as modernism becomes conscious of its own strategies—and it cannot fail to do so if it is justified ... in the name of a concern for the future—it discovers itself to be a generative power that not only engenders history, but is part of a generative scheme that extends far back into the past.... Only through history is history conquered; modernity now appears as the horizon of a historical process that has to remain a gamble. Nietzsche sees no assurance that his own reflective and historical attempt achieves any genuine change" (*Blindness*, 150–151). One cannot simply link modernity entirely with a force of change, and history with a force of conservatism. Modernity always exists within history since, to inaugurate a better future, it offers a proleptic history of that future by explaining its own ability to generate it. It is the horizon of any historical process because it posits the future as an escape from an entrapment within history, but that positing always gambles since the proleptic history may always be a new entrapment, a new historical specification. But the reverse problem is also true. If historical horizons derive from modernity's attempt to escape pastness, conservative resignation to the traditional lessons history teaches also shares modernity's attempt to escape history. After all, those lessons will always stand apart from the history that teaches them as its horizon. De Man does not make explicit this reverse side of his logic about modernity in his discussion of Nietzsche, but that reverse plays a crucial role in his move from this discussion of history to a definition of literary history.

The confrontation between the desire for modernity and the constraints of historicity does not, in the first instance, pertain especially to the writing or the interpretation of literary history. In Nietzsche's essay, all forms of writing history stood opposed to the desire to begin anew—even if they also entailed that desire and that desire also entailed knowing one's own historicity. De Man discusses history and modernity to preface a discussion of literary history because we find the confrontation between the two forces embedded in the literature in a way that forces a redefinition of literary history. Literature, rather than literary history, feels "the appeal of modernity.... No true account of literary language can bypass this persistent temptation of literature to fulfill itself in a single moment. The temptation of immediacy is constitutive of a literary consciousness and has to be included in a definition of the specificity of literature" (152). Coming at the end of the extended meditation in *Blindness and Insight* on literary language, this occurrence of modernity as an inevitable result of literary language has a certain internal strangeness. First, if modernity arises out of the attempt to begin anew, the sense of immediacy, which would occur in literature in the symbolic coincidence of signifier with meaning, thereby connects with a literary force of conservative mystification even as it causes the literary desire for modernity. The force is literarily conservative in its belief in symbolism, politically conservative in the Coleridgean tendency to justify institutions in terms of their symbolic encompassing of value. Moreover, the literary language we saw defined in "Criticism and Crisis," as well as in other essays, recognized the noncoincidence of signifier with meaning, a denial of symbolism. The modernity that occurs in literature, despite its source in a desire to escape history, is then a force of traditionalism. Since modernity carries the generation of history within it, however, its conflicted identity reconstitutes the internal contradictions that comprise antisymbolic literary language: "Assertions of literary modernity often end up by putting the possibility of being modern seriously into question. But precisely because this discovery goes against an original commitment that cannot simply be dismissed as erroneous, it never gets stated outright, but hides instead behind rhetorical devices of language" (152). In other words, the contradictions within the desire for modernity both correspond to and cause the contradictions of literary language. One finds the same analysis carried out in reverse when de Man addresses historical valuing of tradition. A regard for tradition would obviously be conservative, but it assumes its literariness by recognizing the value of decorum in tradition, decorum being defined by its artifice and thus reproducing the subversive literary recognition of the signifier's noncoincidence with meaning (153–154).

Through an analysis of Baudelaire, de Man works out in more detail how the conflicting desires for modernity and decorum, and the conflicts within those desires, create narrative sequence in literature and thus the form of temporal sequence in historical writing.[9] He sees literary language, not as denying historicity, but as embodying the internal activity that constitutes its temporal sequence. Nevertheless, literary language enacts this embodiment in its structure rather than by referring to historical event, and thus the history it possesses has noticeably little historical specificity; it merely abstracts impulses to transform and impulses to conserve. And that abstraction raises the historical problem for the literary historian. On the one hand, "it is generally admitted that a positivistic history of literature, treating it as if it were a collection of empirical data, can only be a history of what literature is not" (162–163). This could be translated into the formalist's or structuralist's argument that, if that which makes literature literature is some particularly literary aspect of its form or language, then the literary history that concerns itself with thematic developments would concern itself with what literature is not. But if the literary historian ignores the central structure of the literary, the formalist, by ignoring the historicity embedded in that structure, repeats rather than explains the problems of both literary form and its historicity: "on the other hand, the intrinsic interpretation of literature claims to be anti- or a-historical, but often presupposes a notion of history of which the critic is not himself aware" (163). The formalist, like the modernist, would be entrapped in a history he tried to deny, thus repeating the constitutive conflict of the literary rather than explaining it.

De Man thus sets up two criteria for a reformed literary history. First, since sequence derives from the narrativity that literary language creates from the internal contradictions of its historical and antihistorical impulses, and does not form part of history itself, a narrative literary history would be another literary artifact rather than a history (163). Second, the vital content and form of both history and literature arise in a conflicted moment of self-questioning in which literary language accepts its own nonrepresentation, modernity generates the history it wants to escape, and conservatives value the decorous, formal, and thus antihistorical aspect of history and tradition. Thus the non-narrative literary history ought not evade that self-questioning either in a thematic literary history or in a formalism that assumes the synchrony that can exist only after self-questioning has been resolved. The essay's last sentences seem almost impossibly sanguine in their identifying this renovated literary history with good interpretation of literature and further in identifying this interpretation-as-literary-history with a reformed general history. But if we take the various turns of this essay as exemplifying the interpretation de Man calls for, it will seem neither simplifying nor a formalism that tries to close itself off from a history it sees either as threatening or vulgar. The literary language that constitutes literature also arises precisely from historical impulses. The reading it calls for must comprehend those impulses rather than attempt to formalize them. If the essay ends by identifying the events of history, "wars or revolutions," as textual, this identification would hardly drain them of their effect or importance. It assumes that their conflicts exist in texts rather than that texts merely refer to those conflicts, that the literary is an oddly intensified version of those conflicts, that the conflicts may thus be better read through an adequately reformed mode of interpretation. In effect, as Pater's artistic view of life becomes culturally redemptive because it includes cultural conflict within itself, de Man's literary history as literary interpretation, rather than being "merely" literary, claims for the literary experience, as constructed by literary language and the vexed interpretations it calls for, an enhanced implication in history.

If "Literary History and Literary Modernity" may claim for its own interpretive maneuvers the structure of a history, the persuasiveness of its conclusion cannot rest on any historical explanations the essay offers. Although it refers to numerous texts or "events" in intellectual or literary history, it never reads the historicity of those texts or events but rather interprets them to discuss what they show about the issue of historicity. We would accede to the argument that literary interpretation is the best form of literary history only if we could see an act of interpretation as simultaneously an act of history. Otherwise an argument in favor of their identity becomes a reduction of one to the other, regardless of the intention of the argument. In the difficulty of imagin-

DECONSTRUCTIVE AESTHETICS   139

ing a literary historical statement that might meet the two criteria for adequate literary history stated above and thus count as good literary interpretation, we can immediately see how de Man has transposed Derrida's conflict between philosophy and historicism to the field of literature, thus making his literary history a way of addressing that problem. De Man argues that since narrativity is a literary effect, history ought not to operate as a narrative since it would then reduce to that effect. But any denotation of change in history would entail a temporal sequence, thus a narrative. And yet without a consideration of change, we lack any historic specificity to the text or to the event we are discussing. Further, de Man thinks that since literature always puts itself in question, we cannot infer a stability to the entity whose history we describe; that entity's self-questioning entails its having no stability. But, although we could analyze a process without stable events, we could not easily give it a history, since its instability would always exceed any historical category we might give it. In effect, de Man wants a philosophic perspective capable of seeing through history's narrative effect without dissipating the whole discipline that depends on that effect; and he wants a historicism that fully recognizes the instability of historical event without losing the philosophic perspective that that historicism questions. The project of rewriting the history of Romanticism, begun in "The Rhetoric of Temporality" and recounted in *Allegories of Reading* and *The Rhetoric of Romanticism*, corresponds precisely to these criteria, and thus attempts to enact the interpretation as history outlined by "Literary History and Literary Modernity."

De Man opens "The Rhetoric of Temporality" by noting a shift of terms in modern criticism from "a subjectivist critical vocabulary" back toward "traditional forms of rhetoric" (187). He then notes a difficulty with this critical turn in "the association of rhetorical terms with value judgments that blur distinctions and hide the real structures" and offers as a way out of this difficulty a history of the generation of those value judgments: "One has to return, in the history of European literature, to the moment when the rhetorical key-terms undergo significant changes and are at the center of important tensions. A first and obvious example would be the change that takes place in the latter half of the eighteenth century, when the word 'symbol' tends to supplant other denominations for figural language, including that of 'allegory'" (188). He does more there than identify the importance of the historical subject he chooses. As the second preface to *Blindness and Insight* and, indeed, the very title of this essay make clear, de Man's argument here will partake of the critical shift that his history claims to explain. Thus its history of a literary self-questioning also creates a critical self-questioning. Further, at least in the first instance, his history of "symbol" and "allegory" in Romanticism does not entail identifying how these forms of rhetoric occur in Romantic literature but determining how the Romantics evaluated these terms. And yet, in order to determine how the Romantics evaluated these terms, he must also interpret how they used the forms of rhetoric they label. In effect, then, the issue the essay sets out for itself is an interpretive one, the value of rhetorical as opposed to subjectivist terms, but to recognize it as such, and not construe the change from one mode to another in terms of an evaluative narrative of progress from one to another, it must be discussed through the historically specific case of Romanticism. Further, we can only write the history of those terms precisely by interpreting their use. The narrative de Man determines in Romanticism, then, questions the narrativity of prior histories that evaluated the movement, while his attempt to understand the workings of that movement cannot escape it into a position of stability outside the history since the movement's history comprehends the critical moment that addresses it.

As with Derrida's critique of Rousseau, this literary history, dependent for its abstract formulation on the absolute historical specificity of Romanticism, can be written only once. The historical distinctness of Romanticism arose from its concern with the conflict between rhetorical and subjectivist vocabularies. While one might understand the works of any other period through rhetorical criticism, one would not in that understanding be discussing their historically distinguishing features. This situation follows from de Man's further historicizing of Derrida's philosophized version of historicism.

Pater, Derrida, and de Man all share a formulation that combines the mutually contradictory forces of historicism and an abstracting philosophy, but their identification of that formula drives them in different directions. Pater could transfer the historical uniqueness of the Renaissance indefinitely because its specific significance entailed defining the ahistorical value of completely individuated sensations, and these sensations in turn created the historical specificity of any period. In effect, Derrida, as we have seen, further philosophized this historicism. Rousseau was historically unique because he represented perfectly a deconstructive situation that applied across the history of philosophy. His example could be infinitely repeated; each repetition would leave an inexplicable surplus, some historical differentiation; but the existence of that surplus was that which deconstruction would always fasten upon as the essential. De Man further historicized that situation by locating the uniqueness of this formulation within Romanticism. The criticism that de Man tried to contain Derrida within a literary transcendence founders upon the status of Romanticism in his writing as the historical figure of the literary in his work. This intensified historicism, however, forces some distortion in its further articulation. If Romanticism both theorized and exhibited the breakdown of subjectivist philosophy into disarticulated forms of rhetoric, how could one write a history even of that period through those disarticulated forms without falling into the threat of articulation? Even the argument of "The Rhetoric of Temporality" will follow only to the extent that the rhetorical analysis de Man outlines will follow for language in general. As Gasché notes with regard to de Man's treatment of philosophical texts: "such analysis of the autonomous potential of language has no relation whatsoever to the meaning that this language appears to transport. Indeed, a rhetorical reading of a text is not geared toward revealing anything regarding the meaning of that text. It is not *about* a text, and thus cannot be measured against it" (Waters and Godzich, 273). From this perspective, all literary history, including this exemplary one, must embody its own disarticulation.

De Man's solution to this problem in the books that follow *Blindness and Insight* entailed thematizing the failure to achieve historical articulation. The prefaces to the very works that critics have identified as attempts to escape history into the aesthetic describe the projects as failed historical attempts, not as triumphant overcomings of history. And each failed attempt has its own historical implication. Thus *Allegories of Reading* opens by declaring a critical shift:

> *Allegories of Reading* started out as a historical study and ended up as a theory of reading. I began to read Rousseau seriously in preparation for a historical reflection on Romanticism and found myself unable to progress beyond local difficulties of interpretation. In trying to cope with this, I had to shift from historical definition to the problematics of reading. This shift, which is typical of my generation, is of more interest in its results than its causes. I could, in principle, lead to a rhetoric of reading reaching beyond the canonical principles of literary history. (ix)

In effect, this opening seems to recast "The Rhetoric of Temporality" from a literary history to the discovery of a new critical method, the discovery indeed which that essay's opening paragraph proposed to explain historically. Changing that essay's history into a rhetoric, however, transforms this book's rhetoric into a historical example of a movement typical of his generation and a historical possibility of disarticulating the literary canon. The attempt to identify literary criticism with literary history extends even to a passage that seemingly admits the failure to write a history. But the failure in *The Rhetoric of Romanticism* reproduces the shape of the literary history de Man forecast in *Blindness and Insight*: "Laid out diachronically in a roughly chronological sequence, [the essays in *The Rhetoric of Romanticism*] do not evolve in a manner that easily allows for dialectical progression or, ultimately, for historical totalization. Rather, it seems that they always start again from scratch and that their conclusions fail to add up to anything" (*Rhetoric*, viii). The refusal to add up, of course, was an aspect of the literary history that de Man sought earlier. Thus, by noting the failure of rhetorical criticism to achieve totalized history, he marks the historicity of its attempt. He also clearly ties his book's structure to the theme of disarticulation that comes to recur more and more clearly in de Man's later works. Far from evading history, he tried with greater deliberation to write essays whose criticism would be both historically and ideologically significant.

III

The constant obstacle to de Man's project of claiming rhetorical criticism as historical, as I said in opening, is the notion that an equation between language and history means reducing history to "mere" language. We can specify this further. While there may be nothing intrinsically threatening in ascribing constructions of the temporal to linguistic structures, or at least one rarely finds de Man criticized for this gesture, the ascription of historical articulation to linguistic articulation seems to entail a skepticism about the significance or the reality of the political and ideological forces operating within history, as if their effectiveness depended on the distinctiveness and coherence of their historical articulation. At points—most particularly in *Allegories of Reading*—his delineation of a rhetorical criticism led de Man to consider an abandonment of the historically revisionist concerns that coincided with his first uses of that criticism. But the other concern that coincided with rhetoric and history—the attention to the cultural role of the critic mentioned in the previous chapter—emerged more prominently as he addressed the institutional response to deconstruction. With this theme, his concern to read both the historical and the political, without reducing them, through his theory of literary language became more evident. In effect, de Man wanted to historicize Derrida's deconstruction. By this I do not mean, obviously, that he wanted to explain it away by calling it a last-ditch version of bourgeois subjectivism or a justification for political inactivity.[10] Even if both these claims were true, they would in fact not explain the specific content of the philosophy or its mode of criticism, but merely connect it to some other coinciding effect. Rather, he wanted both to see deconstructive methodology as caught within the history it deconstructs, as he caught his rhetorical criticism within the Romantic literature he turned it toward, and to see how deconstruction accounted for the contemporary response to itself, historical and ideological, and also took shape from that response. His final essays on aesthetics accomplish this historical and ideological extension of deconstruction in two ways. First, they respond to the mistaken notion that the aesthetic ever claimed or desired, much less achieved, a total separation from the political or the ideological. Showing the interdependence of the aesthetic and the ideological implied by extension that the literary language that he had so constantly connected to the historical would not operate as a reduction of history to language. Second, he used the disarticulations deconstruction finds within the historically separate but generally significant case of nineteenth-century aesthetics to comment upon the response of both literary and political critics to deconstruction.

Pater, as we have seen, used Hegel's *Aesthetics* because its historicized view of art, combined with its transcendental organization of its history from the perspective of philosophy, allowed him to replace philosophy with aesthetics in Hegel's structure (their roles were structurally similar; they are differentiated only by the pastness of art), thus combining a comprehensive historicism with a culturally explanatory perspective. The very contradictions Pater found within the experience of art allowed aesthetics this dual role. De Man deploys a version of the same contradiction between the centrality of aesthetics to systems of philosophy in nineteenth-century philosophy and the dependence of that centrality upon its marginalization, either as past in Hegel or as separated from matters of interest in Kant, to offer literary readings of aesthetics, aestheticizations of philosophy, as explanations of ideological situations surrounding current critical debates. Once again, by accepting the accusation of a link between aestheticism and deconstruction, I want to change the understanding of each one's significance.

Both Pater and de Man respond to a persistent misunderstanding in the readings of aesthetics that has shaped the misreading of their own works as well. This misunderstanding starts with a frequent claim that Kant separates aesthetic experience out into a special realm. This claim results from Kant's well-known insistence on the disinterestedness of aesthetic judgment.[11] In fact, as de Man in the opening to his essay on Kant ("Phenomenality," 122–124) and Derrida in his discussion in *Truth in Painting* (35–42) both point out, Kant places his *Critique of Judgment* and its aesthetic theory at the center of his critical philosophy. Kant, at first, divides mental activities into the cognitive, those that understand objects in nature, and the faculties of desire, those that, through reason's working through the principle of freedom, determine moral laws. But since the understanding can only know the laws of nature and the reason can only legislate through a consideration of the supersensible, there is a gap between our knowledge and our ethics that makes the one purely determined and the other groundless. Kant, therefore, proposes a third faculty, judgment, which deals with pleasure and pain, and which connects his other two:

> We may therefore suppose provisionally that the judgment likewise contains in itself an *a priori* principle. And as pleasure or pain is necessarily combined with the faculty of desire (either preceding this principle, as in the lower desires, or following it, as in the higher, when the desire is determined by the moral law), we may also suppose that the judgment will bring about a transition from the pure faculty of knowledge, the realm of natural concepts, to the realm of the concept of freedom, just as in its logical use it makes possible the transition from understanding to reason. (Kant, 15)

The judgment of pleasure and pain binds understanding to reason because of the pleasure one takes in a certain kind of patterning, a purposiveness, which, although it attaches to objects, is not in fact itself a sensible phenomenon. Purposiveness per se is thus a transcendental concept, but it is perceived only in nature or natural objects (17–25). Aesthetic pleasure is the model for this pleasure in the fact of purposiveness because one cannot take any interest in an aesthetic object, as a matter of definition rather than constraint, except to appreciate its patterning, its quality of purposiveness without purpose: "*Taste* is the faculty of judging of an object or a method of representing it by an *entirely disinterested* satisfaction or dissatisfaction" (45). One could take other kinds of satisfaction in art objects, of course, having personal desires or ends in mind, but in doing so, one's attitude would cease to be a matter of aesthetics. As a direct result of this disinterestedness, aesthetics binds understanding and reason in that it offers a model of a transcendental cognition. Thus, far from being an enclosed sphere, aesthetics, precisely in its disinterest, creates the capability of moving from an understanding of nature to an articulation of just laws.

The case is somewhat more complex with Hegel, in ways that make de Man's reading of him equally complex. On the one hand, as we have seen in the earlier discussion of Pater's transformation of Hegel's aesthetic theories, Hegel thought of art as a superseded mode of the spirit's self-expression. Art, for him, thus, was not disinterested, but simply surpassed. On the other hand, the structure of spiritual self-expression, as Pater's transformation also shows, accorded well with nineteenth-century notions of aesthetic expression. Hegel's opening statement in *The Phenomenology of Mind* on the working of philosophy makes this clear: "because philosophy has its being essentially in the element of that universality which encloses the particular within it, the end or final result seems, in the case of philosophy more than in that of other sciences, to have absolutely expressed the complete fact itself in its very nature" (67). Philosophy operates by a coinciding of universal with particular that partakes of Romantic theories of symbolism, as de Man's discussion makes clear. Thus, Hegel's *Aesthetics* becomes, through de Man's reading, a central way of understanding the articulations within his philosophy and indeed of understanding the connections between aesthetics generally and other discourses that both literary critics and political critics deny. In the case of each philosopher, de Man applies what he describes as a literary reading ("Reply to Raymond Geuss," 384), more particularly a version of the rhetorical reading worked out in essays from "The Rhetoric of Temporality" through *Allegories of Reading,* to show the eccentric centrality of the aesthetics that reading outlines to matters of political and institutional debate.[12]

De Man begins his discussion of Kant by insisting on the relevance of Kant's aesthetic to his critical philosophy and by explaining the pertinence of that issue to the more general one of the relationship between ideology, which is concerned with empirical application, and critical philosophy, which addresses pure concepts. Like the most skeptical of political critics, de Man immediately challenges this division, though: "Ideological and critical thought are interdependent and any attempt to separate them collapses ideology into mere error and critical thought into idealism. The possibility of maintaining the causal link between them is the controlling principle of rigorous philosophical discourse: philosophies that succumb to ideology lose their epistemological sense, whereas philosophies that try to by-pass or repress ideology lose all critical thrust and risk being repossessed by what they foreclose" ("Phenomenality," 122–123). Half of this statement repeats precisely the Marxist critique of idealist philosophy. In trying to purify themselves of empirical and political concern, of any ideological significance, these philosophies not only become pointless, "lose all critical thrust," but they ultimately allow ideology to determine them; ideology takes possession of that which tries to avoid it. De Man also argues that the accuracy of ideological critique equally depends on its grounding in a transcendental system. Just as philosophy without the empirics of ideology is mere idealism, ideology without some philosophic structure collapses into mere error. The question de Man then raises is what constitutes the substance of the transcendental system. And to answer that question, he also repeats Kant's claim for the centrality of the aesthetic, precisely in the context of the concern for ideological pertinence: "One sees again how the *Third Critique* corresponds to the necessity of establishing the causal link between critical philosophy and ideology, between a purely conceptual and an empirically determined discourse. Hence the need for a phenomenalized, empirically manifest principle of cognition on whose existence the possibility of such an articulation depends. This phenomenalized principle is what Kant calls the aesthetic" ("Phenomenality," 124). The connection we have seen Kant define between the sections of his critical philosophy here operates to make aesthetics primary in including rather than expelling ideology. But the second concern of this opening section is the issue of articulation itself. What substance connects philosophy with ideology? If aesthetics articulates the two fields, what is the status of its articulation? This theme of articulation connects de Man's discussion of aesthetics with his deployment of rhetoric in that discussion, thus connecting his ideological analysis with his earlier discussions of literary language.

De Man proceeds to outline a series of disarticulations, connecting links that are necessary to the argument but don't quite connect. He starts with the status of the section on the sublime within the rest of the work (124–125). On the one hand, to the extent that *The Critique of Judgment* addresses the theme of teleological judgment, the appreciation of purposiveness without purpose, "the consideration of the sublime is almost superfluous." Because the sublime results from an attitude in the subject and not from any aspect of the object perceived (Kant, 88–89), it cannot be precisely a teleological judgment of an object, a proper connection of the supersensible with the sensible, and thus is in excess of the work's theme. But, on the other hand, the sublime "informs us about the teleology of our own faculties" ("Phenomenality," 125), and since our faculties, in their perception of the supersensible in the sensible, connect the understanding with the practical reason, thus connect philosophy with ideology, the sublime, like aesthetics as a whole, becomes central in its very disarticulation.[13] De Man proceeds, in a brief analysis of Kant's logic in this section, to argue that the elements of the sublime are connected according to the logic of grammatical structures:

> In order to make the sublime appear in space we need, says Kant, two acts of the imagination: apprehension ... and comprehension or summation. ... Apprehension proceeds successively, as a syntagmatic, consecutive motion along an axis, and it can proceed ad infinitum without difficulty. Comprehension, however, which is a paradigmatic totalization of the apprehended trajectory, grows increasingly difficult as the space covered by apprehension grows larger. The model reminds one of a simple phenomenology of reading, in which one has to make constant syntheses to comprehend the successive unfolding of the text. ("Phenomenality," 129)

From this, de Man can conclude that "the sublime cannot be grounded as a philosophical (transcendental or metaphysical) principle, but only as a linguistic principle" (130). This linguistic articulation has the internal coherence of linguistic systems, but it cannot be "translated back, so to speak, from language to cognition" (130) without the articulations disintegrating.

De Man frequently ascribes the philosophical to the linguistic, and that maneuver, as we have seen, has led to the recurrent charge that he argues that philosophy is merely language or literature. Nor is his logic as compelling here as it is in other, more finished essays. The ascription to the linguistic depends on an analogy between the workings of apprehension and comprehension and certain grammatic and reading structures, and analogy hardly proves identity.[14] This flaw seems particularly problematic in the light of his insistence that the linguistic cannot be translated back to the cognitive: if the translation from the cognitive to the linguistic occurs by way of analogy, why will not the same analogy get us back? Moreover, the refusal to allow a translation back, at this point, does assert a reduction to language rather than an equivalence between linguistic and philosophic structures. But de Man's argument is only half over at this point. And the transition to the second half is somewhat jarring: "The *Critique of Judgment* therefore has, at its center, a deep, perhaps fatal, break or discontinuity. It depends on a linguistic structure ... that is not itself accessible to the powers of transcendental philosophy. Nor is it accessible, one should hasten to add, to the powers of metaphysics or of ideology, which are themselves precritical stages of knowledge. Our question then becomes whether and where this disruption, this disarticulation, becomes apparent in the text, at a moment when the aporia of the sublime is no longer stated" (132). This transition seems less than inevitable. If de Man has made his case about the logical reduction of the philosophical to the linguistic, why do we need to see its textual embodiment in some aspect other than the logical articulation of the sublime? What will this textual analysis add?

If we assume that de Man knows the logical problem with his argument, however, the situation becomes considerably more complex. A textual embodiment of the aesthetic theory disarticulating into discrete materiality would demonstrate at a concrete textual level the abstract dependence of the Kantian sublime on a linguistic element that could not be translated back up. The demonstration would work, however, by using a literary critical gesture, delineating a text's formal embodiment of an argumentative structure, to rearticulate de Man's logic. Although this procedure is not logically problematic at this point, since de Man does not criticize Kant for such a procedure, it provides a model for a constitutive deconstructive gesture in the essay, an enacted rearticulation within an analysis of disarticulation, whose enactment the analysis must redefine. More particularly, looking for the embodiment of an argument within a textual structure, as opposed to working through the argument the text expresses directly, matches well with the aesthetic gesture of apprehending purposiveness within the structure of an object. Thus if de Man's analysis deconstructs (in the banal understanding of that word) Kant's aesthetics to show its reduction to language, the mode of his analysis enacts the central moment in that aesthetics. My point here, we will see, is not to deconstruct deconstruction but to lay the groundwork for what I take to be the full significance of de Man's analysis of aesthetics.

To summarize the balance of de Man's argument briefly, the essay proceeds to point to a textual moment of aporia in Kant's definition of a sublime perception of nature, one that sees the sea and the sky not in terms of their organic or life-bearing qualities but in their pure materiality. De Man describes this as an "architectonic world" (135) because it is perceived completely in terms of its material structure. But this materiality, void of any internal significance, de Man notes, is "also purely formal . . . reducible to the formal mathematization or geometrization of pure optics. The critique of the aesthetic ends up, in Kant, in a formal materialism that runs counter to all values and characteristics associated with aesthetic experience" (136). Since the example of how to perceive nature sublimely is, in itself, a detachable aside in Kant, de Man does not end his demonstration of textual disarticulation here but asks what the passage is doing in the argument. He ascribes it to Kant's sense that human beings need the material for the subjective aesthetic experience of sublime tranquility to occur. That experience of tranquility he then analyzes as resting on various figural, organic personifications of the mind. De Man notes that this is the second time that the text has broken down into linguistic tropes. He then focuses on the juxtaposition of this passage, setting up what he describes as an organic architectonic in its discussion of the mind, with the disarticulated formal materialism in the earlier architectonic of the sublime perception of nature. He concludes by citing the example following that of sea and sky through which Kant explains sublime perception: "The like is to be said of the sublime and beautiful in the human figure. We must not regard as the determining grounds of our judgment the concepts of the purposes which all our limbs serve, and we must not allow this coincidence to *influence* our aesthetical judgment (for then it would no longer be pure)" (Kant, 111; "Phenomenality," 142). In effect, the organic architectonic rests on a material architectonic that transforms its organicism into weirdly disassembled parts, as the body in the original example becomes, by implication, merely a set of limbs: "We must, in other words, disarticulate, mutilate the body" ("Phenomenality," 142). The melodrama of this image de Man finally reascribes to a disarticulated linguisticity:[15] "The bottom line, in Kant as well as in Hegel, is the prosaic materiality of the letter and no degree of obfuscation or ideology can transform this materiality into the phenomenal cognition of aesthetic judgment" (144). In effect, de Man supports the logical reduction of the sublime to the linguistic in the first half of his essay with an analysis of a formal disarticulation in the second half that can only be described linguistically.

But the form of de Man's argument realigns its conclusions. De Man's conclusion in the linguistic does not rest here on the tropic quality of the organic architectonic. Indeed, not tropic disarticulation but material disarticulation confirms the first half of the essay's ascription of the sublime to the linguistic. And while the juxtaposition of the organic architectonic with the material architectonic reduces one to the other, it does not reduce the organic to its own inherent trope of personification. The materiality of the letter, then, is as much material as letter. Moreover, the juxtaposition between the two architectonics itself works architectonically, and through both types of architectonics at once. On the one hand, this argument is not merely analogic. De Man works carefully through the sequence of Kant's argument, which leads from the vision of the void materiality in the sublime to a tropically described sublime tranquility. The argument he works out, however, does not account for the juxtaposition of one architectonic with the other in Kant, since, though the tropic description of the mind occurs in close proximity with the examples of sublime perception of nature, it occurs *before* those examples. Thus the juxtaposition of the two architectonics with which de Man concludes his argument is in Kant a matter of pure spatial proximity within the text. Using one architectonic to disarticulate the other construes such textual juxtapositions in simultaneously organic and dismembered terms. Closeness between passages may indicate a natural connection that underlies the seeming artificiality of their physical juxtaposition. But de Man uses the physical juxtaposition to dismember any other connection between the two passages. Above, I noted that the logic of the essay's first half demands a literary, aesthetic demonstration in its second. Actually, de Man's argument rests on a logic, his opening analysis of the sublime, placed next to an alogical organic architectonic, his reading of an intrinsic connection between two passages juxtaposed spatially but not logically. In *Allegories of Reading*, when the meaning implied by the rhetorical form of a statement, argument, or narrative conflicted with its expressed content, one had to entertain both possible meanings at once under the more general rubric of rhetoric. By that model, the ambiguously structured articulations of de Man's argument force us to reread the significance of his final reduction of aesthetics to the materiality of the letter. His disarticulation of the aesthetic that would connect philosophy with ideology does not reduce to the letter as if there were nothing else; it reduces to a letter that labels an alternative aesthetic, de Man's own, that recognizes its own willed, empirical, ideological gestures. Not a foundational ground for connecting ideology with aesthetics, perhaps, this disarticulation certainly could not intend to separate itself from the ideological.

I would like to stress, before concluding with a discussion of de Man's reading of Hegel, the ways in which this reading reproduces the earlier concerns with literary language and its historical ills and promises. The definition of aesthetics as an embodied articulation that, through being about articulation and embodiment, becomes disarticulated and disembodied of course reproduces the concentration of literary language on the problem of its own representation. Aesthetic articulation here works, in fact, as literary language does in Derrida's "Double Session." It is not a polar opposite to ideology or critical philosophy any more than literary language is a polar opposite either to truth as presence or its determined negation. It is, rather, a necessary "between," both functioning to connect philosophy to ideology and constantly determining that connection in terms of the lack of connection that any reflection of articulation upon itself reveals. Moreover, just as literary language's problematic status carried within it a problematic both historiographic and historic, thematized as the conflict between and within impulses toward modernity and toward establishing historical placements, de Man's discussion of aesthetics, as we will see more clearly in the treatment of Hegel, tries to capture historical conflicts within it rather than expelling them from the realm of some transcendental position. The connection between this aesthetics and history works in two ways. First, just as the reading of Kant stresses the connections among philosophy, aesthetics, and ideology by making the problem of connection itself central, de Man places the aesthetics he creates in its historical context, paradoxically, as we will see in the discussion of Hegel, by denying the historical separation of it that Hegel's historicism created. Second, he uses the philosophical and aesthetic implications he draws from his reading, again more explicitly in the case of Hegel, to read the historical and ideological situation of literary criticism. In each case, he reproduces his and Derrida's sense of the contradictory interdependence of historical specificity and philosophic foundation.

In order to understand de Man's reading of Hegel's *Aesthetics*, we must first deal with two related misreadings. The first takes the essays—and particularly "Sign and Symbol in Hegel"—to connect Hegel's aesthetics with a valorization of the symbol and Romantic interiorization and to criticize him for that position.[16] De Man explicitly denied this reading: "I am not giving a reading of 'the sensory appearance of the idea' which 'assimilates Hegel to Wordsworth and the English Romantics'.... What is being discussed in these sections is not Hegel's definition of 'beauty' but what is called 'the ideology of the symbol' as a defensive strategy aimed against the implications of Hegel's aesthetic theory" ("Reply to Raymond Geuss," 390). As in "The Rhetoric of Temporality," de Man sees the ideology of the symbol as a defensive response, expressed variously in some Romantics and in recent critics of Romanticism, to the more rhetorically, philosophically, and aesthetically complex position of Romantics such as Hegel here, Rousseau and Wordsworth in the earlier essay. This misreading, however, grows out of a more complex problem. De Man's reading of the *Aesthetics* is distinctly idiosyncratic. Indeed some aspects of it, taken in isolation from the project as a whole, seem egregiously incorrect. In particular, de Man's connection of art with symbol as opposed to sign ("Sign and Symbol," 763) runs directly counter to the clear definition within the *Aesthetics* of the symbolic as one stage of art, and that indeed the earliest one. Far from art being symbolic in Hegel, the symbolic period in art can only be described as preartistic. Similarly, de Man's assertion that "the sublime for Hegel *is* the absolutely beautiful" ("Hegel on the Sublime," 144) sounds distinctly odd given that Hegel's discussion of the sublime locates it specifically in the preartistic period of the symbolic. Moreover, if we define the symbol as the correspondence between the sensory and its significance, the sublime stands in direct contrast to the symbol—as de Man recognizes in an immediately subsequent sentence—and it is hard to see how the beautiful can be both symbolic ("Sign and Symbol," 763) and sublime. Finally, de Man's reading of Hegel's statement that "art is ... a thing of the past" (*Aesthetics*, 11) as meaning that art is a matter of memory ("Sign and Symbol," 773–774; "Hegel on the Sublime," 142–143) seems almost a willful misreading. The paragraph preceding the quoted fragment states clearly enough that we can no longer achieve the aesthetic level of Greek art or even the art of the Middle Ages because our culture no longer has art as its highest expression. Hegel means precisely what de Man questions, that art is a surpassed form of cultural expression, that the spirit has moved beyond it.[17] If we take the obvious willfulness here as a sign that de Man knows that he is interpreting against the text, that he is trying to articulate an aspect of Hegel's system that Hegel wants to repress, however, all these misreadings take on a different light, and de Man's interpretation of Hegel's definition of symbolic discourse and its relationship to Romanticism and to current critical and ideological situations becomes more understandable.

Indeed, all of de Man's "errors" in reading Hegel are so egregious as to be obvious even upon the most preliminary exposure to the *Aesthetics*, and de Man even calls attention at times to the seemingly forced quality of his readings. His previously cited definitions of the pastness of art, for instance, note their sources outside the *Aesthetics* and their difference from the traditional interpretation of the sentence. If we ask why de Man makes these "mistakes" in fairly clear awareness of making them, we can start to put together a fuller sense of what he does with Hegel's text. We should note that all of the mistakes amount to taking statements with historical location in the *Aesthetics* and interpreting them as ahistorically linguistic or epistemological, using aspects of Hegel's epistemology and his philosophies of history and of Right. Thus Hegel offers his distinction between sign and symbol (*Aesthetics*, 304–305) fairly specifically to explain his labeling of the first period of art as symbolic. He stresses both the symbol's approach to a binding of its significance with its sensory form and its partaking of the sign's conventional relationship between the two in order to have it identify the preartistic quality of the first period of art: the symbolic approaches the identity of sensuous form with meaning but does not achieve it; thus it is only symbolic. De Man takes this definition of the symbolic to identify the signification implicit in all forms of art by identifying the definition of beauty as the sensuous manifestation of the Idea with a rather different discussion elsewhere of the symbolic imagination.[18] The expansion of Hegel's remarks on the sublime to a general theory of the beautiful takes its justification from the placement of that issue in the context of Hegel's philosophies of law and religion. And finally, and most obviously, de Man's reading of the meaning of art's pastness explicitly detaches that sentence from the aesthetics to place it in certain psychological and epistemological contexts. By de-historicizing the *Aesthetics*, both by taking some of its periodically located definitions as descriptive of the whole definition of art and by taking the workings of art in the *Aesthetics* to correspond to other branches of Hegel's philosophy despite his claim that the time of art is past, de Man effectively claims to be able to read Hegel's philosophical and ideological statements through his aesthetic ones and vice versa.

Rather than simply mistaking Hegel's meaning, de Man makes an interpretive claim about the connection between his aesthetics and his philosophy. Both essays claim that artistic expression and its correspondence between sense and meaning, which de Man labels symbolic, are necessary aspects of Hegel's philosophies of spirit and Right, his epistemology and his ideology, even though these philosophies rest on the sublative structure of the sign, which both conventionalizes and defers meaning, thus making it available for reappropriation in a higher form by the spirit.[19] The basis for this connection occurs in the analysis of Hegel's connection of memory with thought and sign in "Sign and Symbol," which concludes: "the synthesis between name and meaning that characterizes memory is an 'empty link [das leere Bande]' and thus entirely unlike the mutual complementarity and interpenetration of form and content that characterizes symbolic art.... It is not aesthetic in the ordinary or in the classically Hegelian sense of the word. However, since the synthesis of memory is the only activity of the intellect to occur as sensory manifestation of an idea, memory is a truth of which the aesthetic is the defensive, ideological, and censored translation" (773). The embeddedness of the symbolic, as it is understood in the *Encyclopedia*, inheres in the working of memory; that form of symbolic imagination corresponds to the definition of beauty in the *Aesthetics*. But the memory represents the location par excellence of thought through conventional signing and naming. If the symbolic imagination inheres in it, and the symbolic imagination enacts the form of art as the embodiment of the Idea in sensuous appearance, then a primitive form of thought, a past form of cultural expression, embodies thought at the moment when it is supposed to transcend those forms. Thus the *Aesthetics* is symbolic and is of the past as a matter of memory because it inheres in the supposedly extra-aesthetic, philosophic analysis of mind.

The ultimate justification for reading the *Aesthetics* according to the categories of Hegel's epistemological and political texts would be the correspondence of such a connection to the structure of Hegel's dialectic, as this interpretation construes it. At various points, de Man makes the analogy he sets up between the *Aesthetics* and Hegel's other works explicit. For instance: "the relationship between pantheism and monotheism in the history of art and religion (since up to this point, it would be impossible to distinguish between them) is like the relationship between natural science and epistemology: the concept of mind ... is the monotheistic principle of philosophy as the single field of unified knowledge" ("Hegel on the Sublime," 145). Within that analogy, the *Aesthetics* functions as the symbolic expression of the epistemology's logical form of signification. Hegel tries to keep these forms of signification separate by historically circumscribing the symbolic within the past of an art that is itself of the past. By detailing the working of the symbol within the philosophy of mind that replaces art and religion, de Man argues the contradictory correspondence of the aesthetic and epistemological theories as an external manifestation (both symbol and sign) of contradictory forms of expression and cognition within each theory. De Man, of course, recognizes that his reading does not accord with Hegel's explicit arguments: "It is true, to take the most vulnerable point, that Hegel nowhere says, in so many words, that the aesthetic is structured like a linguistic inscription in a memorization. It is also true that he does not exactly tell the story of a threatening paradox at the core of his system against which his thought has to develop a defense in whose service the aesthetic, among other activities, is being mobilized. No one could be expected to be *that* candid about his uncertainties: Hegel could hardly openly say something like this and still be Hegel" ("Reply to Raymond Geuss," 389). Had de Man written in the mode of a philosophic refutation, critics would not have called posited reconstructions misreadings, even if they did not assent to the validity of the reconstruction. De Man, however, offers his reconstructions as literary critical comments on the structures and figures of a text. His arguments on Hegel's aesthetics effectively give us a fuller way of construing this mode of using literary criticism to produce philosophic responses and the reverse: the differences between the discourses inform the conclusions made by their mixing in precisely the way that the differences between aesthetics and epistemology, between sign and symbol, inform their moments of including each other.

It might seem an aside to add that the notion of self-deconstructing texts becomes in this context not a methodological defense of canonical propriety but a description in intratextual terms of the critic's relationship to his texts. Literary commentaries are reconstructions, and philosophic reconstructions are also commentaries. The modesty of the former and the pride of the latter are both forms of mastery that exclude the opposing textual relationship. In fact, this reconstruction of self-deconstruction clarifies the critical misapprehensions of de Man's point in his discussion of Hegel's aesthetics and finally the role of history in this de-historicized art theory. If one reads the essays as purely commentary on Hegel's *Aesthetics*, then de Man's definition of symbolism as central to aesthetic expression will necessarily seem preparatory to his long-standing critique of symbolism as a defensive reaction to Romantic allegory or to deconstructive philosophy. One can make the symbol constitutive of Hegel's theory of art, however, only by construing the historical categories within the *Aesthetics* according to the logical analyses of those categories within Hegel's epistemology. Such a reading has the paradoxical effect of embedding the symbolic within a philosophy that, as de Man notes, extols the "greatness" of the sign ("Sign and Symbol," 767). Thus, as we have seen, far from embodying "the ideology of the symbol," Hegel, for de Man, represented the position that that ideology responded to as a defensive strategy. De Man wants neither to defend the symbolic nor the purely aesthetic through some deconstructive reformulation, nor to attack the symbolic through deconstructive skepticism. Taking him as trying to reduce the philosophical to the literary derives from the assumption that self-deconstruction must be a philosophical presumption grounding the literary criticism. Taking him as attacking the symbolic derives from the assumption that his literary commentary, in the stance of rearticulating a textual self-deconstruction, imagines the *Aesthetics* to be saying that which he is able to construe it as signifying. De Man's point, though, is neither to reduce philosophy to the linguistic nor to attack the mystification of symbolism. Rather, as all three of his essays on Kant and Hegel state, he wants to articulate the relationship between ideology and philosophy. Aesthetics is neither the hero nor the villain of this piece. As the territory through which the movement from ideology to philosophy occurs, it is rather the place in which philosophers claim transcendence and the place in which, by offering a literary critique of the philosophy of aesthetics, de Man can show the ideology of the philosophic claim and thus, oddly, the centrality of the aesthetic as a discourse to an understanding of the relationships among the philosophical, the political, and the aesthetic. Self-deconstruction functions as the contradictory ground, defining the dual role of a literary construction as a philosophical remark and vice versa, on which de Man's contradictory commentary as analysis can occur.

One can accurately accuse de Man here of de-historicizing both Hegel's historical definition of the periods of art and his circumscription of art within a superseded past. But this ahistorical aesthetics turns out to be the cost of reading more fully the embeddedness of Hegel's whole philosophy within the historical context of Romanticism. De Man's reading sees the very principle and structure of the dialectic, the dual working of sublation as sign replacing aesthetic symbol and as distorted symbol of aesthetic sublime, as partaking of the Romantic conflict between symbol and allegory, thus further explaining the traditionally articulated connections between Hegel's phenomenology and theories of Romantic internalization. Thus, in the conclusion to "Sign and Symbol," de Man claims that Hegel's philosophy, as a result of the symbolic *Aesthetics*, functions as a disjunctive allegory: "Hegel's philosophy which, like his *Aesthetics*, is a philosophy of history (and of aesthetics) as well as a history of philosophy (and of aesthetics)—and the Hegelian corpus indeed contains texts that bear these two symmetrical titles—is in fact an allegory of the disjunction between philosophy and history or, in our more restricted concern, between literature and aesthetics, or, more narrowly still, between literary experience and literary theory" (775). If we assimilate, somewhat reductively perhaps, symbol in this argument to aesthetics and sign to epistemology, what status has the allegory that the philosophy as a whole forms? The literary history of "The Rhetoric of Temporality" makes clear the specific historic significance of that term as a transformation of epistemology into rhetoric. De Man's literary analysis of Hegel's philosophy in his *Aesthetics* shows that it functions precisely in the Romantic mode of allegory, moving through the categories of epistemology and aesthetics. The circle in de Man's movement from literary history through rhetoric to an aesthetics that functions as a history is now complete. Self-deconstruction as a methodological protocol may de-historicize, but as a description of a critic's relationship to a text, as we have seen, it depends on the historical specificity both of the text's significance and of the critic's interpretation of it.

If the above passage describes the historic functioning of an aesthetics read literarily rather than philosophically, it also indicates the historical functioning of that criticism within its own ideological context. As de Man's essay on Kant begins with an assertion of the connections among critical philosophy, aesthetics, and ideology, proving in the end the impossibility of using any category to transcend the others, his essays on Hegel begin by referring to the current ideological situations of aesthetic theory. "Hegel on the Sublime" reads attacks upon Derrida as consequences of his concomitant concerns with philosophy and aesthetics: "Reactionaries deny [Derrida] access to the aesthetic because he is too much a philosopher, while proponents of political activism deny him access to the political because he is too concerned with questions of aesthetics. In both cases the aesthetic functions as the principle of exclusion" (139). "Sign and Symbol" opens with a reference to the first of these attacks by referring to the conflict within literary studies between "literary experience and literary theory" (761). Each essay ends by referring that conflict to the analysis of aesthetics that it has offered. The reference never indicates the reduction of the ideological to the literary or the aesthetic, but rather it demonstrates their interdependence. We have seen the closing of "Sign and Symbol," with its reference of the relationship between literary theory and literary experience to philosophy as allegory. In "Hegel on the Sublime," having assimilated the poetic to the prosaic through the sublime, de Man concludes by assimilating this relationship to Hegel's analysis of the master-slave relationship and using that analysis to re-place the *Aesthetics*:

> Hegel summarizes his conception of the prosaic when he says: "It is in the slave that prose begins." ... Hegel's *Aesthetics*, an essentially prosaic discourse on art, is a discourse of the slave because it is a discourse of the figure rather than of genre, of trope rather than of representation. As a result, it is also politically legitimate and effective as the undoer of usurped authority. The enslaved place and condition of the section on the sublime in the *Aesthetics*, and the enslaved place of the *Aesthetics* within the corpus of Hegel's complete works, are the symptoms of their strength. Poets, philosophers,

and their readers lose their political impact only if they become, in turn, usurpers of mastery. One way of doing this is by avoiding, for whatever reason, the critical thrust of aesthetic judgment. (153)

The above last sentence should serve as ample corrective to anyone who would read the last sentence of "Phenomenality and Materiality in Kant," which refers aesthetic judgment to the prosaic materiality of the letter, as reducing the ideological to the linguistic. De Man claims here, precisely, that such an argument involves an attempt to usurp mastery because linguistic relationships and ideological relationships describe each other, even as philosophical relationships, between, for instance, aesthetics and epistemology and politics, describe and are describable by linguistic and ideological relationships. Charging Derrida as aesthetically irrelevant because of his philosophic concerns has, then, as little validity as charging him with political irrelevance because of his concern with the aesthetic. His relevance to both resides precisely in his acceptance of the conjunction of aesthetics, philosophy, and politics outlined in this essay's description of the disjunctive ground of the sublime. Equally, the ideological relevance of this essay's analysis of aesthetics resides precisely in its articulation of aesthetic and ideological disarticulation.

De Man has described these essays as his broaching the problem of his theory's ideological reference by analyzing the topic of ideology from the perspective of linguistic reference (*Resistance to Theory*, 121). The most ideological topic in contemporary literary debate is precisely the question of the ideology of literary criticism and its connections to political grounds or political ends. Thus, through a self-descriptively literary commentary on the philosophical and ideological implications of aesthetics, de Man comments by extension on the ideological situation of his own literary criticism. We may now connect de Man's thinking on literary language, literary history, aesthetics, and ideology. I have argued that literary language, in Derrida and de Man, by reflecting the act of reflection—a linguistic act that is both impossible and necessary to any system dependent upon comprehensive reflection—comments upon the foundational philosophy that marginalizes it by embedding itself within that philosophy. In this chapter, I have argued that one version of that forcing upon philosophy of that which it excludes for its own systematic coherence entails accepting the impossible necessity for deconstruction of both absolute historical specificity and absolute philosophic comprehensiveness. In de Man, this version entailed the embedding of a historical problematic within the rhetorical problematic of literary language while working out how that rhetorical problematic made a comprehensive literary history incoherent, a series of failed starts. This stuttering literary history, extrapolated from the self-contradictions of literary language, de Man extends to an aesthetics whose ideological relevance he indicates by analyzing the various disarticulations in its system. We may see the relevance of this commentary to a direct comment upon the ideological situation of literary theory by comparing the previously quoted conclusion to "Sign and Symbol" with the essay "Resistance to Theory," which describes the institutional reaction of literary critics against theory as a necessary concomitant of theory, a need for resistance embedded within it (*Resistance to Theory*, 3–20). "Sign and Symbol" shows the workings of precisely this resistance by explaining the resistance to literary theory of those who value literary experience in terms of necessary disjunction between and within philosophy and history, aesthetics and literature, literary theory and literary experience. De Man analyzes this disjunction in the terms of his literary criticism and literary history as the contradictory interdependence in the mode of allegory of philosophical sign and aesthetic symbol.

Once again, if one does not assume at the outset that setting up an equivalence between a linguistic or aesthetic structure and a historical or ideological situation entails reducing the latter to the former, then the common ground between deconstruction and Pater's aestheticism emerges as the definition of that equivalence as a mode of reading ideology and history rather than avoiding either. Pater confronted the criticism that aestheticism involved an ahistorical flight from the social by noting the dependence of historicism upon a transcendental perspective. Binding his aesthetics with an empirical process of history, he replaced Hegel's philosophic perspective with an aesthetic acceptance of the historic process and used that process to interpret culture. Starting with the same awareness of the interconnectedness of historic specificity and philosophic abstraction and the contention that that interconnectedness enacts both Derrida's critique of foundational philosophy and his own consequent analysis of literary language, de Man uses aesthetics—the aesthetic theories he analyzes and the one his analysis enacts—both to embody his own binding of the philosophic with the historic and to claim an ideological significance in that binding. For both Pater and de Man, the binding must always be paradoxical. For Pater, the historical specificity upon which aesthetics rests also carries within itself the idealization entailed by having aesthetics perform the function of Hegelian philosophy. For de Man, the very binding rests on an analysis of disarticulation, an analysis itself constructed and troubled by the problematic relationship between literary criticism and philosophic critique. But paradoxical binding repeats the paradox in Pater, Derrida, and de Man of using foundational comprehensiveness to question foundational exclusions. The ideological significance detailed by this paradoxical binding no more disappears as a result of paradox or reduces to merely language than the meaning of specific statements or their validity disappears as a result of detailing problems within concepts of meaning or validity. These four chapters have argued the philosophic and political relevance of both Pater's aestheticism and deconstruction through an analysis of their connections among philosophic foundation, literary language or artistic experience, and ideological and historic relevance. The final chapter will specify the ideological implications of both theories.

Five

Aesthetic Analysis and Political Critique

PATER's aestheticism as a form of cultural critique ended in Wilde's prison cell. The reading I have been offering of his theories has had to counter critical reductions that read them as espousing a solipsist's flight into an art that functioned in determined opposition to reality. This reduction, which conditioned his influence—broad as it was—in the twentieth century, became possible through the separation of his epistemology from his statements about art.[1] Thus one can find echoes of the perceptual situation the "Conclusion" describes, though without the aesthetics, in William James. James sees Pater's world of endless variety: "the world of concrete personal experiences to which the street belongs is multitudinous beyond imagination, tangled, muddy, painful and perplexed" (*Essays in Pragmatism*, 17). And he sees perception as arising out of what I have called friction: "all feeling whatever, in the light of certain recent psychological speculations, seems to depend for its physical condition not on simple discharge of nerve-currents, but on their discharge under arrest, impediment, or resistance" (*Essays in Pragmatism*, 3). Separated from this epistemology, the aestheticist view of art as intensified sensation can then become the higher ordering of the imagination Stevens describes in the introduction to *The Necessary Angel* (Stevens, vi–vii), which seems to have Pater in mind. Placing Pater's aestheticism and deconstruction in each other's light, as well as helping articulate the relations between philosophy, literary language, history, and aesthetics in Derrida and de Man, by restoring the connections between those discourses in Pater, may also help to restore his claims upon us as a cultural critic. But, more, to see the reasons for his repression may also allow us to see why he and Derrida and de Man threaten both their critics on the left and those critics who consider themselves defenders of tradition.

This chapter, then, will work out the political practices and implications of Pater's, Derrida's, and de Man's theories and end with a discussion of the actual repression of Pater and what it reveals about the social fears that lie beneath many critiques of aestheticism and deconstruction. The political readings here grow directly out of the contentions of the past four chapters. Neither aestheticism nor deconstruction, I argued, construed their placement of aesthetic sensation or literary language at the center of philosophical discourse as either solipsism or relativism. Rather, they analyzed the contradictions entailed by the exclusionary practices foundationalism must establish in its project of grounding all knowledge. That analysis worked not by denying the existence of true statements, nor even by attempting to exclude the concept of truth from its discourse, but by showing the inclusion within that concept of aspects that it could neither do without nor do with. By noting the common ground between the practice of grounding knowledge in philosophy and the explanations various political forces and institutions may offer for the right to rule that grounds specific rulings, the philosophical discourse practiced by aestheticism and deconstruction can extend to a political analysis that, from a position within specific institutions, can undo not their foundational categories themselves but the ability of those categories to make rulings, to include and exclude. I also claimed earlier that extending the problems and characteristics of aesthetic interpretation into a way of interpreting history and politics did not reduce the historical and the political to the aesthetic, construed as an absolutely enclosed alterity to the category of the Real. Rather, Pater's and de Man's analyses of aesthetics and historicism worked precisely to open out the categories of aesthetic interpretation, Pater's frictional sensation and de Man's literary language, so that they became ways of analyzing political and historical situations. Pater's, Derrida's, and de Man's explicit consideration of various political and historical topics, I will argue here, likewise should not be seen as reduction of those topics to an aesthetic spectacle for solipsistic delectation but as an application of aesthetic interpretation to those problems. Indeed, that aesthetic interpretation, with which I will start, leads to a proper understanding of the analyses of political foundations with which I will proceed.

Before going on to develop these political extensions, I want to refute two inaccurate versions of them that reproduce the misinterpretation discussed earlier of transforming deconstruction into a method for producing specific interpretations of literary texts. These problematic methods, I think, lead to charging deconstruction with an ineffectual relativism and both deconstruction and Pater's aestheticism with either an intentional or de facto conservative quietism. Corresponding to my claim that deconstruction establishes the value of analyzing historical and political questions with certain techniques of literary and aesthetic interpretation is the contention or hope that deconstruction will provide an exit from all political, institutional, and conventional constraints.[2] This version of deconstructive politics bases itself on Derrida's claim that since all conventions are violable, they can be enforced only by some form of police, combined with the suggestion that one could simply not invoke conventions and step outside the police state. Thus Derrida ends his argument with Searle: "I will not claim the copyright because ultimately ... there is always a police and tribunal ready to intervene each time that a rule [constitutive or regulative, vertical or not] is invoked in a case involving signatures, events, or contexts.... If the police is always waiting in the wings, it is because conventions are by essence violable and precarious" (*Limited Inc*, 105).[3] If Derrida were proposing an opposition to all political structure by constructing some absolute negative alterity to all conventional discourse, he could indeed be criticized for a relativism that, by criticizing all positions, ends up criticizing none.[4] The literary form of deconstruction that argues the indeterminacy of all texts and the misreading of all interpretations, even if it is self-contradictory in its relativism, at least does not cease to have literary relevance. Indeterminacy carried into the realm of the political, however, by contending for the repressiveness of any political position or contention, leaves no basis for resisting any repressive authority, since any resistance must be political.

I argued in Chapter 3 that Derrida shows any attempt to escape foundational discourse absolutely to be the establishment of another foundational discourse, that the attempt to step into an alternative criticism of joyful free play was itself a version of the centered discourse it attempted to escape. The analogy to the political situation here should be clear enough, but a closer look at Derrida's own explanations of his notion of a police makes it inescapable. As Derrida insisted that the fact of foundational contradictions did not entail that one could step outside that discourse into some noncontradictory form of knowledge, he also argues that the police, construed as any arbitrary protection of a convention, cannot be assimilated with straightforward repression and cannot be escaped. Thus, in response to Gerald Graff's questioning him on this point, he argues that the fact of policing does not equal repression, at least normally so understood: "Every police is not repressive, no more than the law in general, even in its negative, restrictive, or prohibitive prescriptions. A red light is not repressive. If one insists on considering its prohibitive force as being 'repressive' ... then this repressive character must be distinguished from that associated, in an evaluation that is never neutral, with the unjust brutality of a force that most often violates the very law to which it appeals" (*Limited Inc*, 132–133). The example of the red light has particular force. Derrida does not argue that some laws are not repressive because they are natural or transcendentally just, obviously. Red lights may not be repressive, but neither are they laws of nature or embodiments of an idea of justice. But the mere fact of artifice and intervention does not entail injustice, could not do so unless there were a state of justice prior to all intervention. Equally, when Derrida refuses to claim copyright against Searle, he does not intend that refusal to place him in some absolute opposition to the difficulties of copyrighting. The claim would obviously be disingenuous since his publishers copyright his works in any case and he frequently also holds copyright to his own. Rather, he refers back to the difficulties of claiming copyright discussed in the opening of the essay, in which he connects the claim to copyright with the possibility that what one says is original enough to be copyrighted only if it might be false (30). In this context, his refusal to claim copyright can be interpreted only as an ironic claim to obvious truth, just the kind of claim that he argues always needs the protection of the police. Derrida does not look for a discourse outside of politics, beyond the police, but a discourse that recognizes the absence of any position of external neutrality from which to make political judgments: "if the police as such is not politically suspect a priori, it is never politically neutral either, never apolitical" (135). The absence of a position outside political determination does not entail the absence of valid political claims. But it does entail the absence of a neutral foundation, even in terms of an aesthetic opposition to foundation, from which to make or govern any political claims.

The second, far more common and, I think, equally unsuccessful application of deconstruction to political ends involves thinking of the practice of deconstruction itself as a powerful method of exhibiting the inbuilt prejudices, biases, and injustices of ruling political concepts of thought. Since Derrida's foundational analyses seem to destabilize in powerful ways central and long-held philosophical and literary modes of thought, it would seem to follow that the method applied to political concepts—and some of Derrida's philosophical oppositions, such as nature and culture in his discussions of Lévi-Strauss and Rousseau, already have clear political ramifications—could lead to an equally powerful destabilization of material, political power structures that rest on those concepts. Michael Ryan makes one of the most forceful and influential articulations of this position: "One of my primary assumptions, then, is that there is a necessary relationship between conceptual apparatuses and political institutions. The domain of philosophy articulates with the various ways power is exercised; concepts are also forces. But equally, the deconstructive critique of absolutist concepts in the theory of meaning can be said to have a political institutional corollary, which is the continuous revolutionary displacement of power toward radical egalitarianism" (8). Depending on how one takes Derrida's deconstruction of philosophical concepts, however, this extension raises some serious problems. If, contrary to the argument I have been making up to now, one takes deconstruction as a mode of disproving and doing away with those concepts, then Ryan's extension will make sense, but at the cost of renewing charges of an all-inclusive relativism that can ground only a politics of quietism. To respond to this problem and distinguish himself from what he takes to be the quietism of Yale deconstruction, Ryan reconceives deconstruction as resting on a provisional grounding: "there is a difference between the angelic disinterestedness accompanying the hypothesis that no truth is determinable, no text readable, and the provisional limitation of a potentially unlimited and indeterminate textuality in the name of the political interest of countering ... structures of power" (41). This qualification will make deconstruction politically effective, but at the cost of internal incoherence: what is the basis for that provisional limitation and why could it not equally be made from any alternative political, philosophical, or literary position? More important, Ryan makes deconstruction distinguishable from any other radical political critique only in terms of a politically unnecessary philosophical complexity.

One can see the problem with this form of politicization more clearly in a specific version of it, Christopher Norris's reading of Derrida's article on nuclear discourse, "No Apocalypse, Not Now." Norris distinguishes his reading of deconstruction from what he sees as the fallacies of much American literary deconstruction by insisting on the internal rigor with which Derrida and de Man reason toward their deconstructions (see particularly *The Contest of Faculties*, 72–74), but he also sees deconstructive conclusions as forms of logical disproof and particularly reasoned disproofs of the workings of reason. Consequently, he takes "No Apocalypse, Not Now" to be showing the special validity of deconstruction in a critique of the illogic involved in the concept of deterrence. He first notes that, no doubt, one hardly needs deconstruction to show that illogic; it has been exhibited quite thoroughly by more traditional attacks. He concludes, however, that "Derrida wants to argue a much closer, more vital and productive link between 'nuclear criticism' and the strategies of deconstruction. If the latter possesses any special competence ... then this has to do with precisely that absence of 'original meaning', the 'logic' of alogical transgression and the effects of 'rhetorical escalation' as against the 'measure' of enlightened reason" (*Derrida*, 167). If Norris means that deconstruction, by carrying within it the special illogic of deterrence, performs its best critique, then his argument falls into precisely the flaws of relativism from which he usually so carefully tries to distinguish himself: from a logical perspective, an illogical argument disproves only itself, not the argument it counters, even if that opposing argument is also illogical, even illogical in the same way. Norris's version of Ryan's provisional limitation, however, applies to the Kantian concept of reason (this is the argument of the chapter in which his reading of "No Apocalypse, Not Now" appears), which he sees deconstruction as reproducing even in its specific critiques of it. Construing deconstruction as a practice of reason carried out to its ultimate conclusion, he would be arguing here that its analysis of deterrence, though more tortuous than that of traditional logic, would be a kind of final statement particularly competent to the form of finality that statements about nuclear war take. This position is little better, however, since deconstruction's formal appropriateness remains logically superfluous to the case Norris imputes to Derrida. In short, if deterrence is wrong because it is deconstructive, it is hard to see why deconstruction is right, but if deconstruction is showing us from some special position the illogic of deterrence, it is hard to see why we need that special position when the workings of standard logic work to clearer effect. Struggling to extricate themselves from what they see as the quietism created by American literary deconstruction, both Norris and Ryan make a political version of the same mistake by turning Derrida's foundational analysis into a method of practical interpretation.

Taking deconstruction as a radical critique of particular political structures and institutions becomes even more clearly problematic if one does follow my earlier reading of Derrida as particularly concerned with the problems of foundational discourse. Thus in an analysis my own argument draws from, Jonathan Culler argues that Derrida does not do away with such traditional concepts as truth, logic, and value but displaces them in some strategic way (*On Deconstruction*, 150). At the level of foundational logic, this displacement has a certain concern, but if the traditional concept at issue is, say, the validity of patriarchy, the situation changes. Even if doing away with patriarchy were merely a utopian ideal, its value as an ideal from which to criticize specific historical manifestations of sexism would seem to be greater than some abstract new comprehension of the patriarchal concept resulting from a deconstruction that still left it operational. Thus a deconstructive displacement does not really effect positive change as a direct consequence of its skeptical analysis of constraining institutions. And even if this were not the case, it would remain true that one hardly needs to confront problems of foundational philosophy to offer a critique of patriarchy, its logical flaws and injustices being empirically evident in ways that no ontological argument either changes or furthers.[5]

Behind both of these methodological transformations of deconstruction lies, I think, a fear of aestheticization that leads these theories to reproduce the very problems of literary deconstruction that they react against. In simple terms, they fear that unless one can see deconstruction as a consequential critique from outside structures of power or authority, its forceful analytic will become merely the creation of an aesthetic spectacle for the delectation of critics and their readers (thus Lentricchia's previously quoted analogy, in *After the New Criticism* [186], between American poststructural literary criticism and interior decoration). One of my constant themes, however, has been that aestheticization does not create an artificial spectacle opposed to a consequential, material reality. If one accepts that an application of the categories of aesthetic interpretation can work only by accepting a position within the system one interprets, even as one asserts the boundaries of the system to be unmarkable, the problem of its relativism disappears. That interpretation cannot deny that if the system's borders are infinitely inclusive it cannot exclude either possibly real objects or possibly just procedures, nor can it posit an outside to those borders from which a just critique or a real statement could be made. Thus Derrida explains that his claim that all conventions are policed does not imply that all policing is unjust or repressive. Nor does he imagine that one could operate in an unpoliced system: he merely claims the absence of neutrality, and thus the possibility of analyzing how the policing works in all its variety. Equally, by accepting that an analysis of foundational discourse can operate only from within that foundation, one may not be able to do away with foundational concepts, but one may disable them from governing and excluding. Deconstruction becomes an effective political critique at the moment that it recognizes the system in which it is enclosed as artificial, but it remains effective only as long as it accepts that enclosure.

When a critic both perceives and accepts this enclosure, the acceptance will become political—and hardly resigned or quietist. Thus Barbara Johnson, describing her own perception of her first deconstructive book, *The Critical Difference*, states:

> It was when I realized that my discussion of such differences was taking place entirely within the sameness of the white male Euro-American literary, philosophical, psychoanalytical and critical canon that I began to ask myself what differences I was really talking about. To say, for instance, that the difference *between* man and woman is an illusion created by the repression of differences *within* each may to some extent be true, but it does not account for the historical exclusion of women from the canon.... if you tell a member of the Ku Klux Klan that racism is a repression of self-difference, you are likely to learn a thing or two about repression. (*A World of Difference*, 2–3)

As a critique of her earlier situation, this passage may seem like an empirical discovery of politics. If its content claims a realization of a previously unseen limitation to the freeing powers of deconstructive analysis, however, it has the form of a deconstructive discovery of an artificial limit within what one thought to be a transcendental analysis. Since Johnson's discovery of the Klan probably does not refer to any actual experience between her two books—at least I hope not—that discovery images the deconstructive surprise at finding that one's subject included what one had hoped to exclude (here racism and sexism) by excluding that which it ought to have properly included (here historically specific manifestations of the categories of sexual difference that she was deploying). Rather than giving up deconstruction, Johnson tries to formulate a way of keeping the moment of surprise at the ignorance embedded in one's own analysis as a motivating force of deconstruction (16–17). And this turns out to mean accepting deconstruction as an act of self-resistance, even perhaps resistance to the assumptions behind one's own reformist discourse, without abandoning the acts of reform themselves (45–46). Deconstruction achieves its political realizations not by stepping outside a system to criticize it, but at the moment its own mode of analysis leads to the discovery that what one thought was its knowledge was part of the system it was supposed to be analyzing.

Pater shows the connections between the extension of aesthetic interpretation to the analysis of political and historical issues, the acceptance of an enclosure within the system one analyzes, and the political implications of that acceptance in his second major work, *Marius the Epicurean*. In "The Resistance to Theory," de Man addresses the ramifications of those connections for the contemporary debate over the relevance of theory in a structurally similar form of self-resistant analysis. Pater himself connected *Marius* with his position statement in the "Conclusion" in the footnote he appended to its reprinting in 1888, after its suppression in 1877: "this brief 'Conclusion' was omitted in the second edition of this book, as I conceived it might possibly mislead some of those young men into whose hands it might fall. On the whole, I have thought it best to reprint it here with some slight changes which bring it closer to my original meaning. I have dealt more fully in *Marius the Epicurean* with the thoughts suggested by it" (*Renaissance*, 186). This chapter will address later the political issues behind Pater's self-censorship and the implications of the first sentence of the footnote. If we take the footnote to declare a desire to accommodate those who criticized the "Conclusion" as skeptic hedonism, however, the inference follows easily that *Marius*'s extension of aestheticism into a consideration of relationships between individual and state and of the claims of religion partakes of that accommodation. And certainly critics have long read the book as indicating Pater's opening of himself to the consolations of Christianity, his relaxation of the skepticism that made *The Renaissance* so antagonistic to his contemporaries. More recently, other critics have been claiming an essential uniformity to Pater's position, one that does not substantially lessen his skepticism, his insistence on not going beyond experience.[6] The debate in its current terms, however, posed almost purely in terms of Pater's belief in Christianity and the formal problem of interpreting the significance of Marius's death—taken as Christian by those around him even though he has not in fact converted—by ignoring the contemporaneous political ramifications of that debate, has occluded the genuine political effect of the book.

As a purely theoretical matter, the notion that Pater changes his ideas in any essential way in *Marius* ignores the value of inclusiveness of experience. My opening chapters have already argued that Pater makes central to his aestheticism the recognition that abstract thought is not only necessary to experience but is itself a necessary experience. Extending that inclusiveness to the experience of religious sensibility would be precisely the kind of self-resistant moment of analysis that we saw in Johnson: realizing an exclusion in the middle of an attempt at inclusion, an ignorance in the middle of what one thought was one's knowledge. That self-resistant inclusiveness characterizes the extension of aesthetic interpretation into the areas of the cultural and the political. And *Marius* establishes early on the ambition of inclusiveness, at the cost of contradicting any limiting abstraction, even the abstraction that establishes the value of inclusiveness:

> Not pleasure, but a general completeness of life, was the practical ideal to which this anti-metaphysical metaphysics really pointed. And towards such a full or complete life, a life of various yet select sensation, the most direct and effective auxiliary must be, in a word, Insight. Liberty of soul, freedom from all partial and misrepresentative doctrine which does but relieve one element in our experience at the cost of another, freedom from all embarrassment alike of regret for the past and of calculation on the future: this would be but the preliminary to the real business of education—insight, insight through culture, into all that the present moment holds in trust for us, as we stand so briefly in its presence. (*Marius*, 1: 142)

Although the language here is more abstract, Pater could aptly claim that this passage describes what a few pages later he calls "this 'aesthetic' philosophy" (*Marius*, 1: 149). Thus, it is a fuller explanation of his original meaning in those moments in the "Conclusion" that call for the attuning of all our capacities to the capture of the present, at the cost of, but also with the use of, philosophical abstraction. By analogy, in his description of Flavian's Euphuism, Pater explains even the changed language, the shift from impassioned metaphor to complex, artificed,

Latinate abstraction, in terms of a comprehensive inclusion of aesthetic sensation:

> The popular speech was gradually departing from the form and rule of literary language, a language always and increasingly artificial. While the learned dialect was yearly becoming more and more barbarously pedantic, the colloquial idiom, on the other hand, offered a thousand chance-tost gems of racy or picturesque expression, rejected or at least ungathered by what claimed to be classical Latin.... The literary programme which Flavian had already designed for himself would be a work, then, partly conservative or reactionary, in its dealing with the instrument of the literary art; partly popular and revolutionary, asserting, so to term, the rights of the *proletariat* of speech. (*Marius*, 1: 94–95)[7]

Euphuism, in these terms, seeing the need for artifice to preserve the "chance-tost gems" of popular speech, combines Latinate form with a content open to popular speech. Once again we see the internal conflict necessary to sensation, redescribed as a contradictory inclusiveness in linguistic form.

The near receptiveness at the end of *Marius* to the supernatural, thus superexperiential, hopes of Christianity occurs explicitly within the terms of this aesthetic philosophy and its coincident literary language: "For himself, it was clear, he must still hold by what his eyes really saw. Only, he had to concede also, that the very boldness of such theory bore witness, at least, to a variety of human disposition and a consequent variety of mental view, which might—who could tell?—be correspondent to, be defined by and define, varieties of facts, of truths, just 'behind the veil'" (*Marius*, 2: 90–91). From the perspective of the book as a whole, we can thus see Marius's ambiguous death as precisely the aesthetic construction of an experience of the religious, for the narrator and the reader, that remains aesthetically inclusive rather than exclusively Christian.

The real problem with Pater's further explanation of his aestheticism is not how it squares with Christianity per se but how it squares with the late Victorian debate over religion in which it participated. Obviously there is no space for anything like a full analysis of that debate.[8] The tone of the reactions to Pater's *Renaissance* indicates, though, that his type of skepticism evoked fears of loss of social control and raised hopes of cultural liberation, both of which were connected with the role Victorians gave Christianity in maintaining the established order.[9] Pater's aestheticized Christianity in *Marius* thus evoked from reformist figures precisely some of the reactions that deconstruction evokes from Marxist and historicist critics. Here the criticism of Mrs. Humphry

Ward in her review of *Marius* becomes particularly pertinent, since Pater in effect answered it three years later in his review of her novel *Robert Elsmere*. Ward first identifies the extension of aestheticism into a justification for adhering to certain ethical rules as essentially utilitarian: "Mr Pater now presents obedience to this same morality as desirable, not because of any absolute virtue or authority inherent in it, but because practically obedience is a source of pleasure" (Seiler, *Walter Pater, The Critical Heritage*, 134). She has no real argument with this extension—utilitarian ethics presented a frequent alternative to Christian dogma, and Ward was thus disposed in favor of its liberating tendencies. But she takes the extension of aestheticism to religion with less equanimity: "Such an appeal has an extraordinary force with a certain order of minds.... But with another order of minds in whom the religious need is not less strong, it has not, and never will have, any chance of success, for they regard it as involving the betrayal of a worship dearer to them than the worship of beauty or consolation, and the surrender of something more precious to them than any of those delicate emotional joys, which feeling, divorced from truth, from the sense of reality, has to offer" (Seiler, *Walter Pater, The Critical Heritage*, 136). One critic has seen it as ironic that "this tailored argument for Pater's return to the fold should have come from a critic of Christian orthodoxy as outspoken and vocally agnostic as Mrs. Ward" (Court, 52). In fact, what Ward objects to, though, is not that Pater takes Christianity aesthetically rather than believing in it fully, but that he entertains a religion aesthetically that he believes to be empirically false, rather than simply abandoning it. Thus, in her novel *Robert Elsmere*, she has her protagonist insist on leaving the Church of England when he can no longer subscribe to all of its beliefs rather than continue to operate within it to forward its moral ends, as some characters suggest he ought to do. In effect, her criticism is precisely the accusation critics level at deconstruction's aestheticism: it implies a quietist participation in authoritarian structures.

Pater's implied response to Ward in his corresponding review of *Robert Elsmere* indicates sharply the difference between self-resistance and a quietist cooperation in a reigning authority. Pater criticizes Elsmere for having taken so long to realize historical problems with Christianity and then for having reacted so absolutely to them as to immediately leave the Church. He concludes, "Robert Elsmere was a type of a large class of minds which cannot be sure that the sacred story is true. It is philosophical, doubtless, and a duty to the intellect to recognize our doubts.... It may be also a moral duty to do this. But then there is also a large class of minds which cannot be sure it *is* false" (*Essays*, 67–68). This passage has been taken as an indication of Pater's growing acceptance of religion. Certainly Ward would have taken it that way. But Pater's complete formulation is far more complex. Pater does not quite identify with the second large class of minds, but immediately takes an inclusive view: "their particular phase of doubt, of philosophic uncertainty, has been the secret of millions of good Christians, multitudes of worthy priests. They knit themselves to believers, in various degrees, of all ages" (*Essays*, 68). Pater chooses neither Elsmere nor those positive skeptics who cannot be sure that Christianity is false. Rather he pictures religion as comprising both believers and skeptics, making Elsmere's definition of the Christianity he rejects the act of partial and exclusive dogmaticism. The point of this new opposition becomes clear when he contrasts to "the purely negative action of the scientific spirit, the high-pitched Grey, the theistic Elsmere, the 'ritualistic priest,' the quaint Methodist" (*Essays*, 68) and then quotes approvingly Ward's definition of the scientific spirit as "for ever making the visible world fairer and more desirable in mortal eyes" (*Essays*, 69). Both dogmatic Christians and Elsmere equally oppose the comprehensive scientific spirit by insisting on a narrow formula—dogmatic or positivist and theistic—and thus excluding some aspect of a reality it cannot accommodate. Pater insists neither on doubting Christianity's truth nor on doubting its falseness. As in the "Conclusion," he insists on "the scientific spirit," which, by attuning us to the beauty of all experience, of the visible world, opposes any rejection, either that of dogmatists or that of hasty positivists.

If we take Ward and Pater to be arguing opposing views of Christianity here, Pater's position would look quietist; and that was indeed what Ward accused him of. But, in fact, as both Ward and Pater realized, and as the generally positive tone of both their reviews indicates, their positions had more in common than not. Indeed Ward's view of Christianity had connections with the same Oxford Hegelianism of which Pater's aesthetics partook (she dedicated *Robert Elsmere* to T. H. Green, one of the central figures in that movement at Oxford). Pater's response then, in *Marius* and in his review, has more the character of self-resistance than of critique from the outside. And he does not resist the process of agnosticism—he defines his religious impulse as a version of it—but the moment in which agnosticism, becoming a positive force, insists on its own exclusions. The case of Ward amply indicates that the constraining force of that exclusiveness extended further than a mere theoretical disbelief; Elsmere goes on to establish a positivist church in working-class East London, thus still seeking social control, though from a changed position of authority. In *Marius*, Pater turns his aestheticism upon his own—and Ward's—skepticism, not to turn aestheticism into a refined enjoyment of the powers that be, but to insure that the skepticism remained self-resistant rather than transforming itself into a force of control. Indeed he could not coherently do otherwise, since self-resistance inhered, as we have seen, in his definition of that aestheticism as philosophy, as linguistic representation, as religious apprehension.[10]

Pater's contradictory acceptance of religious apprehension and rejection of its exclusionary theology, his acceptance of scientific apprehension and his rejection of a positivist's scientific claim to dispense with Christianity as decisively false, no longer create much polemic spark in contemporary theoretical debates (though one can easily think of circles in which, if it were read, *Marius* would create much more heat than those theoretical debates). For that reason, while perceiving Pater's relevance, a recent critic has, in a noticeably forced reading, connected Marius's aesthetic philosophy to a quietist attitude toward the Roman imperial state, and by extension, toward the Victorian imperial state.[11] We do not need to resort to this kind of forced relevance in order to extend the pertinence of Pater's self-resistance to contemporary theory's political situation; de Man's "Resistance to Theory" addresses the question of that self-resistance directly. The essay begins with a near perfect example of the dual meaning of its title. De Man, having been asked to write a section of the MLA's *Introduction to Scholarship in Modern Languages and Literatures*, responded that "the main theoretical interest of literary theory consists in the impossibility of its definition. The Committee [on Research Activities of the Modern Language Association] rightly judged that this was an inauspicious way to achieve the pedagogical objectives of the volume and commissioned another article" (*Resistance to Theory*, 3). The MLA's judgment can of course be construed as the profession's resistance to theory in general and to deconstructive theory in particular that is one of the title's referents and an obvious political as well as theoretical concern. But the rest of de Man's anecdote specifies two other equally significant resistances. The first is theory's own resistance to self-definition, which is, according to de Man, also a resistance to theory in the sense of a resistant quality that theory has. But second is de Man's own resistance in proposing an essay so obviously at odds with the aims of the theoretical section offered him. This may be taken as de Man's own resistance to theory and thus to the discourse that has offered him the possibility of this institutionalization by the literary critical profession.[12]

At this point, the standard view of de Man's theories would lead us to expect a critique of the opponents of deconstruction based on their fear of and hostility to the negative truth about language that deconstructive theory teaches. And certainly the essay does diagnose some critical resistance in this manner. And it insists, as de Man does elsewhere, on a resistance in the density of linguistic structures to easy interpretability. But such a view of the essay must radically shear away the various contexts in which this claim is placed and to which it appeals. When de Man first identifies literary theory in terms of its affinity with the structuralist determination of language "as a system of signs and of signification rather than as an established pattern of meaning" (9), he specifies that he does *not* intend this theoretical self-constitution to imply a complete alterity between language and reality:

> The most misleading representation of literariness, and also the most recurrent objection to contemporary literary theory, considers it as pure verbalism, as a denial of the reality principle in the name of absolute fictions, and for reasons that are said to be ethically and politically shameful. The attack reflects the anxiety of the aggressors rather than the guilt of the accused.... Literature is fiction not because it somehow refuses to acknowledge "reality," but because it is not *a priori* certain that language functions according to principles which are those, or which are *like* those, of the phenomenal world. ... What we call ideology is precisely the confusion of linguistic with natural reality, of reference with phenomenalism. It follows that, more than any other mode of inquiry, including economics, the linguistics of literariness is a powerful and indispensable tool in the unmasking of ideological aberrations, as well as a determining factor in their occurrence.... we begin to perceive some of the answers to the initial question: what is it about literary theory that is so threatening that it provokes such strong resistances and attacks? It upsets rooted ideologies by revealing the mechanics of their workings. (*Resistance to Theory*, 10–11)

As if to bear out his description of those who attack literary theory as "pure verbalism," one of de Man's persistent critics has cited a sentence from this section, out of context of course, to show that de Man does argue that literature and reality have nothing to do with one another.[13] In fact, de Man argues for not a presumed alterity but a refusal to presume absolute identity between linguistic *structures* and the structures of phenomenal reality. He identifies the recognition of this theoretically possible difference with the ability to specify the ideological because ideology results from an incorrect claim of correspondence between a linguistic and a natural structure or "reality." Rather than separating literary criticism from commentary on the social, the historical, or the real, de Man here claims its centrality to that commentary. That identification, far from being a Derridean or de Manean resistance to arriving at ideological criticism, allows a standard mode, in Marxist and Foucaultian critics, of specifying the ideological.[14] Thus, in claiming the profession's resistance to theory's disturbing claims about language as ideological, de Man identifies that claim, and his own rhetorical criticism, with ideological criticism.

Only at this point does de Man turn toward a more specifically linguistic diagnosis, and he clearly intends to explain more than the polemical heat of his or other theorists' opponents. He starts by noting that explaining professional resistance to theory as a hostility to theory's power to unveil ideology, however accurate a diagnosis, is "not a satisfying answer to the question. For it makes the tension between contemporary literary theory and the tradition of literary studies appear as a mere historical conflict between two modes of thought that happen to hold the stage at the same time" (*Resistance to Theory*, 11). The purely contingent historical answer might well be the correct one, but it has no theoretical element, precisely because of its absolute contingency, and thus has "limited theoretical interest." But the essay starts by noting the coincidence of theory's rise to prominence and the resistance against it, a coincidence that at least seems to indicate a closer link than contingency. Thus de Man turns the question: "rather than asking why literary theory is threatening, we should perhaps ask why it has such difficulty going about its business and why it lapses so readily either into the language of self-justification and self-defense or else into the overcompensation of a programmatically euphoric utopianism" (12). Here finally de Man seems to turn to a strictly linguistic answer: "the resistance to theory is a resistance to the use of language about language. It is therefore a resistance to language itself or to the possibility that language contains factors or functions that cannot be reduced to intuition" (12–13). De Man offers linguistic opacity as an explanation of a resistance *in* theory to its own insights not to prove that politics reduces to language but to argue that theory cannot write off the resistance to itself as merely a matter of external politics: the structure of that external resistance follows the structure of a resistance within theory. De Man does not deny any validity to the specific political explanations theory may offer for instances of linguistic opacity any more than he denies validity to many of the specific interpretations produced by pedagogic methods pragmatically opposed to all theories. Rather he denies that the results of theory may be sufficiently transformed into a methodology to account, within its own terms, for political resistance as something entirely external to itself, without itself offering versions of that political resistance: self-justification, self-defense, euphoric utopianism. Given the context in which this self-resistance is placed, an anecdote recounting an institutionalized rejection by the profession of a proposed theoretical interest, de Man's response seems the opposite of a flight from the political. Rather than blaming the enemies of theory for an ideological animus that the transcendent truth of his theory does not merit, he turns his analysis upon his theory, in the terms of his theory, to determine the source of the politics within it, the resistance in it as well as to it. If he ends with the difficulties of language and reading with which he began, he presents these difficulties neither as transcendent ground nor as ultimate explanation of all other errors but as the medium in which political resistance of all kinds may be read. My afterword will show clearly the political implications of this self-resistance in the light it casts on the self-protectiveness of de Man's adherents in their responses to his *Wartime Writings*. But de Man here seems to be addressing that self-protectiveness as it had already developed prior to his death.

The recurrence of attacks upon de Man for seeking a pure self-enclosure in an absolutely nonreferential literary language at precisely the moments in which he denies that position is marked enough to consider it a symptom of the real political effect of his own self-resistance. In addition to the critique cited above, one might note the contention that the final sentence of "Shelley Disfigured" "enshrine[s] nihilism as the principle of critical activity in our culture at this time" (O'Hara, 233–234). That final sentence claims that "to monumentalize this [de Man's] observation into a *method* of reading would be to regress from the rigor exhibited by Shelley which is exemplary precisely because it refuses to be generalized into a system" (*Rhetoric*, 123). Again this sentence argues against a systematization of the reading activity worked out through the essay into a method of reading that would reach certain stable evaluations, nihilistic or otherwise. It thus argues precisely against enshrining, thus monumentalizing, nihilism. Given his italicization of the word *method* in his final sentence, one might wonder why it would be taken as critical of all theoretical statements rather than critical of the way in which his own reading might be transformed into a method reproducing within his theory, as any method would, the naivete he argues against. If these critics cited the moments in which de Man does argue for the productive activity of linguistic structure, however, they would be hard put to read them as constructing a rarified aesthetic activity. As we have seen in previous chapters as well as here, these arguments occur persistently as extensions of political and historical situations and interpretations. To argue that de Man seeks to turn away from the political, critics must constantly transform precisely the moments in which he recognizes its activity—either in his own interpretation or in general critical or professional response from which he does not exclude himself—into moments claiming a pure alterity to any reference. Because de Man questions the political element in the linguistic turnings of any theory, a theorist who wants to attack a political situation from an outside that would be free of the tainting of the political must resist his self-resistant analysis, it seems, by living out the turnings it describes.

Even if we grant the political effect of taking aesthetic interpretation as a mode of analyzing from within the political and historical determinants of one's own position, rather than construing it as a claim to exit politics into some pure realm of either language or truth, that effect might seem particularly limited in its purview. Barbara Johnson, for instance, in the definition of its value discussed above, notes that self-resistance has assured women's "lack of authority and their invisibility." One might hesitate to prescribe self-resistance to women as a political program. At first, then, Johnson seems to limit its value to those in power: "Self-resistance, indeed, may be one of the few viable postures remaining for the white male establishment" (*A World of Difference*, 45). Even her extension of its value to feminists at the moment in which they presume to generalize their experience into appropriative theories still limits its use to the self-chastening of the powerful or potentially powerful. While one would not want to write off that value too hastily—moments of theoretical self-satisfaction being far more common than moments of genuine self-criticism or inquisition—still it seems essentially subsidiary to any genuine attempt to reform. Feminists, no less than other theorists, perhaps ought to guard against their own self-aggrandizement, but if they practice only self-resistance, they will no doubt be participating in their own co-option by the authority they started out to resist. In fact, though, when we turn aesthetic interpretation back to the foundational analysis from which it starts, while it is not a more effective critique than less self-resistant skeptical responses to false authoritarian self-justifications, it may become the basis for the effect that those attacks upon various authoritarian forms of self-protection have. My instance here will be the literary canon and what I take to be deconstruction's participation in the feminist attack upon it.

Before outlining what I take to be the connection between the deconstructive analysis of foundations and the feminist work of canon revision, and thus the political effect of self-resistance as turned upon foundations, I must somewhat ruefully admit that that connection has not been persuasively worked out by deconstructive critics themselves. Many of those who consider themselves de Man's followers simply do not question the validity of the literary canon as it has been traditionally defined. Most notoriously, as we have seen, J. Hillis Miller has claimed deconstructive priority for the standard line of great works of literature ("Deconstructing the Deconstructers," 31) and connected deconstruction with a desire "to rescue and make functional again aspects of our three-thousand-year-old culture" ("Theory and Practice," 612). While de Man himself argues that his "shift from historical definition to the problematics of reading... could in principle, lead to a rhetoric of reading reaching beyond the canonical principles of literary history" (*Allegories of Reading*, ix), and his critique of monumentalization in "Shelley Disfigured" certainly extends at least implicitly to a critique of the exemplary monumentalizing activity of canonization, no very specific canonic questioning goes on in his work. Although the authors he addresses cross disciplinary boundaries—or did prior to the canonic acceptance of his and Derrida's work—most were canonic writers in one discipline or another. Thus he admits canonic principles in *Allegories of Reading* "as the starting point of their own displacement" (ix). Moreover, while some critics have explicitly extended deconstructive analysis to a political critique of authoritarian structures and principles, I have already argued the unsatisfactoriness of that extension in the opening of this chapter. In order to see the connection between deconstruction and feminism on this issue, following my general resistance to articulating deconstruction as a knowledge founding a method that would encompass a particular politics, in this case, feminism, I want to consider instead how the deconstructive project explains a certain feminist success that in turn explains the effective political consequence of that project.

I want to propose then that an analogy operates between criticizing deconstruction as politically ineffectual and quietist and criticizing feminist attacks upon the canon as internally inconsistent. Accordingly, explaining the way the deconstructive analysis of foundations may operate as a form of political discourse also provides a justification for a skeptical mode of feminist argument and an analysis of how that mode works. The political case against deconstruction and the logical case against broad feminist attacks upon the value bases of the literary canon boil down to the claim that skepticism or nihilism, by undercutting all ground, also denies itself any ground from which to criticize political, social, or literary institutions. We have seen that in the case of deconstruction this argument leads to its being identified with quietist conservatism. The case against feminist criticism is rather more complex because of the evident success of some of its most skeptical attacks upon the canon. Here critics claim logical inconsistency rather than ineffectuality. There may be a theoretical basis for claiming a place within the canon for specific works by women writers based on those works having met some positively existing criteria of literary value. But certain feminists argue for a more inclusive canon or a differently constructed canon by attacking the concept of literary value itself as a culturally determined category rather than a set of objective criteria, thus contending either that literary value is in and of itself a sexist concept or that, since all concepts of value are culturally determined, any concepts operating within our culture will reflect their sexist bases.[15] Either argument seems to undercut the basis for offering a revised canon. If the very concept of literary value is itself sexist, on what ground will feminists base their revised canon? Similarly, if all concepts of value are culturally determined, even if feminists have a revised set of criteria for literary value to propose, why won't those values be as self-interested or culturally determined, as partial, as the sexist criteria they have replaced? I want, for a moment, to look at this difficulty in more detail, since I will be claiming that, to the extent that it has not stopped the success of feminist canon revision, we can explain the difficulty and account for the success only in terms of a deconstructive analysis of foundations.

More refined theories of value as culturally or communally constructed—most notoriously Stanley Fish's *Is There a Text in This Class?* and more recently, in a more flexible and detailed articulation, Barbara Herrnstein Smith's *Contingencies of Value*—have responded persuasively to these charges of maintaining a self-contradictory relativism. Rather than opposing subjectively determined, individually variable tastes to the notion of value as an objective quality, they oppose values held in common by larger and smaller communities as a result of a range of contingent beliefs and experiences that may or may not be persuasive to other communities. Consequently, they claim no contradiction in trying to persuade others of what we believe while not claiming that any case could be universally persuasive. These theories account persuasively for what we take to be values without having recourse to concepts of either universal objectivity or relative subjectivity. But one finds one cannot marshal them any more easily in the service of specific arguments over the values or interpretations of given works than more naively relativistic theories.

As purely descriptive accounts, these theories of contingent value are at least more persuasive than objectivist accounts in describing how, in for instance our own interpretive community in which such theories are frequently articulated and widely held, specific debates over interpretations of works and inclusions of works in the canon manage to take place and get won or lost. Objectivist accounts often seem to suppose that all of us are simply giving way to radical inconsistency as a result of some unaccountable virus of subjectivism that has somehow infected our minds. But there seems some trouble in turning these revised theories of values into an argument in favor of a specific value. Thus Fish, in a concluding remark to *Is There a Text in This Class?* that continues both to vex and to motivate his theories, claims that his theory "is not one that you (or anyone else) could live by ... because to live by it you would have to be forever analyzing beliefs, without ever being committed to any" (370). In making this claim, Fish has been criticized, with some force, for holding to an unadmitted concept of knowledge that stands outside communally constructed beliefs.[16] Smith falls into no such difficulty because she suffers no embarrassment in maintaining her theory on the only basis on which she says anything can be maintained: "my reply to the charge of self-refutation consists of everything I have already said here, from which my own *saying* of it is, of course, *not* exempt. Having designed this verbal/conceptual construct to be of value—interest, use, and perhaps even beauty—to the members of a certain community, I exhibit it here for sale, hoping that some of its readers will, as we say, 'buy it,' but by no means expecting all of them to do so" (Smith, 113). While she can maintain her own theory comfortably on this basis, and could maintain specific claims about interpretation or value as comfortably, in the immediate context of the theory such specific claims, while not being self-contradictory, would lose a certain force. The theory itself, regardless of its replacement of truth-terms with terms like "alternate description," demands the concept of contingency as a kind of ultimate perspective of description from which we will always see specific evaluations as demanding less from us than total assent. Not surprisingly, she early on admits that, as a result of knowing them too well, she can no longer evaluate Shakespeare's sonnets (5); while she does not state explicitly that what she knows too well are, in fact, the various contingencies of her own past responses and evaluations, those contingencies are what she describes in recounting her past experiences. Thus while Smith's theory may in fact be the most adequate account of value, it is not an account feminists could use any more easily than less refined, relativistic accounts to espouse particular revaluations.

Despite the difficulty of holding such theories of value and revising the canon, their political attraction and the reasons for their deployment toward the end of canon revision become evident when one considers the implications of more modest claims. One might, for instance, accept that there are objective values but propose new ones for determining canonic inclusion or, even more modestly, one might accept that the values in place are valid but argue that they have been misapplied in the specific case of a given excluded or included work. Marxist critics have been active in proposing different systems of evaluation, but those systems all too frequently end up supporting the same old canon in the terms of the new values. The logical reason for this is fairly clear: if one proposes a new system of values, the best evidence that those values are really connected with our experience of literature will be their connection with works we already value.[17] Proposing new values to undergird a canon containing completely new works, while logically possible, has too much and too obvious potential for circularity or complete randomness (why not a canon including only works that accord with the theories of quantum mechanics?). On the other hand, arguing for or against a specific inclusion or exclusion on the basis that in that case sexist, racist, or class-elitist prejudice obstructed the proper functioning of our ability to fit general principle of value to specific instance has an inevitable tendency to move toward questioning of that general principle. After all, if specific works are valued negatively or positively as a result of a sexism that contradicts the explicit values we hold, then the activity of canon formation must be open to the intervention of accidental and contingent beliefs and prejudices that would make our explicitly held principles irrelevant to an understanding of the process of that formation. Arguing on the basis of principles that have never functioned, even while they have always been ostensibly held, will quickly come to seem as irrelevant as the principles themselves since, quite evidently, we can hold those principles and contradict them again and again in our actions and beliefs. And so we will return to pointing toward the politically determined nature of the values that have actively formed the canon.

So we have a situation in which only by questioning canonic foundations can we revise the canon, but the perspective we need for that questioning either undercuts the possibility of revision or simply makes us too aware of contingency to undertake the evaluative judgments necessary for that revision. This is the kind of double bind that critics frequently find deconstruction glorying in. The mode of exit in this case, however, is only too empirically evident: regardless of the logic of the situation, feminist criticism has had noticeable success in the project of canon revision in tandem with its critique of the foundations of literary value.[18] The question remains, however, how we can account for or describe the workings of that success. The deconstructive analysis of foundations, I think, both recuperates the seeming contradictoriness of the situation and provides a descriptive model for what has occurred. I stress that the model is descriptive because I do not mean to suggest in what follows that feminists must learn to follow deconstruction in order to be successful—it is only too evident that they need do no such thing. Rather, in the situation of the success of feminist revision, we can see a manifestation of the political workings of deconstruction.

In Chapter 3, I argued that deconstruction is not relativist or nihilist because it does not question the possible existence of true statements or successfully meaningful ones. Rather it questions the constitution of concepts such as truth and meaning to show the necessary and contradictory inclusiveness of their make-up. Because deconstruction functions in this way, it cannot be used to critique from the outside authoritarian concepts. If the concepts are contingent prejudices, deconstructive critique will have less relevance than the array of critical techniques we have developed to attack prejudice. If the conceptions are foundational, deconstruction will not do away with them.[19] Thus, to criticize patriarchy or nuclear deterrence, deconstruction is either superfluous or genuinely quietist. To see deconstruction function in its philosophical position as a corrosive element within foundational thought, I would like to return to Derrida's essay on nuclear politics. This essay can easily seem a classic exercise in overreaching, an attempt to use literary criticism to support a critique of nuclear policy that is more than strong enough without it. We have seen the problems with Christopher Norris's analysis of the essay as an attack on the logic of deterrence. This would be a critique of Derrida, however, only if his point were to show, in the terms of the essay, the competence ("No Apocalypse," 22) of his particular argument against the concept of nuclear deterrence. But he does not make any argument for or against deterrence in the article; nor does he argue for the special competence of deconstructive criticism in particular. Rather he argues precisely the competence of literary criticism in the nuclear debate. To the extent that he addresses deterrence, it is to identify as rhetorical Leslie Gelb's critique of the Reagan administration's position on the winnability of a nuclear war ("No Apocalypse," 25–26). This clearly does not produce a conservative defense of the Reagan position. But it also does not produce a new attack upon his position in particular. Derrida's issue of competence, though, reaches much further than the best way to make a certain argument. It is addressed to the whole critique of literary critics entering the nuclear debate. He argues that since there never has been a nuclear war (the use of a nuclear weapon at the end of World War II being the end of a conventional war, but not the process of a nuclear war), the concept of such a war is in the strict sense fabular, not because nuclear weapons are not real or their danger is not real, but for the simple reason that any description of what a nuclear war would be cannot refer to any real event or reach that event through some logic we might test. The event to which the logic of the nuclear debate attaches itself is fabular, and the discipline that analyzes fabular discourse is precisely literary criticism. The threat Derrida addresses is not a particular position within the nuclear debate but the impulse shared by all participants within that debate to specialize it, to make it unreachable by ordinary discourse. Those modes of specialization may be internally coherent and indeed outside the purview of those who do not have the specialized knowledge, but their specialization cannot be grounded by a particular appropriateness to the fact of nuclear war since relation to a nonexistent ground raises questions of rhetoric and linguistic relevance that are either outside the purview of those specializations or are inside that purview only to the same extent as is all literary criticism, indeed all fabulation. Derrida may have proved nothing about deterrence, but by eliminating the special placement of a certain discourse about it, he has eliminated the real power of that discourse, its claim to be the only way to talk about a threat we all share. When politics becomes foundational, an equalization of all positions to regional positions becomes a political position and an anticanonical one at that.

In the case of literary canons, Derrida also proves the truth of the reverse: not only are foundational statements kinds of regional statements, but regional statements can co-opt the position of foundational ones. His description of literary canons comes almost as a side effect in the essay. In order to clarify further his sense of the dependence of technocratic modes of thinking about nuclear war upon literary modes, he argues that the concept of total destruction, of destruction without remainder, rests on the peculiar ability literature has to be totally destroyed, even to the eradication of its own concept, through the destruction of the literary canon:

> Now what allows us perhaps to think the uniqueness of nuclear war, its being-for-the-first-time-and-perhaps-for-the-last-time, its absolute inventiveness, what it prompts us to think even if it remains a decoy, a belief, a phantasmatic projection, is obviously the possibility of an irreversible destruction, leaving no traces, of the juridico-literary archive—that is, total destruction of the basis of literature and criticism. Not necessarily the destruction of humanity, of the human habitat, nor even of other discourses (arts and sciences), nor even indeed of poetry or the epic; these latter might reconstitute their living process and their archive, at least to the extent that the structure of the archive (that of a non-literary memory) implies, structurally, reference to a real referent external to the archive itself. ("No Apocalypse," 26)

As later statements make clear, Derrida distinguishes between the literary archive and all others, at least at the conceptual level, because the archives in other disciplines refer in principle to things that stand independently of the existence of the archive. Thus, at least in principle, if every element of the present archive of some science were eradicated, we could rebuild the archive and the discipline by rediscovering the objects to which the archive referred. Literature, in contrast, is created by the very existence of the literary canon. There are individual works, of course, but their existence *as literature* is determined by the prior existence of a literary canon, which, as a result of the rise of the principle of reason in the seventeenth century, came into being to define a contrary principle.

The implications of Derrida's description for questioning the canon immediately become clear if we turn to a statement by Allan Bloom opposing canonic revision. In an exemplary statement of what is at issue, Bloom complains of a turn of attention away from "a classic's content," the ideas that made it great, to a historical concern with how it got into the canon (51). In principle, one of these concerns would not negate the other, one would think. There might be historical reasons for one kind of attention, and ethical, philosophical, and literary reasons for the other, and those reasons might even be coincident. Bloom clearly fears that the reasons will not be coincident and that that noncoincidence will be destructive. In other words, if we discovered that Shakespeare's works became canonical for extra-literary, historical reasons, even if those reasons were not ideological in root, we would have no more reason to study his works for the literary values they contained—even if they did objectively contain them—than any other works. Derrida shows, however, that even if we found that the historical reasons for a work's entering the canon were coincident with the reasons we value that work, this could hardly prove that the values were objectively there in some verifying extra-literary sense. Shakespeare's literary value just is part of his comprehension within a literary canon, since before the inception of a concept of canonicity, while the individual works might have existed, they did not exist as literature. If we look outside of the canon and literary value for reasons for canonical inclusion, those reasons will be extra-literary and thus destructive in their implications for the value of the work. If we refuse to accept an extra-literary cause, we are condemned to saying that, while any particular work may belong to the canon because it embodies certain literary values that other works do not, the values it embodies, rather than being reasons for inclusion in the canon, are constitutive of it. By reconstituting the canon, then, rearranging the works that comprise it, we will automatically be reconstituting the values it preserves in the only way possible. We do not need to worry about the contradiction between questioning foundational value and arguing for specific canonic revisions. In the light of the deconstructive analysis of foundations, both activities come to be versions of each other.

In the case of philosophical foundations, I argued that Derrida showed that foundational discourse had a certain, self-destructive inescapability that implied not that we could not know the truth or falsehood of particular statements but that we could not set up a foundational system for determining from the outside the rules for knowing when something is true or false. This logic does not make foundational discourse disappear—its logical necessity is part of its logical contradiction—but questions its claims upon us. Any political force that operated as a foundation would be open to the same deconstruction. We cannot prove or disprove the value of deterrence, but we can undercut the claim of a certain technical discourse to have special purview in that debate. The same thing happens to patriarchal modes of canonic or political justification. To the extent that they do not operate with the self-destructive comprehensiveness of a foundational value, they become just another historical event, and questioning them does not question all value. To the extent that, in the case of literature at least, questioning them does question all value, it could do so only because they operate with the kind of foundational logic that will never quite succeed in governing our decisions about the values of particular works. We can now see why the deconstructive project explains the empirical event of the feminist success in both calling the foundation of the canon into question and in inserting new works into the canon, despite the seeming contradiction of those two projects. The relativist justifications of certain feminists may be logically contradictory, as indeed the more traditional foundational bases of more conservative feminists for confining themselves to local justifications of particular works often are. The local justifications stand in the face of these contradictions precisely because of the failure of any foundational logic to control method or empirical result. From this perspective, the feminist analysis of noncanonical, ideological elements within the concepts of canon formation would not produce in a consequential way reasons for inclusion of alternative works within the canon. It produces, instead, the breaking of a canon's exclusionary power, opening us to other voices. If deconstructive analysis provides an explanation of the recent feminist successes in the literary debate, one may also reverse the situation and see those feminist successes, in their very inaccessibility to explanation by the alternatives either of relativism or foundationalism, to be the particular kind of exorbitant political event that clarifies deconstruction's consequence.

The two political extensions of aestheticism and deconstruction specified here—using aesthetic interpretation as a form of political self-resistance and the corrosive internal analysis of foundations—actually form part of a unified political effect. Self-resistance becomes something more than the self-negation of the powerful when placed within an institutional structure. At that point the deconstruction of a conceptual foundation enables the participation of previously excluded positions, thus allying with the shifts those inclusions entail. To claim that

AESTHETICS AND POLITICS   185

this is an opening without a sufficiently detailed objective to achieve anything, that it allows conservative oppression as easily as reformist activity, fails both to grasp the philosophical content of the act of opening itself and, more surprisingly, to deny the evidence of how that opening has worked. By now, the philosophical argument should be clear at least: whereas neither aestheticism nor deconstruction can engage in the kind of refutation of institutional or oppressive forces from the outside that critics sometimes want from literary criticism, the philosophical and political environment created by their open-ended inclusion from within is not very hospitable to those forces. While Mrs. Ward may have found in Pater's aesthetic response to religion a capitulation to dogma, there is little evidence that the Anglican Church, or literary figures like T. S. Eliot who wanted an alliance between literary and religious traditions, found his opening one they either wanted or could use. Equally, if de Man's deconstruction is a form of quietism, one wonders why the traditional literary criticism for which he was supposed to be covertly re-creating a space did not find aid and comfort there. In contrast, deconstruction does work in evident alliance with reformist movements. The coincidences between and alliances among feminists and deconstructive critics I have tried to show here are a matter of theoretical interdependence as well as historical contingency.

Given Lentricchia's contention that, regardless of abstract theoretical possibility, ideas manifest their reality only in their actual historical context (*Ariel and the Police*, 129–130), one might have expected him to interpret Derrida's and de Man's theories in the light of their evident influence not only on those who account themselves of their party but on all the theories creating professional turmoil recently, even on the Marxism that criticizes it so vehemently. Since he does realize that de Man's immediate influence has been upon those "with committed interests in criticism" and those with "activist experiences within the socially wrenching upheavals of the 1960s and 1970s" (*Criticism and Social Change*, 39, 41), perhaps the question is not how so many have been so deluded but why aestheticism and deconstruction evoke such antagonism not only from those whose tenure it threatens but from those with whom, regardless of its antagonism, it remains in implicit alliance. Here again, and finally, we shall turn to Victorian aestheticism and the responses to it to clarify the reasons for the contemporary hostility.

The ambiguity in the criticism of *The Renaissance* points toward the real hostility to aestheticism. That ambiguity manifests itself in the reasons for Pater's suppressions and revisions of his text. When he restored a revised version of the "Conclusion" to the third edition, after excising it entirely from the second, he explained the earlier omission, as we have seen, in a footnote specifying that "it might possibly mislead some of those young men into whose hands it might fall." Since then, critics have argued over whether Pater was actually trying to make his ideas clearer or was trying to protect himself from the disapproving response to the aura of homosexuality that surrounded the work.[20] That such an aura existed has long been known: W. H. Mallock's portrayal of Pater as the sexually ambiguous Mr. Rose in *The New Republic*, although it was published in book form after the second edition of *The Renaissance*, circulated widely in manuscript well before it.[21] Recent scholarship has made it clear that Pater was in fact responding to the homophobia around him. In particular, evidence has come to light showing that someone, perhaps Mallock, had given incriminating letters from Pater to a younger man to Benjamin Jowett, the master of Balliol College. Those letters may have influenced Jowett's decision to oppose Pater's candidacy for a university proctorship (he became a fellow of Brasenose College in 1864 but was never elected to any higher office).[22] Surprisingly, though, the revisions to the text of *The Renaissance* seem to show more concern with questions of philosophy and theology than with homosexuality. Pater excised and revised sentences concerned with the threats of theological and philosophical abstraction. But he never changed passages that referred sympathetically to the sexual ambiguity of some of da Vinci's paintings or to Winckelmann's homosexuality. The implication is unmistakable: somehow, as far as society's antagonism or the possibility of misleading young men was concerned, Pater's criticism of religious dogma and his concern for building a philosophy upon sensations and particularly aesthetic sensations were more homosexual than were his more explicitly homoerotic passages.

We can see the connection between homophobia and aestheticism and the real politics behind the response to Pater in Catherine Gallagher's distinction between two forms of literary theory: "the gender distinction in literary theory is not between male fathers who *can* multiply and female eunuchs who *cannot*, not between male language and female silence, but between the natural production of new things in the world and the 'unnatural' reproduction of mere signs. According to the father metaphor, the author generates real things in the world through language; according to the whore metaphor, language proliferates itself in a process of exchange through the author" ("George Eliot and *Daniel Deronda*," 41). Gallagher uses this distinction to analyze the image of the female writer in George Eliot. But the concept of natural and unnatural writing activity extends to Pater quite easily. To the extent that Pater's philosophy suggested indulgence in sensation, even if it was the fairly intellectualized sensation of aestheticism, it represented a turning inward away from the world, thus an "unnatural" inversion—inversion rather than perversion was the Victorian judgment of the psychological flaw they thought inherent in homosexuality—a turning away from outwardly productive and reproductive sexuality toward inverted enjoyment of and repetition of private sensations. Thus masking homophobia was a fear of the unnaturally private and inward, the symptom of which would be a writing skeptical of forms of asserting external value, what Pater refers to in an excised phrase from the "Conclusion" as "political or religious enthusiasm, or the 'enthusiasm of humanity' " (*Renaissance*, 274). Such writing would offer instead a philosophy based on physical sensation, which will then be labeled inverted, unproductive, and solipsistic, regardless of the logic of that philosophy or the illogic of the criticism.

Enclosure and the acceptance of enclosure form the common ground holding together aestheticism, homosexuality, and an unnatural writing that reproduces through the sterile proliferation of signs. Sign proliferation is sterile, of course, because it does not break out of its system and refer to a world of real things. Homosexuality as inversion shares that enclosure; thus both homosexuality and sign proliferation, being essentially sterile and enclosed, can reproduce only through an unnatural tainting process. Art, to the extent that it is defined by its inescapable alterity to the real or the natural as artificed reproduction, will, of course, share all these qualities. If art and language must be entirely other, then a theory that asserts the centrality of aesthetics to perception, of literary language to the workings of truth and the interpretation of history and politics, must obviously be reducing perception, truth, history, and politics to the aesthetic and the literary, enclosing them within its unnatural, artificed boundaries. More strangely, a critic who asserts the centrality of the literary or the aesthetic must share its unnaturalness, must have been tainted by the strange, unnatural reproductive power of art, literature, and signs.

Pater makes these connections easier to see because critics have started to make homophobia visible for us as ideology.[23] Where the ideological connecting element is not homosexuality, however, it may be harder to see this distorting system in the opposition to an aestheticist theory. One can see it, however, in the contradictory responses of de Man's critics. Thus, as we have seen in the earlier chapters, though Lentricchia accuses American deconstruction of passively conservative quietism because its skeptical formalism offers no grounds for opposing any structure or institution of power, he oddly accuses de Man not of being passively quietist but of having this quietism as an explicit political project. He construes de Man as having ambitions that go beyond being merely a formalist literary critic and as constructing an allegory depicting the futility of political action. One can see in Stanley Corngold the same awareness that de Man claims reference in his essays to a field broader than the strictly literary, bound with a contrasting claim that his message is nihilist and thus undercuts the ability to achieve political understanding or power. In his first essay, Corngold noted that "de Man, hard foe of metropolitan meliorism, is ... intent on driving the act of reading off the sofa and out of the ivory carrel into the dusty arena of combat" ("Error in Paul de Man," 491). When it reaches that arena, however, according to Corngold, de Man's theories then destroy the ability to make coherent political judgments ("Potential Violence in Paul de Man," 122–124). Were these critics able to show that de Man actually contended for the inability of literary language in particular and thus of language in general to refer to anything outside itself or to communicate any meaning at all, this contradiction would have been de Man's rather than theirs. But, as I have been arguing, the passages they cite in defense of that position actually claim that the opacity of literary and linguistic structure indicates the ideological, the political, the external. But if aestheticism is always enclosed, always unnatural, that position is simply impossible. Thus they transform de Man into an unnatural entity, a literary critical vampire, actively preaching a passivity whose infection must be sterile and unnatural since how can passivity preach?

If art and literature are ineluctably other, the literary critic will fear becoming paralytic by contact with their artifice, will fear becoming socially irrelevant. To ward off that danger, literary critics must transmogrify the theory that espouses aesthetic or literary centrality into an essence of otherness, passivity, the socially irrelevant, and thus, finally, the antisocial. The popularly understood meaning of "art for art's sake" and the way Pater's theories were distorted by the modernists who followed finally indicate that fear which his theories evoked as much as the homophobia surrounding them. That process of distortion continues in the current attempt to rationalize deconstruction away as an aestheticist wave that is thankfully passing from the scene. And indeed, in terms of its explicit influence, that may well be what is happening. But if in fact, as aestheticism, deconstruction offers a way of making sense of political and institutional activity, then the passing of its explicit influence will not lessen the accuracy of its analysis. As an indication of that accuracy, one might note that Derrida first outlined Catherine Gallagher's opposition between natural and unnatural writing—which she poses as a historically specific ideological contradiction, and which I have been using to analyze the political situation behind the reception of aestheticism and deconstruction—in a description of our thinking about writing dating back to Plato: "Writing and speech have thus become two different species, or values, of the trace. One, writing, is a lost trace, a nonviable seed, everything in sperm that overflows wastefully, a force wandering outside the domain of life, incapable of engendering anything, of picking itself up, of regenerating itself. On the opposite side, living speech makes its capital bear fruit and does not divert its seminal potency toward indulgence in pleasures without paternity" (*Dissemination*, 152). Derrida extends this opposition to the one between good and bad writing and asserts its recurrence in Western thought since Plato (149). He, of course, does not himself contend for the unnaturalness of writing any more than he does for the naturalness of speech, but details what we may call a persistent ideology. My point is not to give Derrida's philosophical analysis priority over Gallagher's ideological analysis. The recurrence of his contrast in historically specific moments that are nevertheless not completely explainable in their specificity gives his philosophical analysis, as I argued in the previous chapter, a medium in which it becomes both visible and meaningful. When we stop worrying about priority, we can see the relevance of that analysis. If, as we have seen Derrida argue elsewhere, the police are always around us, we can choose to pretend that they are not or that they might not be and claim that an acceptance of their constant presence is an acquiescence in what might be eliminable, but we cannot by that choice do away with the fact of their being around us, any more than we can do away with the accuracy of deconstructive analysis by distorting it. By analyzing foundational systems of institutionalized power instead of denying that power, by facing the reality of our placement within them in the kind of self-resistant analysis this chapter has been detailing, we can direct their operations toward the corrosion of foundational power, if not of foundations per se. And while this acceptance may disallow the belief in a conceptual escape from these systems, it does not disallow particular critiques or revisions of any given aspect of them. This will seem a quietist resignation only to those who need their resistances to be conceptual and foundational as well as material.

Afterword

Aestheticism, Journalism, and de Man's *Wartime Writings*

NEWS OF Paul de Man's collaborationist journalism and his now notorious anti-Semitic article broke early enough in the writing of this book for an analysis of the issues that discovery raises for my argument, if any, to have been incorporated into the body of my text. Indeed, many of the responses printed in both academic and more widely disseminated journals have already been reprinted in books.[1] Originally, I had pointedly refused to deal with the subject, since I felt that de Man's wartime writing, regardless of its content, had no relevance to literary theory he wrote forty years later. The argument surrounding those early newspaper reviews, I thought, was essentially a journalistic controversy that interrupted theoretical debate rather than forwarding it. Sympathetic readers of the manuscript—including one of Princeton's readers, who supported publication—nevertheless insisted that a book that addressed the politics of deconstruction had also to address the controversy, if only out of a prudent regard for currency. Having no antipathy to prudence, I nevertheless wondered why literary theory had to be journalistically timely in order to be prudent. Working through the arguments in the controversy, and particularly my dissatisfaction with the positions of those with whom I usually find myself aligned, especially Derrida's, I realized that I was resisting the intrusion of the journalistic into the aesthetic; and my argument for the political effectiveness of deconstruction needed to address that resistance—regardless of currency or prudence.

In order to address that matter, I want first to detail the kinds of responses that critics have offered so far and why they in fact fail to make a case for the relevance of de Man's early writings to his later ones. Then, in this afterword, which is neither entirely a part of my original argument nor simply a pendant to it, I want to show how this book's redefinition of aestheticism elucidates that failure. As a reviewer for *Le Soir*, writing journalism for a collaborationist editorial board, de Man, I will argue, tried to articulate a safe place within a fascist state for a pure and self-contained literature and literary criticism. Later, as a theorist who has often been criticized for his rarified lack of general accessibility, paradoxically, de Man both became a matter for journalism and gave us the means to analyze that event.

The controversy over de Man's *Wartime Writings* has been less than edifying partially because the positions taken in it have been so schematically predictable. Breaking down its elements into positions on the early journalism and positions on the later theories, one can predict four possible permutations. The *Wartime Writings* may be either totally condemned as completely fascistic and anti-Semitic in intent and effect, or their clear fascistic and anti-Semitic positions may be placed within the context of de Man's possibly more central concern with defining an aesthetic position. In turn, critics either find de Man's later writings implicated in the politics of the earlier writings or they defend de Man by describing his late work as a critical response to those early writings.[2]

Only three of the four possible combinations of these positions have actually been taken. First, one can contend for the entirely fascistic and anti-Semitic content of the early writings and a consequent suspect quality in the later ones. Second, one can contend that the early writings, while complicit in fascism and anti-Semitism (no one has actually argued that they are free of any fascism or anti-Semitism), have a primary concern with aesthetics that makes their significance more complex and that, further, de Man's later writings were a deliberate critique of his earlier, fascist ideology. Third, one could assent to the fascism and anti-Semitism of de Man's early writings but still argue that the late writings were a critique of those early positions. Predictably, de Man's critics have taken the first position, while most of his supporters have taken the second.[3] As we will see, these are, though the most predictable, also the most internally illogical positions. Consequently, some of de Man's supporters have taken the third position. Although logically consistent, this position, I will argue, has no real ground other than the fact that both bodies of writings exist and need to be explained. Moreover the urge to make such connections runs obviously afoul of de Man's own warnings against that procedure in his critique of "monumentalism" in "Shelley Disfigured." This leaves a fourth position that has particular pertinence for this book: de Man's early aesthetic concerns are troubling not so much because they are explicitly fascist but because they coexist too easily with support for fascist and anti-Semitic positions. That coexistence is troubling because it could extend as easily to his later theories, different as they might be. Although no critic has actually taken this position, if it could be maintained, it would suggest that aestheticism, or deconstructive aestheticism at least, is potentially politically quietist in precisely the way I have been arguing against. In working through the possibilities of this fourth position and why no one has taken it, I will make my final case for the political effects of deconstruction.

Since no one has really denied that, as Jonathan Culler puts it, "whatever interpretation one gives [the wartime writing], de Man is guilty of having written an anti-Semitic article and of working in the collaborationist press" ("'Paul de Man's War' and the Aesthetic Ideology," 780), the argument about the extent of de Man's commitment to fascism has frequently been over merely how strongly to *label* his writing as fascist and anti-Semitic.[4] Thus Stanley Corngold complains about Norris's formulation that some passages "can be read as endorsing what amounts to a collaborationist line" and Hartman's description of de Man as moving "closer to being explicitly collaborationist," labeling such descriptions as "plain enfeeblement" and wondering "what would it take to occupy an *explicitly* collaborationist position" (Hamacher, Hertz, and Keenan, 81). Once one has determined that de Man wrote for a newspaper whose editorial board was under Nazi control and that his articles at least conformed to the ideological demands of such a situation, of course, the question of collaboration is already settled. For such a settlement, however, one does not actually have to read any of de Man's articles. In order to describe the extent and shape of his collaboration, though, such a reading will naturally entail describing various positions, and Norris's and Hartman's language simply describes positions it finds more or less iniquitous. Unless Corngold simply demands vituperative rhetoric, one wonders what the complaint is about.

Moreover, to connect deconstruction with simple condemnation of anti-Semitism and fascism is no easy task. As we have seen, critics generally accuse deconstruction of relativism or nihilism. Even if such accusations were true, though, de Man's formulations of fascist ideology in his *Wartime Writings* do not base themselves on relativism. Thus Jon Wiener, to get deconstruction to sound fascist, must slide in his characterization of it from "nihilistic" to "implicitly authoritarian" ("Deconstructing de Man," 22), without arguing how to get from one to the other. And Roger Kimball, after struggling manfully to connect de Man's early writings with what he takes to be the radical nihilism of academics, finally just gives up: "Not that those early anti-Semitic articles exactly *prove* that deconstruction is nihilistic; but it is a rum thing when the patron saint of a literary movement that has so arrogantly proclaimed itself a champion of freedom is brutally exposed as having trafficked with a political force whose very essence was the denial of freedom" (103). The news of de Man's wartime writings surely is a rum thing; the interest of the press clearly focuses precisely on the rumminess of it. But we are still left wondering about the theoretical implications of that rumminess.

Somewhat more logically, some critics have connected de Man's ostensible deconstructive relativism with his early writings in terms of an alibi. By proving that all morality or all history is merely language, they argue, de Man tries to excuse his early writing as merely language. The constantly cited passage in this argument comes from de Man's analysis of confessions and excuses in Rousseau: "it is always possible to face up to any experience (to excuse any guilt), because the experience always exists simultaneously as fictional discourse and as empirical event and it is never possible to decide which one of the two possibilities is the right one. The indecision makes it possible to excuse the bleakest of crimes because, as a fiction, it escapes from the constraints of guilt and innocence" (*Allegories of Reading*, 293).[5] Without even addressing the misreadings this connection entails, one ought to note the obvious overadequacy of deconstruction to the service it is being turned to. An excuse for every crime, no matter how bleak, does not actually excuse any particular crime very well, so if de Man really wanted to excuse his past to himself or, implicitly, to others, he chose a singularly ineffective way to do it. De Man's critics here have merely taken the general accusation that we have seen them constantly make against deconstruction, that its relativism gives one no ground for condemning any moral transgression, and have turned it to the specific transgression of de Man's wartime collaboration. We have in fact learned nothing new about deconstruction in this connection but have seen an old accusation reasserted in a different register.[6]

But this objection about the overadequacy of deconstruction as an alibi stands equally against the arguments that the late work is an explicit meditation on and critique of fascist ideology. I am, for instance, entirely persuaded by Cynthia Chase's antitotalitarian reading of de Man's article on Kleist (in Hamacher, Hertz, and Keenan, 44–79). But precisely because the aesthetic ideology Chase shows de Man criticizing involves "expectations and assumptions [that] continue to be those of most practice of comparative literature and of the study of literary history" (Hamacher, Hertz, and Keenan, 71), one cannot very well take the essay as offering "an incisive diagnosis of the conditions of possibility of Nazism" (45). It may be readable in terms of those conditions of possibility. But its reach is too broad to be an incisive diagnosis. De Man has been a powerful force as a critic of conservative ideology because he has shown us how to articulate buried presumptions within the constructs of disciplines to which we have been attracted. One lessens his force as well as misreads him by turning those arguments to the narrower, if now more current, topic of fascism—the skeptical analysis of which we hardly need deconstruction to achieve even if it accords with such skepticism.

The unsatisfactory positions outlined here thus led me to think that, whatever biographical sense will have to be made of the wartime writings, and despite the generally agreed upon belief that we will no longer be able to see the later writings without the earlier ones in mind, nevertheless their context has not been extraordinarily helpful in reinterpreting those later essays. I became troubled about another possible connection only after rereading those essays while working toward writing this afterword. Seeing at first no real connection between early and late de Man, and indeed thinking that the more fascist the early de Man's writings proved to be, the more obvious their distance from the later deconstructive criticism, I was perfectly prepared to accept John Brenkman's contention that Paul de Man "was at that time a fascist and an anti-Semite as well as an active collaborator with the Nazi occupation of Belgium" (Hamacher, Hertz, and Keenan, 21). That position, though, seemed too simplistic a reading of the actual essays and their actual aesthetic concerns. "The Jews in Contemporary Literature," for example, when one actually reads it rather than trying either to excuse or blame it, seems less like the work of a *committed* anti-Semite than the work of one who was only too willing to give lip service to anti-Semitism in order to separate a field from fascist ideology in which literature might continue to flourish freely. The opening of the piece makes clear the accuracy of Derrida's contention that "De Man wants especially to propose a thesis on literature that visibly interests him more here than either antisemitism or the Jews" (Hamacher, Hertz, and Keenan, 144):

> Vulgar antisemitism is readily pleased to consider the cultural phenomena of the post-war period (after the war of 14–18) as degenerate because judaized. Literature has not escaped this lapidary judgment: it has sufficed that one discover a few Jewish writers with latinized pseudonyms for all contemporary production to be considered polluted and injurious. This conception has dangerous enough consequences. First of all, it leads to an a priori condemnation of a whole literature that in no way merits that fate. Moreover, if one is pleased to accord some merit to contemporary letters, it would be hardly flattering to occidental writers to reduce them to being simple imitators of a Jewish culture that is foreign to them. (de Man, *Wartime Writings*, 45)[7]

De Man begins by setting aside the literary judgment of vulgar anti-Semitism, claiming that literature is free of any taint of Jewish influence (thus implying, of course, that Jewish influence would be a taint). The middle of the article then defends literature, and particularly the modernist literature de Man tries to preserve from Nazi condemnation throughout his essays, as self-contained, "developing according to its own great evolutionary laws." From this perspective, the frightening hypothesis of an expulsion of the Jews from Europe is not something de Man actually espouses but something he is willing to contemplate as far as the integrity of literature is concerned.

De Man's direct discussions of other aspects of fascist ideology, particularly in his treatment of collaborationist books he reviews, parallel his handling of anti-Semitism. Describing the conclusions of these books as positive truths, he nevertheless brackets those truths as not of central concern to him. Thus Brenkman can extract a fascist ideology to which he argues de Man is committed by quoting de Man's approving summaries of books, while extracting those summaries from their contexts. For instance, Brenkman quotes de Man's approving summary of Charles Dekeukeleire's call for workers to learn the value of merging themselves in a collectivity—in context distinctly not a Marxist collectivity (Hamacher, Hertz, and Keenan, 23). And though de Man does not deny the value of this, he insists on exempting art from the responsibility of forwarding this goal:

> But one cannot follow [Dekeukeleire] any longer when he assigns to artistic production a social function that does not belong to it. Considering aesthetic emotion as identifiable with social emotion and believing that the two may influence each other profoundly is, at the least, a debatable assertion.... As we have said, the greatness of art depends in the first place on its eternal aspects, and it is only in that function that one may judge it. All attempts to transform it into a utilitarian means, even toward a great and respectable end, risk leading to the worst deformations. (*Wartime Writings*, 208–209)

One can from the passages Brenkman exhibits, even placed back in context, see that de Man effectively assents to a fascist ideology in the course of defining an aesthetic field he wanted to protect. But his commitment remained aesthetic, not fascist.[8]

I want to stress that I do not see this central concern with aesthetics as in any sense an excuse for de Man or a mitigation for what he wrote. As Johnson notes with regard to the anti-Semitism: "the fact that, as Derrida puts it, 'de Man wants especially to propose a thesis on literature that visibly interests him more than either anti-Semitism or the Jews' is ... no comfort. If there had not been people who, without any particular personal anti-Semitism, found the idea of deportation *reasonable*, there could have been no Holocaust" (*A World of Difference*, xv–xvi). To assent to anti-Semitic propositions, even as a hypothesis in order to defend literature, nevertheless assents to anti-Semitism. When de Man asserts that literature, in being free of Jewish influence, is healthy, he presumes that if Jews had had important literary influence literature would be unhealthy.[9] Similarly, to assent to Nazi propaganda in order to defend literature nevertheless assents to Nazi propaganda. J. Hillis Miller's claim that de Man's articles on collaborationist writers express reservations about their work thus seems egregious special pleading (Hamacher, Hertz, and Keenan, 336).

Derrida's reading of "The Jews in Contemporary Literature" seems to me something worse than special pleading, though, and brings me to the reason for insisting on the importance of aesthetic concerns in de Man's wartime writings, even though that does not excuse what he did. Derrida's argument, I think, aestheticizes issues in just the way that I have been arguing in this book—in just the way that Derrida argues in this very article on de Man—deconstruction does not do. One sees this first of all in Derrida's reading of the phrase "vulgar antisemitism": "To condemn vulgar antisemitism may leave one to understand that there is a distinguished antisemitism in whose name the vulgar variety is put down.... But the phrase can also mean something else, and this reading can always contaminate the other in a clandestine fashion: to condemn 'vulgar antisemitism,' *especially if one makes no mention of the other kind*, is to condemn anti-Semitism *itself inasmuch as it is vulgar, always and essentially vulgar*" (Hamacher, Hertz, and Keenan, 143). First, de Man pretty clearly does not mean to condemn anti-Semitism as vulgar. As we have seen, he accepts the anti-Semitic hypothesis to condemn the vulgarity of dismissing literature as "judaized." Moreover, as Alice Yaeger Kaplan points out, Nazi ideology already distinguished between vulgar and more intellectual anti-Semitism, the more intellectual anti-Semites insisting on a racial rather than a social anti-Semitism (Hamacher, Hertz, and Keenan, 273). And, on the same page as de Man's article, the lead piece, "The Two Faces of Judaism," begins essentially with this distinction (*Wartime Writings*, 287). But Derrida's argument is even more disturbing because even if he were right about the phrase, the situation would be no better. Condemning anti-Semitism as vulgar is too much like condemning an axe-murderer for messing up a living room. Indeed, Oscar Wilde specialized in that kind of condemnation of an immoral act, to great social effect but at the expense of narrowing the meaning of aestheticism.

This might be merely a miscalculation in detail except that Derrida's whole argument depends upon taking the rhetorical complexity arising from de Man's aesthetic aims to indicate some deeper duality in his stance. Thus Derrida introduces his analysis of the rhetorical difficulties of de Man's journalism this way: "de Man's discourse is constantly split, disjointed, engaged in incessant conflicts. Whether in a calculated or a forced fashion, and no doubt beyond this distinction between calculation and passivity, all the propositions carry within themselves a counterproposition: sometimes very explicit, always readable, this counterproposition signals what I will call, in a regular and contradictory manner, a *double edge* and a *double bind*, the singular artifact of a blade and a knot" (Hamacher, Hertz, and Keenan, 135). This passage duplicates closely enough the language Derrida employs to deconstruct the philosophical or rhetorical contradictions within a text that his critics have, with some justification, taken him to be deconstructing de Man in order to defend him. And they thus call into question the political effects of a method that allows such a defense.[10] In effect Derrida argues that the contradictions he uncovers indicate a mitigating duplicity in de Man's stance. Timothy Bahti's simplified formulation, which says the article "may be anti-Semitic—*and*, simultaneously, may *not* be anti-Semitic," makes the untenable end of the analysis clear (Hamacher, Hertz, and Keenan, 5). The deconstructive working of literary analysis here moves toward blurring the possibility of a moral judgment. Just as de Man accepted fascist ideology in order to clear a space for the literary culture he valued, Derrida uses his analysis to clear a space for de Man's aestheticism. The charge of totalitarianism has been thrown around too loosely by all parties to this debate. Special pleading for de Man does not remotely resemble special pleading for Nazis. But the model by which de Man thought he could help his aestheticism live with fascism looks uncomfortably close to the political quietism with which deconstruction has been accused. And at least arguably, Derrida acts out that quietism here.

In fact, Derrida's reading is not a deconstruction. Even the reading method incorrectly drawn from deconstruction showed contradictions within specific texts, not contradictory impulses within an author's intentions. Thus, even if one were persuaded by Derrida's analysis, it could at most show that we could not be sure what de Man meant, not that he had mixed meanings. And if my argument is correct that deconstruction as articulated by Derrida and de Man analyzes foundational and theoretical contradictions, not specific texts, then it is even less suited to making specific determinations about de Man's intentions in his wartime writings.

But once we have the model of an aestheticism that lives quietly within an ideology, accepting it as a social practice while claiming to have its own content untouched by that practice, any aesthetic, even a rectified deconstructive aesthetic, will fit equally well. I noted earlier that Cynthia Chase convincingly drew the vital distinctions between the internal coherence claimed by de Man's earlier aesthetics and the disjunctures that determine his deconstructive aesthetics (Hamacher,

Hertz, and Keenan, 44–79). And her further assertion that that disjuncture contradicts totalitarian claims to comprehensive and univocal explanations (though other theories that are not politically totalitarian also make those claims) also seems to me persuasive. But elements of de Man's wartime aesthetics also contradicted fascist values. Accepting the need for social collectivity, for instance, de Man also praised the individuality of French literature and argued that "from a purely artistic point of view, this attitude [French individualism] is distinctly fecund and productive since it encloses literature cleanly within a domain in which it enjoys complete liberty" (*Wartime Writings*, 188). If literature may enjoy the liberty to be individualistic within its domain, protected by the fascist ideology it passively accepts, so might it enjoy the liberty to be disjunctive. Even an implicitly antifascist aesthetic, as aesthetic, could live within a fascist ideology if it claimed de Man's enclosure. The question here is not whether de Man in his later writing or Chase claims that enclosure—neither of them does—but whether anything in their aesthetics disallows it.

As I said, given the frequency with which deconstruction has been criticized as a revivified aestheticism, it is somewhat odd that this correspondence between early and later de Man has not been commented upon. One obvious reason is that such an analysis does not fit the predetermined positions of any party. Those who want to connect the fact of de Man's collaboration with his later criticism do not want to start with the claim that the collaboration served an aestheticism of greater interest to de Man.[11] And while those defending de Man have been attracted to that position, they do not want to explore its uncomfortable ramifications for deconstruction. But for both parties to this debate, this aestheticist connection presents deeper problems. Opponents of deconstruction's aestheticism would need to define an aesthetic that could *not* accept the enclosure created in de Man's collaborationist writing. And, just as the later de Man's disjunctive, antitotalitarian aesthetic could accept that enclosure, so could any definition. Even if one insisted on the political or social content of art, one could protect that content from an inimical reigning ideology by claiming a special realm of literary value. Indeed, de Man, in his journalism for *Le Soir*, frequently discussed the political and social content of the novels he was reviewing and even speculated on the connection between the type of art a nation produced and its national characteristics, but he simultaneously claimed that these aspects of a literature could not be used for judgmental purposes: "Grosso modo, one could say that germanic nations practice an art more 'volkish' than latin nations, France in particular. But one would be wrong to make of that an argument in favor of any supposed superiority" (*Wartime Writings*, 178).

I have been proposing in this book a response to this charge of aestheticism as enclosure by claiming that Pater, Derrida, and de Man defined an aestheticism that functions as a resistant interpretation of political issues. But for de Man's defenders, I think that that critique strikes quite specifically at the rhetoric of their defense, particularly its sometimes shrill self-protectiveness. The force of deconstruction, I think, as opposed to its professional position, is little threatened by journalistic attacks that cannot even accurately define what it is. But it has far more to fear from the rhetoric of even its best practitioners when Derrida can suggest that those who criticize de Man operate with totalitarian logic (Hamacher, Hertz, and Keenan, 154–155) and Timothy Bahti labels "perfidy" any criticism of de Man's early writings further than "juvenile, offensive" (Hamacher, Hertz, and Keenan, 5). The rhetorical and polemical failures in the responses of de Man's defenders have been discussed by others who—like me—consider themselves as normally aligned with the intellectual position of those defenders.[12] Rather than going into them in detail, I would be happy to consider them unfortunate effects of immediate response to an issue that demanded such immediacy.

One aspect of that response, however, has been so recurrent, has indeed caused my own reluctance to address this debate, and partakes, I think, so deeply of a form of the aesthetic enclosure that I have been arguing against, that it must be addressed. Constantly one hears a call to beware hasty journalistic formulations, an insistence on the difference between de Man's late theories and inappropriate journalistic presentations of them in the inappropriate light of a deceptively hot event. This call, oddly, starts—at least in terms of this debate—with de Man's quoting in a review for *Le Soir* the collaborationist writer Henri de Montherlant's criticism of journalistic response: "To writers who have given too much, in the last few months, to contemporary events, I predict, for that part of their work, the most total oblivion. When I open today's journals and reviews, I hear the indifference of the future roll over them" (*Wartime Writings*, 162). De Man immediately turns this statement against its author, criticizing him for too complete a concern for passing events. Derrida quotes the passage ironically, suggesting that oblivion would normally have buried de Man's journalism, but it has been buoyed up by his more lasting, later theoretical work (Hamacher, Hertz, and Keenan, 127–128).[13] Gasché makes the point explicitly, separating de Man's early writing from his later work in terms of "the elevation to thinking" in the latter, which makes it "impossible to make it derive from the writings of the journalistic period" (Hamacher, Hertz, and Keenan, 217). Miller completes the process by stating that "this is not a matter where you would want to let the newspapers do your reading and thinking for you" (*TLS*, 676). First de Man tries in his own journalism to separate lasting literary judgments from transient responses to current events. Then we find his later theoretical writings separated from the early writings on the basis of the former's journalism. Finally, the whole dispute is taken to be too serious to be left to journalism. Instead of an enclosed space for aestheticism, we now have an enclosed space for theory, which journalism can only taint, in which all real serious thought takes place.

This book has articulated a far different, less self-protective deconstruction, I think. We saw in the previous chapter that de Man, in his last essays, placed his analyses of philosophical and aesthetic problems firmly in the context of issues that held contemporary interest for our profession at least. Far from trying to separate his aesthetic theories from journalism, as he had done in his wartime writing, he accepted the connection between current concern and aesthetic analysis as at least one that cannot be escaped. One way or another, de Man has always been writing aesthetic theory only to find that he has been writing journalism. I have meant this afterword to be an application of his later theory's self-resistant analysis to my own reluctance to take the journalistic issue of de Man's early journalism seriously. For all its strange rhetorical effects, the transformation of deconstruction into newspaper stories may yet have much to say about the politics of deconstruction as a theory and the politics of professional aggression and defensiveness. Because of those rhetorical effects, what it says may resist various positions in the dispute. Given the hardening occurring in contemporary critical debates, such a resistance would be a large advance.

May 1990
Washington, DC

Notes

Introduction

1. The most exemplary and earliest (and thus somewhat formulaic) deconstruction is J. Hillis Miller's "Walter Pater, A Partial Portrait." Perry Meisel's *Absent Father* discusses Pater's influence on Woolf but through the medium of a deconstructive reading of Pater. Gerald Monsman's *Walter Pater's Art of Autobiography* claims to write under the aegis of deconstruction, though that shows up mostly in his claiming to elide the difference between Pater's criticism and his fiction. Harold Bloom's "Crystal Man," vii–xxxi, reflects Pater's amenability to Bloom's antithetic alternative to and within deconstructive criticism.

2. Daniel T. O'Hara's *Romance of Interpretation*, by discussing Pater before a series of essays on Bloom, Hartmann, Frye, and de Man, explicitly claims his writing as part of the contemporary debate, but it does so by focusing on the theoretical implications of what Pater discusses for modern hermeneutic debates. More recently, Linda Dowling's *Language and Decadence in the Victorian Fin de Siècle* argues that the decadence in general and Pater in particular, especially in *Marius the Epicurean*, were defined by a skeptical attitude toward earlier Victorian theories of language and linguistics that she compares to the ideas of Foucault and Derrida (xiii). As persuasive and informative as her discussion is, however, its thesis is established at the cost of relegating *The Renaissance* and its "Conclusion" to "an aestheticism of the cultural surface" (4).

3. Seiler, *Walter Pater, The Critical Heritage*, 70. This review is mostly laudatory of Pater, whom, moreover, Morley, as editor of *Fortnightly Review*, frequently invited to contribute to his journal. Early versions of *The Renaissance*'s chapters on Pico della Mirandola, Botticelli, Michelangelo, and da Vinci had already first appeared there. After the review, Pater wrote to Morley thanking him for his "explanation of my ethical point of view" (Evans, 14). In view of these generally friendly relations, the reservation Morley expresses in the conclusion to his review becomes perhaps more significant.

4. Abrams, 458. Since Abrams uses J. Hillis Miller's writing here as a representative rather than an idiosyncratic example of deconstructive theory, one may take his charge to have broader application.

5. Fish's further development of his theory led him to recant this sentence (174).

6. Determining the political significance of the content of works of art and evaluating them accordingly has been such a common aspect of committed criticism, not only of Marxism but of the cultural criticism of figures like Lionel Trilling and of various strands of feminism, that its practice hardly needs evidencing. Connecting literary form with political significance has been a more recent development. Fredric Jameson's *Political Unconscious* offers one of the most detailed theories of how to determine the political causes of literary form and how to construe those causes. In a larger sense, new historicism, following

Foucault, has developed modes and themes for discussing the ideological roots of literary forms. To the extent that they also see the forms themselves as ideological effect, and thus question the alterity of aesthetic form and even the coherence of the concept of the literary or the aesthetic, I would argue that they partake of the deconstructive argument worked out here, rather than oppose it.

Chapter One

1. To an extent this view is seconded by DeLaura, who argues that Pater's ideal is *not* "art for art's sake," which "is an ideal for the artist only" (226).

2. For Pater's label, see Evans, 14. Eliot, 390, agrees, calling it "a theory of ethics." I quote Jowett's epithet from Levey, 143, who describes it only as "attributed to Jowett."

3. The edition of *The Renaissance* used here contains both all textual variants and a section of critical notes by the editor, Donald Hill. Citations of Hill will refer to these notes. I am quoting the passage here as it appeared in 1873, as I will throughout unless I am explicitly discussing revisions. In order to reconstruct the 1873 edition, I will frequently have to use both Hill's main text, the 1893 edition, and the listing of variants printed afterwards. Passages with widely separated page numbers in the parenthetical reference, such as this one, refer both to text and variant. Passages with only one number were either unchanged through the various editions or were omitted and are being cited entirely from the pages containing variants. The phrase "art for art's sake" was changed to "art for its own sake" in Pater's last revision for the edition of 1893. The phrase "political or religious enthusiasm, or the enthusiasm of humanity" Pater changed in 1888 to the marginally less controversial "the various forms of enthusiastic activity, disinterested or otherwise, which come naturally to many of us." Other revisions seem merely stylistic.

4. Pater's taste is eclectic enough to surprise some of his critics. His citation of Hugo's *Les Misérables* at the end of the "Conclusion" leads Harold Bloom (*Selected Writings*, 63) to exclaim, "a most un-Paterian book astonishingly cited, for its greatness, at the end of the essay on 'Style' in *Appreciations*." Indeed, Hugo seems to be a favorite of Pater's, un-Paterian or not. In *The Renaissance* alone, *Les Misérables* is cited in two other places, and Hugo generally, or other works by him, quite frequently. But then Pater is generally much less interested in reevaluating and excluding than is Bloom.

5. Hill, 457–458, locates various early French sources for the phrase, going back as far as Benjamin Constant. But he notes that the phrase gained currency in England in the 1860s and then particularly cites Swinburne's *William Blake*, "a book which Pater must have read."

6. Thus Graham Hough, 143, argues that "there is hardly any kind of conduct which could not be sanctioned by this doctrine, including the conduct of the philosophic or religious ascetic." Hough attributes this openness to "an immense appreciation of the variety and multitudinousness of the world." While I would not deny this aspect of Pater, I am arguing that the refusal to exclude is itself a deliberate philosophic stance as much as, if not more than, a consequence of an appreciation of variety.

7. Locke and Hume still see simple impression or sensation as registered by resistance of or violent striking on the nerves. Thus Locke, in *An Essay Concerning Human Understanding*, defines the idea of solidity—the only simple idea of sense he discusses in detail—by saying that "it arises from the resistance which we find in body to the entrance of any other body into the place it possesses, till it has left it" (1: 151). And Hume opens *A Treatise of Human Nature* by saying that "all the perceptions of the human mind resolve themselves into two distinct kinds, which I shall call IMPRESSIONS and IDEAS. The difference betwixt these consists of the degrees of force and liveliness with which they strike upon the mind, and make their way into our thought or consciousness. Those perceptions, which enter with most force and violence, we may name impressions" (1). By the nineteenth century, definitions of sense no longer included a consideration of a physiological forced entry, but sensation still rested on friction, now defined as change between sensations. Thus, J. S. Mill, in a footnote to James Mill's *Analysis of the Human Mind*, notes that "the necessary condition of sensation is change ... an unchanging sensation instead of becoming latent, dwindles in intensity until it dies away and ceases to be a sensation" (1: 232). Here we have entered Pater's world of sensation as flux.

8. Peter Alan Dale, in *The Victorian Critic and the Idea of History*, offers the most complete articulation so far of Pater's use of empiricism (173–185). DeLaura's reading of Pater's works through the 1870s (192–255), though it does not refer to empirical philosophy in any detail, by stressing Pater's relativism would clearly be in sympathy with Dale's reading. Anthony Ward's *Walter Pater: The Idea in Nature* offers the fullest reading of Pater within a Hegelian and an Oxford Idealist tradition.

9. See, for instance, Mill's famous definition of reality as the permanent possibility of sensation in *An Examination of Sir William Hamilton's Philosophy* (177–187).

10. The self has been a notoriously problematic concept for empiricism at least since Hume's *Treatise of Human Nature* doubted its existence as anything more than a bundle of sensations (251–253).

11. Bloom says of this passage, "this ultimate skepticism is essentially the predicament of all Pater's *Imaginary Portraits*, and presumably of Pater himself" (*Selected Writings*, 62). Given Bloom's sense of the power of subjectivity in Pater, one wonders whether he thinks Pater really experiences this skepticism as a predicament or a liberation. The phrase "relativity of knowledge" I take from Dale's, *Victorian Critic* and his previously cited section on empiricism, in which he argues that Pater draws his relativism from empiricism in general and J. S. Mill in particular.

12. The fullest articulation of this argument is in Meisel, 111–116. Meisel cites J. Hillis Miller's prior argument in "Walter Pater, A Partial Portrait." Billie Andrew Inman, in "The Intellectual Context of Walter Pater's 'Conclusion'" (Dodd, 13), maintains that Pater makes two arguments, a scientific one about the external world and a philosophical one about the internal world, and therefore he does not contradict himself because they are two separate topics. But, even if Pater does intend such a sharp turn in direction, if his two arguments for flux and doubt contradict each other, even if they are drawn from different

fields, one or the other of them must be looked on somewhat askance. Moreover, Meisel argues that contradiction exists within the strictly philosophical argument and its divergent views of the self as bundle of sensation and as thick wall of personality. Meisel does not identify what he calls "Pater's deindividuating phenomenology" (113) with empirical skepticism about the self, since that would threaten the compactness of his deconstruction of Pater.

13. Meisel, in order to deconstruct Pater, must insist that Pater cannot accept this vision of self-loss and so does not discuss the passage imaging its "weaving and unweaving," and he sees the main significance of this passage to be its repression (115). Since I have used Meisel as a counterpoint in my analysis of this passage, it seems only fair to note that his analysis of the role of difference in Pater is close—at least in concept—to mine of the role of contrast and friction.

14. Hill argues that "Pater subverts Arnold's meaning profoundly in what follows" (297). Bloom notes Pater's references to Arnold here and twice more in the "Preface" (*Selected Writings*, 21–22).

15. In his early essay "Coleridge's Writings," Pater found aesthetic value in precisely what he found philosophically objectionable in Coleridge, his transcendental absolutism, because that absolutism contrasted with his age's scientific and moral relativism.

16. William K. Wimsatt, Jr., and Cleanth Brooks, in *Literary Criticism: A Short History*, discuss the idea of art as pure form within the aesthetic movement, attributing this idea to Pater as well as to Wilde and others (484–491). Wolfgang Iser, in *Walter Pater: The Aesthetic Moment*, while he sees art in Pater as in contradiction to its historical placement, also argues that this art operates to smooth the contrasts of history and reality (40–41).

17. DeLaura argues with persuasive comprehensiveness for the pertinence of Arnold's "Pagan and Medieval Religious Sentiment" to "Winckelmann" (202–222). His general outline of the influence of Arnold upon Pater and his resultant interpretation of Pater are both a source and an antagonist for my argument here. Since the details of my argument stress the antagonism, it is worth noting that the antagonism could not have occurred without my use of the source.

18. This depiction starts with T. S. Eliot, "Arnold and Pater." Eliot, however, sees Pater completing what Arnold has begun (388) and thus does not think that Pater narrows Arnold in any real way: " 'Art for art's sake' is the offspring of Arnold's Culture; and we can hardly venture to say that it is even a perversion of Arnold's doctrine, considering how very vague and ambiguous that doctrine is" (390). DeLaura, in particular reference to the idea in "Winckelmann" of the supreme, artistic view of life, contrasts Pater with Arnold on the ground that Pater "*despaired* of changing society as the mature Arnold never did" (229). DeLaura generally finds Pater narrowing and draining Arnold's social and moral force, at least in his writing through *The Renaissance*. Dale's *Victorian Critic and the Idea of History* also follows this general view.

19. Arnold's editor, R. H. Super, notes that Arnold uses this line as a touchstone in his essay "Byron" (Arnold, 10: 469).

20. DeLaura first remarked on the context created by this paragraph for the "Conclusion" (224–225).

21. Inman locates Pater's sources in an article by Lewes summarizing then recent biological conclusions and in Herbert Spencer's *Principles of Biology* (Dodd, 14–15). Dale also notes the context of Spencer's book in discussing Pater (211–212).

22. Eugene Goodheart's *Skeptic Disposition in Contemporary Criticism* analyzes Arnold as a positive alternative. Michael Fischer's *Does Deconstruction Make Any Difference?* sees Arnold as a forerunner of the aestheticism that disables deconstruction from making a difference.

23. I am indebted to Paul Sawyer's incisive discussion of Ruskin's relationship to scientific theories of his day over the course of his career in *Ruskin's Poetic Argument: The Design of the Major Works*, 266–274.

24. In this view, Bloom concludes that Pater's "largest departure from Ruskin was in opposing a darker and hedonistic humanism to the overtly moral humanism of his aesthetic precursor" ("The Crystal Man,"xvi). My objections here are largely to the words "hedonistic" and "moral." Bloom's one-paragraph summary of Pater's revisions of Ruskin remains one of the best discussions of their relationship. Richard Stein, in *The Ritual of Interpretation: The Fine Arts as Literature in Ruskin, Rossetti, and Pater*, offers a less subtle version of this position by implication when he suggests that the distinction between Ruskin and the doctrine of art for art's sake resides only in Ruskin's additional sacramental sense of the landscape (53).

Chapter Two

1. Since this book was written, Carolyn Williams's fine study *Transfigured World: Walter Pater's Aesthetic Historicism* has appeared. In articulating fully Pater's historicism and its tie to his aestheticism, Williams has predicted some of my argument here and carried it further in terms of analyzing *Marius the Epicurean*, *Greek Studies*, and *Plato and Platonism*. Despite the similarities in our approaches to Pater's historicism, though, our analyses diverge over the concept more central to this work—aestheticism. Williams shares the definition I argue against here and therefore makes Pater's historicism a mode of an enclosed aestheticism rather than seeing the aestheticism as opening itself out into a mode of interpreting the philosophical problems of historicism.

2. Dale, *The Victorian Critic*, 173–183, provides a fine discussion of the connection between empiricism and historicism.

3. Thus Richard Stein, in *The Ritual of Interpretation*, argues that "it is clear throughout *The Renaissance* that Pater's subjective aesthetic militates against history, acknowledging the reality of the past only as it survives in vivid 'impressions' in the present" (224).

4. This distinction, deriving from Russian Formalism, has, through French structuralism, become so pervasive in narrative theory that we may now refer to the definitions of overviews. Seymour Chatman, in *Story and Discourse: Narrative Structure in Fiction and Film*, says: "the 'fable' (*fabula*) [is the] basic story stuff, the sum total of events to be related in the narrative, and, conversely, the 'plot' (*sjuzet*) [is the] story as actually told by linking the events together" (19–20). The attachment of the word "plot" to *sjuzet* is slightly deceptive since

"plot" in Anglo-American criticism, as Peter Brooks, 13, notes, often refers to the events as well as their arrangement.

5. I am indebted to Stein's description of the connection here for leading me to think about the relationship in the terms of narrative theory, despite my problems with the lack of specificity in his formulation.

6. Thus Levey's statement in *The Case of Walter Pater*: "For him there is always a grave gaping half-hidden among even the lushest grass on the brightest day. Indeed it was exactly at the point when emotions of beauty or love are most actively stirred that Pater seems to have been seized by a panic fear of death. The 'Conclusion' to *The Renaissance*, especially in its unrevised form, is itself a desperate 'cry on the stair', in which the beauty of life and art is seen inextricably bound up with human evanescence" (31).

7. DeLaura finds Pater's disagreement with the full extent of Hegel's metaphysics and his ultimate subordination of art to philosophy the only explanation for "what would otherwise be an inexplicable change of tone less than two years later" in this passage of the "Conclusion" (224). But Pater already disagreed with this aspect of Hegel when he wrote "Winckelmann" and revised him accordingly, without being any less laudatory. It thus makes more sense to rethink the tone of this passage. Pater always used Hegel rather than simply aligning himself to him, but he does not see using philosophy as an entirely trivial activity.

8. Wright, in his *Life of Walter Pater*, describes Pater as an enemy to Gothic (1: 180). Levey, in *The Case of Walter Pater*, finds the essay a response to Ruskin's ostensibly negative criticism of Leonardo as well (124). But though one can find criticisms and dismissals of Leonardo in Ruskin, as Levey has, his major statements in *Modern Painters* and *Stones of Venice* are all laudatory.

9. For a discussion in this mode, see A. Dwight Culler, 182–184.

10. Sawyer notes *Stones of Venice* as marking a shift from *Modern Painters* whereby art, instead of offering a mode of transcending time, is described in historical terms (77).

11. Thus DeLaura persuasively reads Pater's analysis of Winckelmann's Hellenism as a response to Arnold's ideas of cultural balance in "Pagan and Medieval Religious Sentiment" (202–222).

12. Hill identifies a number of possible French sources for Pater's idea of a renaissance in the twelfth century, particularly Jules Michelet's *Histoire de France* (*Renaissance*, 303–304). The first great work in English on the subject is C. H. Haskins, *The Renaissance of the Twelfth Century*.

13. Pater's use of Hegel has been extensively discussed. I am particularly indebted to Dale's analysis in *The Victorian Critic*, 226–232, and to Hill's detailed location of borrowings in his critical notes to "Winckelmann" (412–443). Ward discusses Hegel's influence upon Pater more generally and extensively but with less critical balance (43–77). Both Dale (241–242) and Hill (440) follow Germain d'Hangest (2: 348, 352–353) in differentiating Pater from Hegel in his refusal to follow the German philosopher's belief in the necessity to transcend art (see also DeLaura, 211). No critic I know, however, has discussed in any detail how Pater's divergence from Hegel shapes his use of him—they generally sep-

arate use from divergence—nor why Pater would use so extensively a philosopher whose ultimate conclusions he shared so little.

14. This is essentially Hayden White's analysis of the narrative structure in Burckhardt's history of the Renaissance, in *Metahistory*, 230-264.

15. For an extensive discussion of Victorian conceptions of a Greek ideal, see Richard Jenkyns, *The Victorians and Ancient Greece*. Jenkyns's discussion of Pater is unfortunately extremely brief.

Chapter Three

1. Although the contexts vary, the significance critics give the terms "Pater," "aesthete," and "aestheticism" remains constant. Thus Paul Bové, citing with approval William Spanos, accuses deconstruction of an aestheticism that creates free-floating texts (Arac, 4-5). Michael Sprinker explicitly connects Pater with Hartmann in order to criticize the hegemony of "aesthetic humanism" (Arac, 54-55, 61). Howard Felperin cites a number of critics who claim deconstruction is a throwback "to the dandyist aestheticism of the nineties, a displaced religion of art" (111). And whenever Pater shows up in Frank Lentricchia's *After the New Criticism*, it is to imprison yet another critic or critical tradition behind his thick wall of personality (66, 78, 329). Daniel T. O'Hara gives the only extended analysis that connects the ills of deconstruction with the ills of Pater in *The Romance of Interpretation: Visionary Criticism from Pater to de Man*. O'Hara's analyses of Pater and de Man, like DeLaura's of Pater and Gasché's of Derrida and de Man, have so forwarded my own that our divergence over the political consequences of their positions has seemed that much more striking to me, and so, of course, I have fastened upon those divergences in the notes that follow.

2. We can see the link such critics make between New Criticism and aestheticism in William Cain's aside on R. P. Blackmur: "When Blackmur acts as a high priest of criticism, his essays are obscure, silly, and seem a throwback to the aestheticism of Pater and Wilde" (155). Once we see New Criticism as a renewed religion of self-referential texts, then we can see deconstruction as only a new New Criticism. So many critics have taken this position that one cannot begin to cite them all. Representative arguments are perhaps those of Gerald Graff's *Literature Against Itself* (151-181), Frank Lentricchia's *Criticism and Social Change* (38-52), and Michael Fischer's *Does Deconstruction Make Any Difference?* (92-97).

3. Rodolphe Gasché has offered the most extended attacks on the use of Derrida in literary criticism in "Deconstruction as Criticism" and, more recently, *The Tain of the Mirror* (255-318). One sees more polemical statements of the same position in Christopher Norris's *Derrida* (18-27) and Michael Ryan's *Marxism and Deconstruction* (37).

4. E. D. Hirsch, particularly in *Validity in Interpretation*, uses Husserl's concept of an intentionality prior to any specific act of perception or any phenomenal moment whatever to ground his claim of the dependence of meaning upon intention. In so doing, however, he redefines Husserl's transcendental moment

into a historically specific moment prior to any speech act. I introduce this distinction here since Hirsch's concept, which is the definition operating for most Anglo-American critics, has caused considerable distortion in the understanding of much of Derrida, particularly the responses to one of the first of his essays that was translated into English, "Signature Event Context." Lentricchia's discussion of Hirsch's use of Husserl (*After the New Criticism*, 270–278) is quite helpful here.

5. Fischer (36–41), among numerous others, takes this to be the point of "Signature Event Context."

6. Leitch (50–51), summarizing J. Hillis Miller, makes both these extensions. We need not here question the accuracy of this summary. Miller has been read this way often enough by friends and enemies to make the point about the extension of Derrida.

7. This accounts for the difficulty Derrida has, even insists on, in answering the seemingly simple question of whether he is a philosopher. In one interview, in the space of a couple of pages, he first says that he has "attempted more and more systematically to find a non-site, or a non-philosophical site, from which to question philosophy," and then he categorizes this questioning as philosophy interrogating itself. And thus, in response to another question, he insists that it would be "naive" to think that one could get outside metaphysics (Kearney, 108, 111).

8. I quote here from the translation in *Speech and Phenomena* because it contains an opening in which this phrase appears that is not included in the translation in *Margins*.

9. In a certain sense, my argument works out more carefully Norris's claim against Rorty's criticism: "Rorty has a strong point here, but one that Derrida himself concedes on numerous occasions. It is only possible to criticize existing institutions from *within* an inherited language" (*Derrida*, 16). But while Derrida does say this frequently enough, and it is one obvious answer to those who criticize him for using logic to destroy logic, it does not really respond directly to Rorty in its generality since Rorty questions the coherence of this counterclaim. Norris's argument is thus, at least formally, circular. I intend these details to break that circle.

10. Approximate as this analogy may be, it is not merely fanciful. When Paul Ricoeur contrasts phenomenology and structuralism in these terms, particularly in *The Conflict of Interpretations*, phenomenology always provides an awareness of consciousness spoken of in religious language that confronts structuralism's concern with abstract, scientific form.

11. This is, obviously, a rather drastically reduced precis of *Cartesian Meditations*. Derrida more frequently addresses those Husserlian texts that complicate the situation with reference to problems of language or purely ideational science. Staten (42–43) offers an exemplary summary of Derrida's handling of Husserl's *Origins of Geometry* that shows how the problems of science from a phenomenological viewpoint reflect the problems of language, both growing out of the necessary impurity of the transcendental reduction.

12. Christopher Norris rightly notes the decontextualized notoriety of this passage (*Derrida*, 140). Proponents of "playful" deconstruction point toward it

as their guide (see, for instance, Leitch, 37-38), while critics inevitably use it to demonstrate all that is wrong about deconstruction (see Donoghue, *Ferocious Alphabets*, 165-166).

13. I should specify here that my identification of the importance of the concept of reflection as foundation in Derrida and my general discussion of him as concerned with the problem owe much to Rodolphe Gasché's *Tain of the Mirror*. The following critique of literary deconstruction is also indebted to that book, particularly in its analysis of "Deconstructive Methodology" (121-142), and to his earlier article "Deconstruction as Criticism," which specifies the importance of precisely the form of reflection that Derrida critiques to the literary criticism that tries to deploy his philosophy as a method. I specify this indebtedness here because, as will become obvious, I do not in fact think his position properly entails, as he does in these two works, the dismissal of all deconstructive literary criticism, nor, in particular, does it pertinently respond to the work of Paul de Man. Gasché's own attitude to de Man is rather more complex than these two works indicate, as a reading of two other articles, "'Setzung' and 'Ubersetzung': Notes on Paul de Man" and "In-Difference to Philosophy: De Man on Kant, Hegel, and Nietzsche," shows.

14. Fischer explicitly takes up Miller's challenge to measure deconstructive criticism by its readings (60) and finds them wanting precisely because they are unfalsifiable (70).

15. Gasché (*Tain*, 121) identifies this dual relationship of method to knowledge, but his discussion is marred by a distinction between "philosophies that scientific thinking patronizes" and that which he labels "any thinking philosophy" or "genuine philosophy." In effect, Gasché shares the Continental presumption that since the only ground of philosophy is the moment of its reflective self-naming, empiricism is an attempted opposition to philosophy rather than another version of it. Since Derrida's own use of the label "empiricism" also shares this flaw—though his criticism of its concept does not—Gasché's analysis does not suffer much from this.

16. Knapp and Michaels define this contradiction with regard to Stanley Fish as one of claiming to know that there is no position outside belief from which one might have knowledge (24-30). Spivak's statements do not precisely fall into this contradiction, although, from a certain reading, they might imply it.

17. Irene Harvey works out the problem of exemplarity in some detail in "Doubling the Space of Existence: Exemplarity in Derrida—the Case of Rousseau." She takes her critique to be directed at a moment of inattentive self-contradiction in Derrida, and yet she virtually summarizes the problems Derrida addresses in his chapter on method without ever referring to it.

18. Barbara Johnson, in this context, enacts a modesty so exemplary that it effectively turns the situation around: "Theoretical pronouncements therefore do not stand here as instruments to be used in mastering literary structures. On the contrary, it is through contact with literature that theoretical tools are useful precisely to the extent that they thereby change and dissolve in the hands of the user. Theory is here often the straight man whose precarious rectitude and hidden risibility, passion and pathos are precisely what literature has somehow already foreseen" (*The Critical Difference*, xi-xii). One might replace the word

"foreseen" with "displayed" to avoid a theoretical implication in the last sentence. But, by giving up the claim to have found a way to read firmly based on theory, rather than one that merely uses it, Johnson gives the reading experience theoretical significance rather than making it an empirical example of value.

19. Jonathan Culler, in the first chapter of *The Pursuit of Signs*, argues against the attempt to turn theories into methods of interpretation.

20. The discovery of and extended debate over de Man's wartime writings have only exacerbated this situation. Since, in Chapter 5, I will be arguing for the reformist political implications of both Derrida's and de Man's theories, I will address the now obligatory problem of de Man's collaboration in an afterword. We cannot know, however, how to construe a connection between the two theories without having a clear sense of what de Man's later theories actually do say. The early writings, after all, by any normal interpretive procedure, do *not* form part of any context that determines the meaning of—as opposed to the genesis of—the later ones.

21. De Man's refusal of the role of practical critic has all too clearly frustrated those who seek to measure him as one. Leitch (48–49) expresses a frustration with him that he diagnoses as de Man's refusal to make "programmatic statements" of theoretical implications, but his relief in dealing with a critic like Miller, who "in the American grain . . . thinks of himself and acts like a 'practical critic' " (51), is so palpable that one can clearly see what he misses in de Man. Critics, used to evaluating theoretical statements by the validity of readings offered in support of them, also comment on the seeming arbitrariness of his statements. Thus Graff complains that "he shows no interest in giving reasons or evidence for his interpretations" (*Literature Against Itself*, 175), and Lentricchia labels his work "The Rhetoric Authority" because of his contention that de Man just declaratively states his thought without feeling the need to defend it (*After the New Criticism*, 283–317). As we will see, frequently de Man does not defend interpretive statements, simply because they are not really interpretive statements and like Derrida's analysis of foundational discourse they are not capable of empirical evidencing. Not surprisingly, these critics also miss the logical articulation he does offer or they merely dismiss it.

22. Lentricchia's chapter on de Man in *After the New Criticism* is the earliest work I know of to delineate the differences between de Man's pre-deconstructive writings and his later positions. The polemical overkill of that essay, which much of my criticism responds to, unfortunately occludes much telling analysis, as is the case with the book as a whole. Norris's more recent *Paul de Man* takes as part of its thesis this difference between early and late de Man. In an attempt to make the later de Man accord with the Kantian Derrida of his book of that title, however, Norris warps de Man as much, though in a different direction, as de Man's critics do.

23. Gearhart, in "Philosophy *Before* Literature," argues with Gasché's " 'Setzung' and 'Übersetzung'" for positing a difference between *Blindness and Insight* and *Allegories of Reading*. To the extent that Gasché does make such a distinction—and he does seem to—my reading follows his.

24. Lentricchia draws attention to the importance of the concept of lucidity throughout de Man's career (*Criticism and Social Change*, 41–42).

25. Stanley Corngold's "Error in Paul de Man" discusses this element of de Man's thought, which is also connected to the theme of lucidity discussed by Lentricchia. Like Lentricchia, Corngold distorts his analysis with a polemical tone and end that seem in excess of his topic.

26. I do not mean to suggest that de Man changed his theory of literary language under the influence of Derrida. Both de Man (*Resistance to Theory*, 117) and Derrida (*Mémoires*, 127) mark their initial common interest to have been Rousseau and his *Essay on the Origin of Languages*. And de Man's dissent from Derrida's deconstruction, based on a claim that Rousseau's literariness constituted the insight Derrida denied to him (*Mémoires*, 130), could not respond to Derrida's treatment of literary language in "The Double Session," since the essays of *Blindness and Insight*, if not the letters Derrida cites in *Mémoires*, predate the publication of "The Double Session" and its analysis of Mallarmé and mimesis in *Tel Quel*. Rather, the congruence of their thinking seems to arise from this common ground in the concern with literary language.

27. Lentricchia, for instance, contends that "de Man everywhere aligns himself with those Continental critics who bring the bad news that a 'literary or poetic consciousness is [not] in any way a privileged consciousness'" (*After the New Criticism*, 301). Not surprisingly, he thus finds de Man's definition of literary language a self-contradiction (302). To the extent that I follow Lentricchia's basic analysis of de Man's pre-deconstructive phenomenology, I will be working out a similar contradiction here. But that contradiction is in de Man's epistemology, not in his definition of the constitutive doubleness of literary language. And it does not extend throughout his career.

28. This may well be the basis for Gasché's critique of de Man's literary criticism as confusing self-reflection with deconstruction ("Deconstruction as Criticism," 206–208).

29. Derrida states his agreement, stipulating that he extends the self-deconstructive quality beyond "so-called literary texts" and qualifying his agreement as dependent upon the definition of the reflexive "itself" in the claim that a text deconstructs itself (*Mémoires*, 124). The first qualification stresses that the self-deconstructive activity of literary language is a linguistic quality, not a feature of the category of literature. The second specifies the reflexiveness to be a feature of language and not any privileged mode of consciousness.

30. Again, my argument may be taken as a working out in detail of Norris's claim that "the word 'reflection' has at least as much weight in this sentence as the idea that literature somehow undoes the truth-claims of philosophy" (*Paul de Man*, 69), but, as with Derrida, Norris wants to use this reweighing to replace de Man in a philosophical *as opposed to* a literary perspective, an opposition that I think both writers want precisely to comprehend. Norris's weight on the word "reflection," in any case, would certainly subject de Man to Gasché's critique in both "Deconstruction as Criticism" and *The Tain of the Mirror*. To repeat, I want to argue precisely the coincidence of the Derrida outlined by his philosophical critics with de Man as a theorist of literary language.

31. Fischer, while disputing the specifics of de Man's reading, for instance, begins by stating that "de Man correctly notes that the questions critics have asked *of* the poem repeat the questions asked *in* the poem" (64).

32. Thus Culler argues that one deconstructive consequence is the treatment of prior interpretations of a text as part of the problem of interpreting that text (*On Deconstruction*, 268). Ellis responds that "traditional criticism too, 'may' (often does?) treat prior interpretation as incomplete rather than simply mistaken and without any important relationship to the text" (73). But Ellis's complaint misses the mark. De Man does not address the completeness of specific interpretations but the problem of the project of interpretation as it emerges within the text. Part of the problem here is Ellis's unspoken assumption that deconstructive criticism must be about the interpretation of specific texts. Surprisingly for one who has argued against that as a sole concern of literary criticism, in the section of his book on deconstructive consequences, Culler's argument sometimes does suggest, though it does not necessitate, such a concern.

Chapter Four

1. Eagleton (*Literary Theory*, 22–30) specifies the importance of Arnold's formulations about literature and religion to the founding of modern literature departments in English universities. To less polemical ends, Graff notes both the influence of Arnold and its creation of an inaugural contradiction between those who wanted the new discipline to have an academically recognizable field of knowledge in philological and historical scholarship and Arnoldians who wanted to teach literary value (*Professing Literature*, 3–5). The contradiction that Graff details was inevitable once one accepted Arnold's distinction between literary value and that of other discourses.

2. Kermode (18–22) clearly outlines the importance of Pater to the concept of what he calls "the artist in isolation."

3. Terry Eagleton has made the same kind of claim more broadly: "Deconstructionism, then, can salvage some of the dominant themes of traditional bourgeois liberalism by a desperate, last-ditch strategy: by sacrificing the subject itself, at least in any of its customary modes. Political quietism and compromise are preserved ... by a dispersal of the subject so radical as to render it impotent as any kind of agent at all, least of all a revolutionary one. If the proletariat can be reduced to text, trace, symptom or effect, many tedious wrangles can be overcome at a stroke" (*Walter Benjamin*, 138–139). Since Eagleton never addresses any deconstructive text with any specificity, much less precision, one cannot work out the leaps in his logic in the same way one can in Lentricchia's more careful argument. It seems to follow the same basic itinerary, however. Barbara Foley, in "The Politics of Deconstruction" (Davis and Schliefer, 113–134), also follows Eagleton's extension of Lentricchia's critique to all of deconstruction, explicitly Derrida's.

4. In addition to the distinctions made between Derrida and Yale deconstruction in terms of the former's political significance—by Lentricchia in *After the New Criticism* and Ryan in *Marxism and Deconstruction*, both mentioned above—even Terry Eagleton, who generally criticizes all of deconstruction as

an extreme manifestation of bourgeois idealism, at times will allow Derrida political effect (see, for instance, *Literary Theory*, 148–150). Suzanne Gearhart also criticizes de Man for draining Derrida of his historical ends by idealizing literature (72–80). Oddly, she concentrates on the moments in which de Man struggles explicitly with his own attempt to engage history in opposition to Derrida's double-edged but essentially philosophical abstractions about the relations between history and metaphysics.

5. Derrida's review of Foucault appears in *Writing and Difference* as "Cogito and the History of Madness." Foucault's response has been translated as "My Body, This Paper, This Fire." Two responses exemplifying the formulation of the debate as over the problem of formal and historical interpretation are John Frow's "Foucault and Derrida" and Edward Said's chapter in *The World, the Text and the Critic* (178–225).

6. On the identification of form, or ideality, with essence, see the discussion in Staten, 23–24.

7. This is the theme of Lentricchia's chapter on de Man in *After the New Criticism* (283–317). Again, in contrast with most of de Man's most vehement critics, Lentricchia often does identify the themes at issue despite his own critical assumptions, which determine his antagonism.

8. Neil Hertz's "Lurid Figures" (Waters and Godzich, 82–104) and Rodolphe Gasché's "In-Difference to Philosophy: de Man on Kant, Hegel, and Nietzsche" (Waters and Godzich, 259–294) both contain instructive discussions of what Hertz terms "de Man's forcing of his texts" (103).

9. Kevin Newmark works out in some detail the connections between arbitrary narrative sequence and de Man's ideas of history in "Paul de Man's History" (Waters and Godzich, 121–135), though with regard to a later discussion of Baudelaire.

10. Eagleton (*Walter Benjamin*, 137–139) and Jameson (124–125) both connect deconstruction, along with various theories grouped together under the label poststructuralist, as both an extreme formulation of and a result of the dissolution of bourgeois liberalism and its ideology of the subject and individualism. I have cited critiques of deconstruction as quietist numerous times.

11. Lentricchia (*After the New Criticism*, 39–44 and elsewhere) sees Kant as reaffirming Plato's original separating out of aesthetics in his sense of its disinterestedness and special role. Interestingly, Christopher Norris (*Paul de Man*, 53) sees Kant's separating out of aesthetics as a politically effective move, protecting the political from aesthetic overreaching. He proceeds to argue that de Man in his late essays defends this sequestering of aesthetics to disengage himself from it. In effect, Norris shares the beliefs of deconstruction's opponents that there is an inside to language and aesthetics and that to draw an equivalence between history, politics, ideology, and the structures of language or literature thus reduces those modes of thought to the mere linguistic or mere literary. He differs from his opponents in arguing that deconstruction does not intend such a reduction because it does not intend such an equivalence. Miller's recent reversal of the normal schema, drawing from Kant's categorical imperative an ethic of respect for a text analogous to respect for an individual (*The Ethics of Reading*, 13–39), tries to restage Kant in such a way that his ethics will

create an enclosed aesthetic space. The problem with the logic is that Kant's ethical imperatives, which are free choices, depend for their grounding on an aesthetic experience that is by definition, not by choice, disinterested. The ethic therefore cannot defend a choice of respecting a text since if the choice exists as a matter of aesthetics the ethic no longer has a ground outside the aesthetic that Miller thinks it rules.

12. By discussing first de Man's treatment of Kant and then his readings of Hegel, I will be reversing the chronological order in which the essays appeared, which might or might not have corresponded to the order in which de Man would have placed them in the book he was planning, in favor of an order that begins with general issues of aesthetics and ideology and moves to specific issues of the connection between aesthetics and the ideology of the ostensible conflict between literary theory and literary experience. I am not of course proposing this order as anything more than a convenience to the argument here.

13. Gasché, in "In-Difference to Philosophy" (Waters and Godzich, 267), faults de Man for his thinking the section on the sublime problematic. He notes that its presence in the book is historically determined, "a concession to eighteenth-century aesthetics," and that Kant broke new ground in his discussion of the beautiful, and he quotes Cassirer on the absolute clarity of the analysis of the sublime. Oddly, this makes rather than refutes de Man's point. If historical context explains the presence of the section, then it is indeed superfluous to the work's theme. And yet if this historical determination allowed Kant to be clear in his analysis, then the clarity would result from the very lack of intrinsic connection.

14. Gasché's complaints about de Man's use of analogy (Waters and Godzich, 272–273) seem more apt where others of his examples of de Man's ostensible misreadings of philosophical texts do not, and verify his general argument about the relationship between de Man's forcing of texts and the strength of his questioning of philosophy.

15. But see Neil Hertz's analysis, in "Lurid Figures" (Waters and Godzich, 82–83), of how this ascription of the melodramatic to the linguistic works.

16. Geuss (378–379) makes this mistake at a local moment in his critique. More noticeably, Norris bases his entire reading of the essay on the notion that de Man deconstructs Hegel's belief in the power of the symbol (*Paul de Man*, 28–35), despite de Man's explicit denial of this to Geuss's charge.

17. Both Geuss (376–378) and Gasché (Waters and Godzich, 269–271) note the problems in de Man's use of the term "symbol." Geuss also contests de Man's interpretation of "art is for us a thing of the past" (380). I have not read any criticism of his treatment of Hegel's sublime along these lines, but de Man's reading of the term follows the same pattern of "misuse" as his reading of "symbol."

18. Gasché (Waters and Godzich, 269–270) notes the correspondence between de Man's application of the symbolic to the *Aesthetics* and Hegel's definition of the symbolic imagination in the *Encyclopedia*.

19. De Man here follows Derrida's argument in "The Pit and the Pyramid" (*Margins*, 71–108).

Chapter Five

1. Pater has fared somewhat better among critics of the fine arts than he has among literary critics. Richard Wollheim, for instance, though his conclusions differ from mine, has argued that Pater's theories of painting must be seen in the light of his epistemology (155–176), reminding us that "by the standards of his time, though barely of ours, Pater lived the life of a professional philosopher" (158).

2. Thus Howard Felperin ends his "deconstruction" of Marxism with the claim that deconstruction's political extension is anarchism, by which one assumes he means that both entail the absence of all laws (73).

3. Derrida also discusses the concept of a necessary policing of conventional rules in "The Law of Genre."

4. Thus Michael Fischer complains, "I criticize deconstructionists ... not for objecting to the academic status quo but for undermining their own objections by questioning the cognitive status of literature and criticism" (xiii).

5. Culler applies deconstructive displacement to an analysis of psychoanalytic definitions of the female to show how it simultaneously marginalizes and centralizes the female (*On Deconstruction*, 167–172). On its own terms, the argument is quite strong, but one wonders why it does not run afoul of his own criticism of Michael Ryan's project of linking deconstruction and Marxism: "Such projects risk bathos—does one need Derrida to unravel the contradictions of right-wing political rhetoric?" (158).

6. Critics who see the book as moving toward Christianity, if not embracing it, have included Pater's first biographer, A. C. Benson (90), and more recently David DeLaura, who argues (165–305) for a long movement toward sympathy with Christianity; Monsman (*Pater's Portraits*, 95–97); Charlesworth (50); and most recently Clyde de L. Ryals (157–174). Critics who see more continuity between *The Renaissance* and *Marius*, a continuity that entails a maintained conflict between skeptical empiricism and idealism, include U. C. Knoepflmacher (189–222), F. C. McGrath (45), and most recently and most sensitively William Buckler (*The Victorian Imagination*, 278–279, and *Walter Pater: The Critic as Artist*, 266–272).

7. Linda Dowling (110–140) gives an admirable analysis of the workings of Pater's style, his theory of Euphuism, and the importance of those formal matters to the place of *Marius* in the decadence.

8. The best extended discussion of debates over religion in the second half of the nineteenth century is Owen Chadwick's *Victorian Church, Part II*.

9. Thus John Wordsworth writes to Pater: "Could you indeed have known the dangers into which you were likely to lead minds weaker than your own, you would, I believe, have paused" (Seiler, *The Critical Heritage*, 62), while John Morley, though with some reservations, writes an appreciative review, praising Pater's doctrine's escape from "the cramped narrowness" of theology (Seiler, *The Critical Heritage*, 70). On the importance of religion as a device of social control in late Victorian England, see McCleod, 24–25.

10. That Pater's self-resistance cannot ground either a conservative reintroduction of religion on cultural grounds or a conservative regrounding of cul-

tural values on a secularized, and even antagonist, psycho-history we may see by noting the responses of two writers influenced by Pater, T. S. Eliot and Harold Bloom. Bloom properly defines the common ground between Pater and Eliot as an interest in moments of poetic illumination (*Ringers in the Tower*, 188). Since Eliot wanted to base his conservative and Christianized version of literary culture on this moment, which Pater had made relentlessly secular and even scientific, he had to dismiss Pater as "incapable of sustained reasoning" ("Arnold and Pater," 390). Since Bloom wants to base on those moments his re-vision of the literary tradition, one that his later works show the explicit conservatism of, he questions whether, by killing off Marius before he would be forced to face "the theological and moral exclusiveness of Christianity," Pater earned the structural irony of the novel's ending (*Ringers in the Tower*, 182). A better and more sympathetic critic of Pater than Eliot, Bloom asks a far more acute question. The answer to it lies in identifying the structural irony with Pater's position as narrator rather than with Marius's final position, and connecting it with his aestheticist reconsiderations of his own aestheticism, as I have been doing here. That answer, however, would not aid Bloom in his project.

11. O'Hara (42), in regard to Marius's extension of his aesthetic philosophy to an at least partial acceptance of "A wonderful order, actually in possession of human life!—grown inextricably through and through it; penetrating into its laws, its very language, its mere habits of decorum, in a thousand half-conscious ways" (*Marius*, 2: 27), claims that "Pater is here talking about the Roman bureaucracy and its 'rhetoric of life' by which the empire imposes its laws and its rituals, some of them quite nasty, upon millions of people," and thus concludes that the argument for accepting this system, "whether in Rome or in Victorian London," as a matter of good taste is rather suspect. His argument breaks upon the unlikelihood that the order Pater is describing has anything even remotely to do with the Roman bureaucracy or its imperial laws. In context, it fairly clearly refers to a culture predating the Empire, even if it extends to include it. Moreover, Marius's critical attitude toward the Stoicism of Marcus Aurelius's court philosopher, Cornelius Fronto, and finally toward Marcus Aurelius himself, indicates that his aestheticist acceptance of a reigning culture does not extend to a support of an imperial government. His acceptance of a Christian community in the end, despite his lack of belief, since that community was in enough resistance to the Imperial government to earn its persecution, further indicates a lack of political quietism, even if Marius always does remain more observer than participant. The comparison between Rome and Victorian England, which Pater draws explicitly, and which had become virtually a cliché of contemporary social criticism of Victorian complacency—see, for instance, T.H.S. Escott's "Two Cities and Two Seasons—Rome and London," which A. Dwight Culler (258) identifies as a source of *Marius*—only furthers a reading of the novel as resistant rather than quietist. O'Hara's reading of *Marius* prepares for his later reading of de Man, but does not really accept the novel on its own terms. Since O'Hara's larger positions prefigure some of my own, perhaps a reading focused on his book would interpret his forcings with the same care with which I attend to de Man's.

12. Peggy Kamuf, in "Pieces of Resistance" (Waters and Godzich, 139–147), has discussed these meanings to de Man's title.

13. See Corngold, "Potential Violence in Paul de Man," 117. Since this article is a review of Christopher Norris's *Paul de Man*, it has a certain looseness to its argument that may be a matter of genre. Corngold's more careful and well-known article "Error in Paul de Man," however, amounts to the same charge.

14. Jameson identifies ideology as a representational structure (30); his formulation of history as an absent cause also finds the evidence of that cause in the formal contradictions of textual representation (35). Lentricchia as well, following an analysis of Foucault, links his work with Derrida's by seeing in "the presiding logocentric urges, rules, and oppositions which have guided the production of meaning from Plato to the present day" (*After the New Criticism*, 208) the manifestation of ideological constraint. Lentricchia has recently distanced himself both from Foucault and the new historicists influenced by Foucault (see *Ariel and the Police*, 30–102), but they would all agree with de Man's basic presumption behind a critique of ideology through literature, even if they might not privilege literature over economics as de Man does.

15. Annette Kolodny, in "Dancing through the Minefield: Some Observations on the Theory, Practice, and Politics of a Feminist Literary Criticism," expresses the clearest and most thorough skepticism toward standards and values as part of a feminist critique of literary values and canons. Patrocinio P. Schweickart's "Reading Ourselves: Toward a Feminist Theory of Reading," in an impressive mediation between radical critiques of inevitable cultural bias and definitions of positive criteria for constructing feminist readings, ends by arguing for giving up deconstructive analysis for a positive hermeneutic based on utopian ideals constructed out of a dialectic between negative and positive readings of texts. The mode by which she argues against a deconstructive feminism, however, shows its clear attraction for her: "The feminist story may yet end with the recognition of the impossibility of reading. But this remains to be seen. At this stage I think it behooves us to *choose* the dialectical over the deconstructive plot. It is dangerous for feminists to be overly enamored with the theme of impossibility" (56). Lillian S. Robinson, in "Treason Our Text: Feminist Challenges to the Literary Canon," clearly charts the possible feminist responses to the canon compressed here.

16. Knapp and Michaels (24–30) and Catherine Gallagher ("Re-Covering the Social in Recent Literary Theory," 42–43) both note Fish's implicit inconsistency here, though from different perspectives.

17. Terry Eagleton, for instance, has worked out Marxist grounds for canon evaluation (in *Criticism and Ideology*, 162–187) that, as Smith (189) notes, wind up justifying "the whole Leavisite canon." Perhaps more pointedly, when Schweickart offers communal values as an alternative system, she evidences them as felt literary values in a justification of Lawrence's *Rainbow*.

18. Both Culler (*On Deconstruction*, 42) and Smith (24) have noted the effectiveness of the feminist critique of the canon. Since I have criticized some of Culler's formulations above, I should note that he argued explicitly for a vital connection between deconstruction and feminist criticism at a time when

most male critics, at least, refused to recognize the significance of feminist approaches.

19. Defining a concept as foundational and refusing to do away with it can itself become a form of political act, it should be noted. Thus, in "Racism's Last World" (Gates, 329–338), Derrida posits apartheid as both the ultimate term for racism and, from the perspective of a futurity that is only a wish at the time of the essay, the last term used to describe it. From this artificed perspective—a political version of the perspective literary language allows him upon philosophy, perhaps—Derrida can both implicate various Western values in the maintenance of apartheid and note the at least ostensible otherness of the practice to those values. Defining a marginal and terminal concept and word here as foundational becomes a political act, one that works toward an end of a practice by fixing upon it the term that defines it. Derrida makes this strategy clear in his response to a critique of the effectiveness of his practice (Gates, 356–359).

20. Lawrence Schuetz's "Suppressed 'Conclusion' to *The Renaissance* and Walter Pater's Modern Image" is probably the most recent case for taking Pater's footnote to the revised "Conclusion" purely at face value. Ian Small, before the new evidence confirming his position, responded to that essay in "Pater and the Suppressed 'Conclusion' to *The Renaissance*: Comment," in which he argued that Pater was responding to surfacing connections between aestheticism and homosexuality. Richard Jenkyns, in *The Victorians and Ancient Greece* (291), argues for the reality of that connection: "Towards the end of the century . . . the cachet of the aesthetic movement gave a certain glamour to what before had been literally unthinkable, and well-educated inverts, who in an earlier generation might have been appalled by their own nature, began to seek carnal satisfaction." The homophobic tone of this description—including even the Victorian term "invert"—may make it less valuable as a historical comment, though, than as a late manifestation of the attitudes surrounding Pater.

21. *The New Republic* was serialized in *Belgravian* between June and December 1876, so its first publication does slightly precede the second edition of *The Renaissance*. Perhaps the most notorious moment in Mallock's caricature is Mr. Rose's statement, "I rather look upon life as a chamber, which we decorate as we would decorate the chamber of the woman or the youth that we love" (27). Oddly, Mallock, in *The New Republic*, seems either unaware of or unconcerned with the skeptical tone of the "Conclusion," which most others reacted to explicitly (Levey, 143, notes this as well). He certainly was concerned with skepticism at Oxford, though, as the book's caricature of Jowett amply shows.

22. The details of these incriminating letters and the role they played in Pater's loss of the proctorship were first discussed by Laurel Brake (Dodd, 39–54) and David Newsome (192). The incident came to light only with the availability of Arthur Benson's diaries detailing his research for his brief biography of Pater. In an attempt to detach Pater from the earlier scandal, Benson falsified his account of this incident in ways Brake details. The relevant passages of Benson's diaries have recently been published in Seiler, *Walter Pater, A Life Remembered*, 253–260. Richard Ellmann (58) quotes portions of one letter

Jowett had. Billie Andrew Inman's unpublished paper "The Estrangement Between Walter Pater and Benjamin Jowett and Its Connection to the Relationship Between Pater and William M. Hardinge" gives the fullest account of the incident, based on substantial new research. Inman verifies the outlines of Brake's discovery but doubts that Jowett blackmailed Pater into never standing for office at Oxford, as Brake, following Edmund Gosse's account to Benson, supposed. I would like to thank Professor Inman for allowing me to see this research.

23. My argument owes an obvious general debt to Eve Kosofsky Sedgwick's *Between Men: English Literature and Male Homosocial Desire*. Regenia Gagnier's analysis in *Idylls of the Marketplace* (137–210) of the workings of homosexuality and homophobia in the writings of Oscar Wilde and public responses to them also needs to be noted here, particularly since Wilde experienced more publicly the persecution Pater avoided almost entirely by keeping his life so private after the blackmailing at Oxford that we still do not have a satisfactory biography of him.

Afterword

1. Geoffrey Hartman's "Blindness and Insight" has been included in his article "Looking Back on Paul de Man" (Waters and Godzich, 3–24). Roger Kimball's rejoinder now appears in his book *Tenured Radicals*. Christopher Norris's response appears as a "Postscript" to *Paul de Man*. Barbara Johnson has added an introduction on the issue to the paperback edition of *A World of Difference*. And the collection of critical reactions *Responses*, including Jacques Derrida's *Critical Inquiry* article "Like the Sound of the Sea Deep Within a Shell: Paul de Man's War," has also come out.

2. Oddly, very few critics have taken the fairly obvious position of claiming that the earlier writings have no obvious theoretical connection with the later ones—whatever their pertinence to a comprehensive account of de Man's intellectual history and biography. To their credit, two of de Man's sternest critics, Gerald Graff, in "Looking Past the de Man Case" (Hamacher, Hertz, and Keenan, 246–254), and Denis Donoghue, in "The Strange Case of Paul de Man," while reiterating their reservations about de Man's theories, have resisted easy retrospective justifications of their positions and have argued that there is no theoretical connection between the politics of early and late de Man. I call such a position an obvious one simply because it recognizes the realities of a large interval of years between the two bodies of writing and the clear differences in their content. One hardly has to contend for "a post-structuralist critique of the unified subject" (Wiener, "The Responsibilities of Friendship," 800) to think that a unified subject might have produced different theories at different times, particularly since no one contended for an explicitly fascist content to the later writings before the revelation of the earlier ones. Possibly so few of either de Man's critics or his supporters have taken this position simply because it leaves one with nothing of interest to say about the early writings and no new position on the late ones.

3. Catherine Gallagher has commented on the absolute predictability of the responses in "Blindness and Hindsight" (Hamacher, Hertz, and Keenan, 204–207).

4. There are exceptions here. J. Hillis Miller, while never actually denying the undeniable, nevertheless in the rather unsavory rhetoric of correcting the inexcusable errors of others, writes as if de Man's position on anti-Semitism were not as bad as it might have been because it is rhetorically complex and as if the aesthetic reservations he makes about collaborationist authors he praises were reservations about their ideologies (Hamacher, Hertz, and Keenan, 335–336).

5. This argument, in one version or another, has been forwarded by Jeffrey Mehlman and Frank Lentricchia (as quoted by Jon Wiener in "Deconstructing de Man," 23), by David Lehman in *Newsweek* (63), and, in a more academic venue, by Stanley Corngold ("Potential Violence in Paul de Man," 133).

6. I have by this time argued sufficiently against the charges of relativism and nihilism by interpreting de Man's criticism so that even those unpersuaded might at least predict what I would say in an extended reading of "Excuses (*Confessions*)," the chapter on Rousseau at issue here. Briefly, de Man argues that, to the extent that an accurate confession operates as a form of self-exculpation, it always becomes an excuse. Thus an accurate confession can always be offered in bad faith as an excuse. Outlining a problem within a rhetorical possibility hardly determines an alibi for de Man's own past or for his failure to confess, though. The passage cited particularly ill suits the argument antagonistic critics want to make of it: excuses in this argument do not mean adequate exculpations but precisely rhetorical alibis. So when de Man argues that one can always excuse a crime, he hardly means that the excuse will be a satisfactory response. In the light of all too many excuses one frequently hears for public crimes, one would have thought that his argument that people always do find excuses for even the bleakest of crimes, far from being "moral idiocy" (Lehman, 65), would have been fairly unexceptionable. In the same terms, those supporters who have argued that, since de Man has shown that all confessions are potentially in bad faith, the only good-faith confession he could make was a restraint from confessing (see Hartman's argument in Waters and Godzich, 22, and Felman, 729–734) confuse the relevance of his argument. Although it may be difficult for others to read the authenticity of a confession—and the essay specifies that it is about a "reading-moment" (*Allegories of Reading*, 278)— that difficulty hardly alleviates whatever responsibility one might have to confess. Hartman seems to realize this when he concludes that "despite his own attitude on 'excuses' such forthrightness might have been more effective, as well as morally clear" (Waters and Godzich, 23).

7. All translations from the French are mine.

8. Numbers of critics, of course, have noted the centrality of aesthetic concern in these articles. Too many of them have used it as a mode of excuse. The best definition of what de Man did seems to me William Flesch's: "De Man made a Faustian bargain, almost literally. The tradeoff meant that he'd do a great deal for the Nazi propaganda machine, as long as the propaganda was inflected in such a way as to convey de Man's own genuinely held aesthetic and

cultural convictions.... This means that he would have toed the line as much as was required.... he did very largely toe it, at least as long as it gave him room to argue his own literary and cultural beliefs" (Hamacher, Hertz, and Keenan, 174).

9. One sees precisely how this argument works in one of the articles with which de Man's appeared. Arguing that contemporary painting was "judaized" (as de Man claims literature was not), one Georges Marlier goes on to claim that Flemish art nevertheless was free of Jewish influence and therefore to be praised (*Wartime Writings*, 289–290). Although de Man does argue that all literature, not just Flemish literature, is free of Jewish influence, the logic of his anti-Semitism is identical.

10. See particularly Marjorie Perloff, "Response to Jacques Derrida" (775), and John Brenkman and Jules David Law, "Resetting the Agenda" (805).

11. Not only is this not a suitably rummy position, but it cannot easily be made into a critique of de Man's activities specifically. Thus Walter Kendrick, who begins by being the only critic I know of who makes the connection I am proposing here, immediately shades off into a lurid and not precisely logical analogy. He starts by claiming that, "sealing literature in its own history and governed by its own rules, the de Man of 1941 sought to exempt poets and novelists from responsibility for the doings of the nonliterary world.... The de Man of the 1980s did exactly the same thing." But he concludes that "if Yale had required its Jewish students to wear a yellow star, no doubt Professor de Man would have gone on writing his dense and difficult essays" (Kendrick, 7). But there would have been nothing to have stopped de Man from protesting Yale's hypothetical oppression in the most vigorous possible terms and still writing the same kind of essays. Indeed, de Man sheltered Jews while he wrote far worse pieces for *Le Soir* (Hamacher, Hertz, and Keenan, 431). Equally, de Man could have written essays on the necessary social commitment of literature without doing anything about Yale's hypothetical oppression. The concept of aestheticism as a connection turns out not to be specific to de Man, troubling as it should be for his adherents. It covers too many different kinds of aesthetic position and says too little about any other beliefs of the person who writes it.

12. See particularly William Flesch's "Ancestral Voices: De Man and His Defenders" (Hamacher, Hertz, and Keenan, 173–184). Both the balance of Flesch's analysis and his specific formulations about de Man's centering upon aesthetics have helped me formulate my argument here.

13. Derrida states that he "will not engage in any negative evaluation of the press *in general*" (Hamacher, Hertz, and Keenan, 128). But all of his evaluations of journalistic treatments of this issue are negative in terms that suggest that journalism has been an intrusion into properly theoretical discussion.

Works Cited

Abrams, M. H. "Rationality and Imagination in Cultural History: A Reply to Wayne Booth." *Critical Inquiry* 2 (1976): 447–464.

Arac, Jonathan, Wlad Godzich, and Wallace Martin, eds. *The Yale Critics: Deconstruction in America.* Minneapolis: University of Minnesota Press, 1983.

Arnold, Matthew. *Complete Prose Works of Matthew Arnold.* Ed. R. H. Super. 11 vols. Ann Arbor: University of Michigan Press, 1960–1977.

Benson, A. C. *Walter Pater.* London: Macmillan, 1906.

Bloom, Allan. "Interview." *New York Times,* December 4, 1988: 51.

Bloom, Harold. "The Crystal Man." Introduction to *Selected Writings of Walter Pater.* Ed. Harold Bloom. New York: Signet, 1974.

———. *Ringers in the Tower.* Chicago: University of Chicago Press, 1971.

Brenkman, John, and Jules David Law. "Resetting the Agenda." *Critical Inquiry* 15 (1989): 804–811.

Brooks, Cleanth. *The Well Wrought Urn.* New York: Harcourt, Brace, 1947.

Brooks, Peter. *Reading for the Plot: Design and Intention in Narrative.* New York: Vintage, 1985.

Buckler, William. *The Victorian Imagination.* New York: New York University Press, 1980.

———. *Walter Pater: The Critic as Artist.* New York: New York University Press, 1987.

Cain, William. *The Crisis in Criticism.* Baltimore: Johns Hopkins University Press, 1984.

Carlyle, Thomas. *Works.* Ed. H. D. Traill. 30 vols. London: Chapman and Hall, 1896–1901.

Chadwick, Owen. *The Victorian Church, Part II.* New York: Oxford University Press, 1970.

Charlesworth, Barbara. *Dark Passages: The Decadent Consciousness in Victorian Literature.* Madison: University of Wisconsin Press, 1965.

Chatman, Seymour. *Story and Discourse: Narrative Structure in Fiction and Film.* Ithaca: Cornell University Press, 1978.

Corngold, Stanley. "Error in Paul de Man." *Critical Inquiry* 8 (1982): 489–513.

———. "Potential Violence in Paul de Man." *Critical Review* 3 (1989): 117–137.

Court, Franklin E. *Pater and His Early Critics.* Victoria, B.C.: University of Victoria English Literary Studies, 1980.

Culler, A. Dwight. *The Victorian Mirror of History.* New Haven: Yale University Press, 1985.

Culler, Jonathan. *On Deconstruction: Theory and Criticism After Structuralism.* Ithaca: Cornell University Press, 1982.

———. " 'Paul de Man's War' and the Aesthetic Ideology." *Critical Inquiry* 15 (1989): 777–783.

———. *The Pursuit of Signs.* Ithaca: Cornell University Press, 1981.

Dale, Peter Alan. *The Victorian Critic and the Idea of History*. Cambridge: Harvard University Press, 1977.

Davis, Robert Con, and Ronald Schliefer, eds. *Rhetoric and Form: Deconstruction at Yale*. Norman: University of Oklahoma Press, 1985.

DeLaura, David. *Hebrew and Hellene in Victorian England*. Austin: University of Texas Press, 1969.

De Man, Paul. *Allegories of Reading*. New Haven: Yale University Press, 1979.

———. *Blindness and Insight: Essays in the Rhetoric of Contemporary Criticism*. Minneapolis: University of Minnesota Press, 1983.

———. "Hegel on the Sublime." *Displacement: Derrida and After*. Ed. Mark Krupnik. Bloomington: Indiana University Press, 1983. 139–153.

———. "Phenomenality and Materiality in Kant." *Hermeneutics: Questions and Prospects*. Ed. Gary Shapiro and Alan Sica. Amherst: University of Massachusetts Press, 1984. 121–144.

———. "Reply to Raymond Geuss." *Critical Inquiry* 10 (1983): 383–390.

———. *The Resistance to Theory*. Minneapolis: University of Minnesota Press, 1986.

———. *The Rhetoric of Romanticism*. New York: Columbia University Press, 1984.

———. "Sign and Symbol in Hegel's *Aesthetics*." *Critical Inquiry* 8 (1982): 761–775.

———. *Wartime Writings*. Ed. Werner Hamacher, Neil Hertz, and Thomas Keenan. Lincoln: University of Nebraska Press, 1988.

Derrida, Jacques. "Discussion." *The Structuralist Controversy*. Ed. Richard Macksey and Eugenio Donato. Baltimore: Johns Hopkins University Press, 1970. 265–272.

———. *Dissemination*. Trans. Barbara Johnson. Chicago: University of Chicago Press, 1981.

———. *Edmund Husserl's "Origin of Geometry": An Introduction*. Trans. John P. Leavey, Jr. Stony Brook, NY: Nicolas Hays, 1978.

———. "The Law of Genre." Trans. Avital Ronell. *Glyph 7*. Baltimore: Johns Hopkins University Press, 1980. 202–229.

———. *Limited Inc*. Evanston, IL: Northwestern University Press, 1988.

———. *Margins of Philosophy*. Trans. Alan Bass. Chicago: University of Chicago Press, 1982.

———. *Mémoires for Paul de Man*. Trans. Cecile Lindsay, Jonathan Culler, and Eduardo Cadava. New York: Columbia University Press, 1986.

———. "No Apocalypse, Not Now (full speed ahead, seven missiles, seven missives)." *Diacritics* 20 (Summer 1984): 20–31.

———. *Of Grammatology*. Trans. Gayatri Chakravorty Spivak. Baltimore: Johns Hopkins University Press, 1976.

———. *Positions*. Trans. Alan Bass. Chicago: University of Chicago Press, 1981.

———. *Speech and Phenomena*. Trans. David B. Allison. Evanston, IL: Northwestern University Press, 1973.

———. "The Time of a Thesis: Punctuations." *Philosophy in France Today*. Ed. Alan Montefiore. Cambridge: Cambridge University Press, 1983. 34–50

―――. *Truth in Painting*. Trans. Geoff Bennington and Ian McLeod. Chicago: University of Chicago Press, 1987.

―――. *Writing and Difference*. Trans. Alan Bass. Chicago: University of Chicago Press, 1978.

d'Hangest, Germain. *Walter Pater: l'homme et l'oeuvre*. Paris: Librairie Didier, 1961.

Dodd, Phillip, ed. *Walter Pater: An Imaginative Sense of Fact*. London: Frank Cass, 1981.

Donoghue, Denis. *Ferocious Alphabets*. Boston: Little, Brown, 1981.

―――. "The Strange Case of Paul de Man." *New York Review of Books*, January 29, 1989: 32–37.

Dowling, Linda. *Language and Decadence in the Victorian Fin de Siècle*. Princeton: Princeton University Press, 1986.

Eagleton, Terry. *Criticism and Ideology*. London: New Left Books, 1976.

―――. *Literary Theory*. Minneapolis: University of Minnesota Press, 1983.

―――. *Walter Benjamin or Towards a Revolutionary Criticism*. London: NLB, 1981.

Eliot, T. S. "Arnold and Pater." *Selected Essays*. New York: Harcourt, Brace, 1964. 382–393.

Ellis, John. *Against Deconstruction*. Princeton: Princeton University Press, 1989.

Ellmann, Richard. *Oscar Wilde*. New York: Alfred A. Knopf, 1988.

Escott, T.H.S. "Two Cities and Two Seasons—Rome and London, A.D. 908–1875." *Macmillan's* 32 (July 1875): 247–258.

Evans, Lawrence, ed. *Letters of Walter Pater*. London: Oxford University Press, 1970.

Felman, Shoshana. "Paul de Man's Silence." *Critical Inquiry* 15 (1989): 704–744.

Felperin, Howard. *Beyond Deconstruction*. New York: Oxford University Press, 1985.

Fischer, Michael. *Does Deconstruction Make Any Difference?* Bloomington: Indiana University Press, 1985.

Fish, Stanley. *Is There a Text in This Class?* Baltimore: Johns Hopkins University Press, 1980.

Foucault, Michel. "My Body, This Paper, This Fire." Trans. Geoff Bennington. *Oxford Literary Review* 4 (Autumn 1979): 9–28.

Frow, John. "Foucault and Derrida." *Raritan* 5 (1985): 31–42.

Gagnier, Regenia. *Idylls of the Marketplace*. Stanford, CA: Stanford University Press, 1986.

Gallagher, Catherine. "George Eliot and *Daniel Deronda*: The Prostitute and the Jewish Question." *Sex, Politics, and Science in the Nineteenth-Century Novel*. Ed. Ruth Bernard Yeazell. Baltimore: Johns Hopkins University Press, 1986. 39–62.

―――. "Re-Covering the Social in Recent Literary Theory." *Diacritics* 12 (Winter 1982): 40–48.

Gasché, Rodolphe. "Deconstruction as Criticism." *Glyph 6*. Baltimore: Johns Hopkins University Press, 1979. 177–215.

―――. " 'Setzung' and 'Übersetzung': Notes on Paul de Man." *Diacritics* 11 (Winter 1981): 36–37.

———. *The Tain of the Mirror*. Cambridge: Harvard University Press, 1986.
Gates, Henry Louis, ed. *"Race," Writing and Difference*. Chicago: University of Chicago Press, 1986.
Gearhart, Suzanne. "Philosophy *Before* Literature: Deconstruction, Historicity, and the Work of Paul de Man." *Diacritics* 13 (Winter 1983): 63–81.
Geuss, Raymond. "A Response to Paul de Man." *Critical Inquiry* 10 (1983): 375–381.
Goodheart, Eugene. *The Skeptic Disposition in Contemporary Criticism*. Princeton: Princeton University Press, 1984.
Graff, Gerald. *Literature Against Itself: Literary Ideas in Modern Society*. Chicago: University of Chicago Press, 1979.
———. *Professing Literature: An Institutional History*. Chicago: University of Chicago Press, 1987.
Hamacher, Werner, Neil Hertz, and Thomas Keenan, eds. *Responses: On Paul de Man's Wartime Journalism*. Lincoln: University of Nebraska Press, 1989.
Harvey, Irene E. "Doubling the Space of Existence: Exemplarity in Derrida—the Case of Rousseau." *Deconstruction and Philosophy*. Ed. John Sallis. Chicago: University of Chicago Press, 1987. 60–70.
Haskins, C. H. *The Renaissance of the Twelfth Century*. Cambridge: Harvard University Press, 1927.
Hegel, G.F.W. *Aesthetics: Lectures on Fine Art*. Trans. T. M. Knox. 2 vols. Oxford: Oxford University Press, 1975.
———. *The Phenomenology of Mind*. Trans. J. B. Baillie. New York: Harper, 1967.
Hirsch, E. D. *Validity in Interpretation*. New Haven: Yale University Press, 1967.
Hobbes, Thomas. *Leviathan*. Indianapolis: Bobbs-Merrill, 1958.
Hough, Graham. *The Last Romantics*. London: Duckworth, 1949.
Hume, David. *A Treatise of Human Nature*. Ed. L. A. Selby-Bigge. Oxford: Oxford University Press, 1938.
Husserl, Edmund. *Cartesian Meditations*. Trans. Dorion Cairns. The Hague: Martin Nijhoff, 1977.
Inman, Billie Andrew. "The Estrangement Between Walter Pater and Benjamin Jowett and Its Connection to the Relationship Between Pater and Jowett." Unpublished manuscript.
Iser, Wolfgang. *Walter Pater: The Aesthetic Moment*. Trans. David Anthony Wilson. Cambridge: Cambridge University Press, 1987.
Jakobson, Roman. Vol. 3 of *Selected Writings*. Ed. Stephen Rudy. The Hague: Mouton, 1981.
James, William. *Essays in Pragmatism*. Ed. Alburey Castell. New York: Hafner Press, 1948.
———. *"Pragmatism" and "The Meaning of Truth."* Cambridge: Harvard University Press, 1975.
Jameson, Fredric. *The Political Unconscious*. Ithaca: Cornell University Press, 1981.
Jenkyns, Richard. *The Victorians and Ancient Greece*. Cambridge: Harvard University Press, 1980.
Johnson, Barbara. *The Critical Difference*. Baltimore: Johns Hopkins University Press, 1980.

―――. *A World of Difference*. Paperback ed. Baltimore: Johns Hopkins University Press, 1989.
Kant, Immanuel. *The Critique of Judgment*. Trans. J. H. Bernard. New York: Hafner Press, 1968.
Kearney, Richard. *Dialogues with Contemporary Continental Thinkers*. Manchester, Eng.: Manchester University Press, 1984.
Kendrick, Walter. "De Man That Got Away." *Village Voice*, April 15, 1988: VLS, 6–8.
Kermode, Frank. *Romantic Image*. New York: Vintage, 1964.
Kimball, Roger. *Tenured Radicals: How Politics Has Corrupted Our Higher Education*. New York: Harper and Row, 1990.
Knapp, Steven, and Walter Benn Michaels. "Against Theory." *Against Theory*. Ed. W.J.T. Mitchell. Chicago: University of Chicago Press, 1985. 11–30.
Knoepflmacher, U. C. *Religious Humanism and the Victorian Novel: George Eliot, Walter Pater, and Samuel Butler*. Princeton: Princeton University Press, 1965.
Kolodny, Annette. "Dancing through the Minefields: Some Observations on the Theory, Practice, and Politics of a Feminist Literary Criticism." *Feminist Studies* 6 (1980): 1–25.
Lehman, David. "Deconstructing de Man's Life." *Newsweek*, February 15, 1988: 61, 63–64.
Leitch, Vincent B. *Deconstructive Criticism*. New York: Columbia University Press, 1983.
Lentricchia, Frank. *After the New Criticism*. Chicago: University of Chicago Press, 1980.
―――. *Ariel and the Police*. Madison: University of Wisconsin Press, 1988.
―――. *Criticism and Social Change*. Chicago: University of Chicago Press, 1983.
Levey, Michael. *The Case of Walter Pater*. London: Thames and Hudson, 1978.
Locke, John. *An Essay Concerning Human Understanding*. Ed. Alexander Campbell Fraser. Oxford: Oxford University Press, 1894.
Macaulay, Thomas. *Critical and Historical Essays*. Boston: Houghton Mifflin, 1900.
McCleod, Hugh. *Class and Religion in the Late Victorian City*. Hamden, CT: Archon Books, 1974.
McGrath, F. C. *The Sensible Spirit: Walter Pater and the Modernist Paradigm*. Tampa: University of South Florida Press, 1986.
Mallock, W. H. *The New Republic*. London: Chatto and Windus, 1879.
Meisel, Perry. *The Absent Father: Virginia Woolf and Walter Pater*. New Haven: Yale University Press, 1980.
Mill, James. *An Analysis of the Human Mind*. London: Longmans, 1869.
Mill, John Stuart. *Autobiography and Literary Essays*. Ed. J. M. Robson and Jack Stillinger. Toronto: University of Toronto Press, 1981.
―――. *An Examination of Sir William Hamilton's Philosophy*. Ed. J. M. Robson. Toronto: University of Toronto Press, 1979.
Miller, J. Hillis. "Deconstructing the Deconstructers." *Diacritics* 5 (Summer 1975): 24–31.
―――. *The Ethics of Reading*. New York: Columbia University Press, 1987.

———. "Stevens' Rock and Criticism as Cure." *Georgia Review* 30 (1976): 5–31, 330–348.

———. "Theory and Practice: Response to Vincent Leitch." *Critical Inquiry* 6 (1980): 609–614.

———. Untitled article. *Times Literary Supplement*, June 17–23, 1988: 676, 685.

———. "Walter Pater, A Partial Portrait." *Daedelus* 24 (Winter 1976): 97–113.

Monsman, Gerald. *Pater's Portraits: Mythic Pattern in the Fiction of Walter Pater*. Baltimore: Johns Hopkins University Press, 1967.

———. *Walter Pater*. Boston: Twayne, 1977.

———. *Walter Pater's Art of Autobiography*. New Haven: Yale University Press, 1981.

Newsome, David. *On the Edge of Paradise: A. C. Benson, the Diarist*. Chicago: University of Chicago Press, 1980.

Norris, Christopher. *The Contest of Faculties: Philosophy and Theory After Deconstruction*. London: Methuen, 1985.

———. *Derrida*. Cambridge: Harvard University Press, 1987.

———. *Paul de Man*. New York: Routledge, 1988.

O'Hara, Daniel T. *The Romance of Interpretation: Visionary Criticism from Pater to de Man*. New York: Columbia University Press, 1985.

Pater, Walter. "Coleridge's Writings." *Westminster Review* (American ed.) 85 (January 1866): 48–60.

———. *Essays from the 'Guardian.'* London: Macmillan, 1910.

———. *Marius the Epicurean*. 2 vols. London: Macmillan, 1910.

———. "Poems of William Morris." *Westminster Review* (American ed.) 90 (October 1868): 144–149.

———. *The Renaissance*. Ed. Donald Hill. Berkeley: University of California Press, 1980.

Perloff, Marjorie. "Response to Jacques Derrida." *Critical Inquiry* 15 (1989): 767–776.

Pratt, Mary Louise. *Toward a Speech Act Theory of Literary Discourse*. Bloomington: Indiana University Press, 1977.

Ricoeur, Paul. *The Conflict of Interpretations*. Evanston, IL: Northwestern University Press, 1974.

Robinson, Lillian S. "Treason Our Text: Feminist Challenges to the Literary Canon." *Feminist Criticism: Essays on Women, Literature and Theory*. Ed. Elaine Showalter. New York: Pantheon, 1985. 105–121.

Rorty, Richard. "Deconstruction and Circumvention." *Critical Inquiry* 11 (1984): 1–25.

———. *Philosophy and the Mirror of Nature*. Princeton: Princeton University Press, 1979.

Ruskin, John. *Works*. Ed. E. T. Cook and Alexander Wedderburn. 39 vols. London: George Allen, 1903–1912.

Ryals, Clyde de L. "The Concept of Becoming in *Marius the Epicurean*." *Nineteenth Century Literature* 43 (1988): 157–174.

Ryan, Michael. *Marxism and Deconstruction*. Baltimore: Johns Hopkins University Press, 1982.

Said, Edward. *The World, the Text and the Critic*. Cambridge: Harvard University Press, 1983.

Sawyer, Paul. *Ruskin's Poetic Argument: The Design of the Major Works*. Ithaca: Cornell University Press, 1985.

Schuetz, Lawrence. "The Suppressed 'Conclusion' to *The Renaissance* and Walter Pater's Modern Image." *English Literature in Transition* 17 (1974): 251–258.

Schweickart, Patrocinio P. "Reading Ourselves: Toward a Feminist Theory of Reading." *Gender and Reading: Essays on Readers, Texts, and Contexts*. Ed. Elizabeth Flynn and Patrocinio Schweickart. Baltimore: Johns Hopkins University Press, 1986. 31–62.

Sedgwick, Eve Kosofsky. *Between Men: English Literature and Male Homosocial Desire*. New York: Columbia University Press, 1983.

Seiler, R. M. *Walter Pater, A Life Remembered*. Calgary: University of Calgary Press, 1987.

——— *Walter Pater, The Critical Heritage*. London: Routledge and Kegan Paul, 1980.

Shklovsky, Victor. "Sterne's *Tristram Shandy*: Stylistic Commentary." *Russian Formalist Criticism: Four Essays*. Trans. Lee T. Lemon and Marion J. Reis. Lincoln: University of Nebraska Press, 1965. 25–57.

Small, Ian. "Pater and the Suppressed 'Conclusion' to *The Renaissance*: Comment." *English Literature in Transition* 19 (1976): 313–316.

Smith, Barbara Herrnstein. *Contingencies of Value*. Cambridge: Harvard University Press, 1988.

Staten, Henry. *Wittgenstein and Derrida*. Lincoln: University of Nebraska Press, 1984.

Stein, Richard. *The Ritual of Interpretation: The Fine Arts as Literature in Ruskin, Rossetti, and Pater*. Cambridge: Harvard University Press, 1975.

Stevens, Wallace. *The Necessary Angel: Essays on Reality and Imagination*. New York: Alfred A. Knopf, 1951.

Swinburne, Algernon. *William Blake*. Lincoln: University of Nebraska Press, 1970.

Ward, Anthony. *Walter Pater: The Idea in Nature*. London: MacGibbon and Kee, 1966.

Waters, Lindsay, and Wlad Godzich, eds. *Reading de Man Reading*. Minneapolis: University of Minnesota Press, 1989.

White, Hayden. *Metahistory*. Baltimore: Johns Hopkins University Press, 1973.

Wiener, Jon. "Deconstructing de Man." *Nation*, January 9, 1988: 22–24.

——— "The Responsibilities of Friendship." *Critical Inquiry* 15 (1989): 800.

Williams, Carolyn. *Transfigured World: Walter Pater's Aesthetic Historicism*. Ithaca: Cornell University Press, 1989.

Wimsatt, William K., and Cleanth Brooks. *Literary Criticism: A Short History*. New York: Vintage, 1957.

Wollheim, Richard. *On Art and the Mind*. Cambridge: Harvard University Press, 1974.

Wright, Thomas. *Life of Pater*. London: Everett, 1907.

Index

Abrams, M. H., 201n.4
Aestheticism, 3, 4–6, 24–27, 61; and deconstruction, 73–74, 160–161, 165–166, 169; and homophobia, 186–187; as artificial enclosure, 122–126; self-resistance as political analysis in, 167–172
Arnold, Matthew, 6, 14, 16, 27, 28, 40, 67, 86, 89, 122; and deconstruction, 34; criticism in, 25; *Culture and Anarchy*, 31; "Literature and Science," 32–33; "On the Modern Element in Literature," 30; theory of Culture compared to Pater's aestheticism, 30–35

Bahti, Timothy, 197, 199
Baudelaire, Charles, 137
Benjamin, Walter, 49
Benson, A. C., 215n.6, 218n.22
Berkeley, Bishop, 18, 22
Blackmur, R. P., 207n.2
Blake, William, 13, 125
Bloom, Allan, 183
Bloom, Harold, 108, 201n.1, 202n.4, 203n.11, 204n.14, 205n.24, 216n.10
Bové, Paul, 201n.1
Brake, Laurel, 218n.22
Brenkman, John, 194, 195
Brooke, S. R., 17
Brooks, Cleanth, 98, 204n.16
Brooks, Peter, 49–50, 206n.4
Browning, Robert, 13
Buckler, William, 215n.6
Burckhardt, Jacob, 58, 207n.14

Cain, William, 207n.2
Carlyle, Thomas, 29
Cassirer, Ernst, 214n.13
Chadwick, Owen, 215n.8
Charlesworth, Barbara, 215n.6
Chase, Cynthia, 193, 197–198
Chatman, Seymour, 205n.4
Christianity, 167–172
Coleridge, Samuel Taylor, 204n.15
Comte, Auguste, 51, 52
Constant, Benjamin, 202n.5

Continental philosophy, 78
Corngold, Stanley, 188, 192, 211n.25, 217n.13, 220n.5
Culler, A. Dwight, 206n.9, 216n.11
Culler, Jonathan, 165, 192, 210n.19, 212n.32, 215n.5, 217n.18

d'Hangest, Germain, 206n.13
da Vinci, Leonardo, 54–60, 186
Dale, Peter Alan, 203nn.8 and 11, 204n.18, 205nn. 2 and 21, 206n.13
De Man, Paul, 3, 7–10, 54, 73–76, 80, 92, 97, 164, 185, 187–188; and aestheticism, 122–126; *Allegories of Reading*, 108, 110, 112, 114–116, 117, 119, 139, 141, 142, 145, 149, 177; *Blindness and Insight*, 107, 108, 109–112, 115, 119, 135, 139, 141; compared to Derrida, 101, 111–114, 116, 120, 134; compared to Pater, 26, 107, 120, 138, 160–161; "Hegel on the Sublime," 156; on Hegel's aesthetic theories, 145, 150–157; and the ideology of aesthetics, 142–159; "Intentional Structure of the Romantic Image," 108; on Kant's aesthetic theories, 145; on the literary canon, 177; "Literary History and Literary Modernity," 135–139; literary language in, 107–120, 126, 127, 134–142; and the literary history of Romanticism, 139–142; "Phenomenality and Materiality in Kant," 157; "Resistance to Theory," 158, 167, 172–175; *Rhetoric of Romanticism*, 139, 141; "Rhetoric of Temporality," 135, 139–141, 145, 151, 155; and the role of the critic, 117–120; self-resistance as political analysis in, 172–176; "Shelley Disfigured," 117, 175, 177, 191; "Sign and Symbol in Hegel," 150, 152, 155, 156, 158; *Wartime Writings*, 175, 190–200

Deconstruction, 3–5; and aestheticism, 73–74, 158, 160, 165–166, 169; foundational analysis as political critique in, 176, 180–184; and the ideology of critical discourse, 142–143, 158, 173–175; as

Deconstruction (cont.)
  literary criticism, 75, 77, 92–95, 96, 100, 117; and the problem of method, 94–97; and self-deconstruction, 113–114, 154–156; self-resistance as political analysis in, 166–176
Dekeukeleire, Charles, 195
DeLaura, David, 15, 204nn.17, 18 and 20, 206nn.7 and 11, 215n.6
Derrida, Jacques, 3, 7–10, 15, 54, 73–74, 108–110, 122, 139, 140, 142, 156–158, 177, 188–189, 190, 199; compared to de Man, 101, 111–114, 116, 120, 134; compared to Pater, 23, 26, 75–76, 79–80, 85–86, 89, 97, 100, 160–161; and Continental philosophy, 76–79; on de Man's *Wartime Writings*, 194, 196–197; "Differance," 82–85; *Disseminations*, 133; "The Double Session," 101–105, 150; on Foucault's *History of Madness*, 128–131; history in, 127–134; and the history of philosophy, 131–134; and literary language, 97, 107, 126; *Margins of Philosophy*, 80–82, 133; "No Apocalypse, Not Now," 164–165, 181–183; *Of Grammatology*, 78, 88, 90, 94–96, 102, 131–134; philosophic argument of, 80–92; political implications of his theories, 161–166, 181–184; "Racism's Last Word," 218n.19; on Rousseau, 95–96; "Signature Event Context," 79; *Speech and Phenomena*, 78, 87–89, 133; "Structure, Sign, and Play," 89–91; *Truth in Painting*, 143; "White Mythology," 79
Descartes, René, 81, 128, 130–132
Deterrence, Nuclear, 164–165, 181, 182
Donoghue, Denis, 219n.2
Dowling, Linda 201n.2, 215n.7

Eagleton, Terry, 212nn. 1, 3, and 4, 213n.10, 217n.17
Eliot, George, 186
Eliot, T. S., 11, 13, 14, 52, 185, 202n.2, 204n.18, 216n.10
Ellis, John, 212n.32
Ellmann, Richard, 218n.22
Empiricism, 18–23, 43, 76; compared to Continental philosophy, 78; and historicism, 44
Escott, T. S., 216n.11
Euphuism, 168–169

Evans, Lawrence, 202n.2

Felperin, Howard, 207n.1, 215n.2
Feminist criticism, 176–180, 184
Fischer, Michael, 205n.22, 207n.2, 208n.5, 209n.14, 212n.31, 215n.4
Fish, Stanley, 5, 178–179, 201n.5, 209n.16
Flesch, William, 220n.8, 221n.12
Foley, Barbara, 212n.3
Foucault, Michel, 128–131, 132, 134, 173, 201n.2, 202n.6, 213n.5, 217n.14
Freud, Sigmund, 49, 50
Frow, John, 213n.5
Frye, Northrop, 13

Gagnier, Regenia, 219n.23
Gallagher, Catherine, 186, 188–189, 217n.16, 220n.3
Gasché, Rodolphe, 141, 199, 207nn.1 and 3, 209nn.13 and 15, 210n.23, 211nn.28 and 30, 213n.8, 214nn.13, 14, 17 and 18
Gearhart, Suzanne, 210n.23, 213n.4
Gelb, Leslie, 181
Geuss, Raymond, 214nn.16 and 17
Goethe, Johann Wolfgang, 29, 40, 61, 62, 64, 65–66, 72
Goodheart, Eugene, 205n.22
Gosse, Edmund, 219n.22
Graff, Gerald, 110–111, 162, 207n.2, 210n.21, 212n.1, 219n.2
Green, T. H., 171

Hartman, Geoffrey, 192, 219n.1
Harvey, Irene, 209n.17
Haskins, C. H., 206n.12
Hegel, G.F.W., 6, 19, 51, 52, 62, 77, 85, 122, 132; *Aesthetics*, 55, 61, 66–73, 125, 143, 145, 150–158; *Encyclopedia*, 153; *The Phenomenology of Mind*, 144–145
Hertz, Neil, 213n.8, 214n.15
Hill, Donald, 52, 60
Hill, Donald, 202nn.3 and 5, 204n.14, 206nn.12 and 13
Hirsch, E. D., 297n.4
Hobbes, Thomas, 18
Hölderlin, Friedrich, 109
Homer, 32–33, 45, 46, 110–111
Hough, Graham, 202n.6
Hugo, Victor, 13, 202n.4
Hume, David, 18, 78, 79, 203nn.10 and 11

INDEX

Husserl, Edmund, 76–79, 86–89, 91, 113, 207n.4, 208n.11
Huxley, T. H., 32–33

Inman, Billie Andrew, 203n.12, 205n.21, 219n.22
Iser, Wolfgang, 204n.16

Jakobson, Roman, 98
James, Williams, 160
Jameson, Fredric, 201n.6, 217n.14
Jenkyns, Richard, 207n.15, 218n.20
Johnson, Barbara, 166–167, 168, 176, 195, 209n.18, 219n.1
Jowett, Benjamin, 12, 186, 202n.2, 218n.21, 219n.22

Kamuf, Peggy, 217n.12
Kant, Immanuel, 23, 77, 81, 127, 155; *Critique of Judgment*, 143–150; *Critique of Pure Reason*, 78
Kaplan, Alice Yaeger, 196
Kendrick, Walter, 221n.11
Kermode, Frank, 212n.2
Kimball, Roger, 192, 219n.1
Kleist, Wilhelm, 193
Knapp, Steven and Walter Benn Michaels, 209n.16, 217n.16
Knoepflemacher, U. C., 215n.6
Kolodny, Annette, 217n.15

Lawrence, D. H., 217n.17
Lehman, David, 220n.5
Leitch, Vincent, 208n.6, 210n.21
Lentricchia, Frank, 5, 123–125, 127, 166, 185, 187–188, 207nn.1 and 2, 208n.4, 210nn. 21 and 22, 211nn.24 and 27, 212n.4, 213nn.7 and 11, 217n.14
Levey, Michael, 30, 202n.2, 206nn.6 and 8, 218n.21
Lévi-Strauss, Claude, 89–90, 132, 163
Literary Canon, 176–180, 182–184
Literary language, 26, 76, 80, 169, 188; compared to art in Pater, 100; in Derrida, 97–107; and disarticulation as ideological analysis in de Man, 146, 149–150, 157–158; as historical analysis, 126, 134–142
Locke, John, 18, 79, 203n.7

Macaulay, Thomas, 44

McGrath, F. C., 215n.6
Mallarmé, Stephane, 102, 104–106, 113, 117
Mallock, W. H., 186, 218n.21
Marlier, Georges, 221n.9
Marxist criticism, 173, 179, 185, 201n.6
Mehlman, Jeffrey, 220n.5
Meisel, Perry, 52, 201n.1, 203n.12, 204n.13
Michelangelo, 56
Michelet, Jules, 206n.12
Mill, J. S., 21, 22, 44, 79, 203nn.7, 9, and, 11
Mill, James, 44, 203n.7
Miller, J. Hillis, 4, 92–95, 96, 113, 114, 176–177, 196, 199–200, 201nn.1 and 4, 203n.12, 208n.6, 209n.14, 210n.21, 220n.4
Mirandola, Pico della, 45–47
Monsman, Gerald, 17, 201n.1, 215n.6
Montherlant, Henri de, 199
Morley, John, 4, 5, 201n.3
Morris, William, 33, 58
Moses, 46

New Criticism, 3, 75, 98, 207n.2
Newmark, Kevin, 213n.9
Newsome, David, 218n.22
Nietzsche, Friedrich, 91, 115, 135–136
Norris, Christopher, 164–165, 181, 192, 207n.3, 208nn.9 and 12, 210n.22, 211n.30, 213n.11, 219n.1

O'Hara, Daniel T., 201n.2, 207n.1, 216n.11

Pater, Walter, 3–4, 6–10, 78, 140, 158–159, 199
—and aestheticism, 122
—aestheticism of compared to Arnold's Culture, 30–35
—aestheticism of compared to Ruskin's aesthetics, 34–40
—aestheticist historicism of, 42–48, 66, 125, 131, 143
—"Coleridge's Writings," 204n.15
—compared to de Man, 107, 120, 138
—compared to Derrida, 23, 75–76, 79–80, 85–86, 89, 97, 100
—compared to Derrida and de Man, 26, 160–161
—and empiricism, 18–23
—his use of Hegel, 67, 70–73

Pater, Walter (cont.)
—and homophobia, 186–187
—*Imaginary Portraits*, 203n.11
—*Marius the Epicurean*, 167–172
—"The Poems of William Morris," 58
—and positivist historians, 73
—*The Renaissance*, 133, 167–169, 185–187; aesthetic criticism in, 24–27; aestheticism and philosophic inclusion in, 27–41; art for art's sake in, 11–16; "Leonardo da Vinci," 54–60, 61; narrative structure of, 50–53 ; "Pico della Mirandola," 45–47; sensation and epistemology in, 16–27; "Winckelmann," 54, 61–67
Phenomenology, 23, 76–79, 86–89
Plato, 67–68, 85, 102–104, 132, 188
Pratt, Mary Louise, 98
Proust, Marcel, 107, 115

Raphael, 59
Reagan, Ronald, 181
Ricoeur, Paul, 208n.10
Robinson, Lillian, 217n.15
Romanticism, German, 29
Rorty, Richard, 78, 81, 83, 84, 208n.9
Rousseau, Jean-Jacques, 91, 95–96, 108, 109, 113, 117, 118, 119–120, 131, 132, 140, 151, 163, 193
Ruskin, John, 6, 14, 16, 27, 28, 86, 89, 122; aesthetic theory of compared to Pater's, 34–40; Gothicism and Renaissance in, 37–39; Gothicism of and Leonardo da Vinci, 54–58; *Modern Painters*, 35–37, 56; *The Stones of Venice*, 56, 57
Russian Formalism, 98, 205n.4
Ryals, Clyde de L., 215n.6
Ryan, Michael, 163–164, 165, 207n.3, 212n.4, 215n.5

Said, Edward, 213n.5
Saussure, Ferdinand de, 132
Savonarola, Girolamo, 65
Sawyer, Paul, 205n.23, 206n.10
Schuetz, Lawrence, 218n.20

Schweickart, Patrocinio P., 217nn.15 and 17
Searle, John, 162, 163
Sedgwick, Eve Kosofsky, 219n.23
Seiler, R. M., 201n.3
Shakespeare, William, 179, 183
Shelley, Percy Bysshe, 107, 117
Shklovsky, Victor, 98, 99
Smith, Barbara Herrnstein, 178–179, 217nn.17 and 18
Spanos, William, 207n.1
Spencer, Herbert, 205n.21
Spivak, Gayatri Chakravorty, 94, 209n.16
Sprinker, Michael, 207n.1
Staten, Henry, 208n.11, 213n.6
Stein, Richard, 48, 205nn.3 and 24, 206n.5
Stevens, Wallace, 160
Structuralism, 78, 86, 89–91, 110, 173, 205n.4
Super, R. H., 204n.19
Swinburne, Algernon, 13–14, 32, 202n.5

Thackeray, William, 13
Trilling, Lionel, 201n.6
Tristram Shandy, 98

Utilitarianism, 44

Ward, Anthony, 203n.8, 206n.13
Ward, Mrs. Humphry, 169–171, 185; *Robert Elsmere*, 170–171
White, Hayden, 207n.14
Wiener, Jon, 192
Wilde, Oscar, 125, 160, 196, 219n.23
Williams, Carolyn, 205n.1
Wimsatt, William K., 204n.16
Winckelmann, Johann, 52, 61, 64, 72, 186
Wittgenstein, Ludwig, 78
Wollheim, Richard, 215n.1
Woolf, Virginia, 201n.1
Wordsworth, John, 215n.9
Wordsworth, William, 151
Wright, Thomas, 206n.8

Yeats, William Butler, 114

GPSR Authorized Representative: Easy Access System Europe - Mustamäe tee
50, 10621 Tallinn, Estonia, gpsr.requests@easproject.com

www.ingramcontent.com/pod-product-compliance
Lightning Source LLC
Chambersburg PA
CBHW061440300426
44114CB00014B/1775